Mannerheim

Mannerheim

PRESIDENT, SOLDIER, SPY

Jonathan Clements

Haus Publishing
London

First published in Great Britain in 2009 by
Haus Publishing Ltd
70 Cadogan Place
London SW1X 9AH
www.hauspublishing.com

Copyright © Muramasa Industries, 2009

The moral right of the author has been asserted

A CIP catalogue record for this book is available from the British Library

ISBN 978-1-906598-26-6

Typeset in Warnock by MacGuru Ltd
Printed in Great Britain by JF Print, Sparkford
Maps by Martin Lubikowski, ML Design, London

Contents

List of Illustrations   viii
Note on Dates   xv

Introduction: Cold Mountain   1
1   Mannerheim's World   9
2   The Field of Vipers   32
3   The Baptism of Fire   51
4   The Tournament of Shadows   79
5   The Horse Reaches China   111
6   The Paper Dragons   142
7   The End of Empire   170
8   The White Devil   190
9   The House of the Four Winds   207
10 The Jaws of Peril   236
11 The Eye of the Storm   255
12 Marski   273
    Afterword: Mannerheim in the 21st Century   285

Note on Names   289
Notes   293
Sources and Further Reading   320
Acknowledgements   332
Index   334

In memory of
Vesa Mäki-Kuutti
1953–2007

List of Illustrations

Pages 4–5
The mountain pass to Mount Wutai.
National Board of Antiquities/Finno-Ugrian Society

Page 11
Mannerheim in the uniform of the Nikolayevskoye cavalry school.
National Board of Antiquities

Page 15
The Mannerheim siblings, 1878: Sophie seated in the centre, with Johan, Carl and August to the left and Gustaf, Annika and Eva to the right.
National Board of Antiquities

Page 22
Mannerheim in the uniform of the Chevalier Guard.
National Board of Antiquities

Page 28
Anatasie Arapova Mannerheim.
Mannerheim Museum

Page 33
Hyökkäys (The Attack), 1905, a painting by Eetu Isto of the Maid of Finland assaulted by the double-headed eagle of russification.
National Board of Antiquities

Pages 38–9
Coronation of Tsar Nicholas II, 1896. Mannerheim is the
Chevalier Guard walking ahead of the Tsar's canopy on the right.
Mannerheim Museum

Page 49
Flanked by a Chevalier Guard, the Tsar and his wife receive a
party of wounded Russian sailors from the war in the east.
Getty Images

Pages 52–3
Lieutenant Colonel Mannerheim (left) leaves for the Russo-
Japanese front, pictured with Captain von Stewen, Colonel
Meissner and Admiral Greve.
Mannerheim Museum

Pages 74–5
A woodblock print depicting a fight between Russian and
Japanese horsemen in Manchuria, 1905.
TopFoto

Pages 82–3
The Pelliot expedition receives its equipment at Andizhan train
station. Paul Pelliot (in bowler hat), Vaillant, Nouette, and four
cossacks are visible.
National Board of Antiquities/Finno-Ugrian Society

Pages 92–3
Mannerheim's ride across Asia.

Pages 98–9
From left: Paul Pelliot, the 'Queen' of the Alai Kirghiz, her
grandson, Mannerheim *sans* moustache.
National Board of Antiquities/Finno-Ugrian Society

Pages 104–5
The game of Tomocha.
National Board of Antiquities/Finno-Ugrian Society

Page 108
Mannerheim outside his residence in Kashgar.
National Board of Antiquities/Finno-Ugrian Society

Page 110
Mannerheim taking hypsometer readings at the Chapchal pass,
8th May 1907.
National Board of Antiquities/Finno-Ugrian Society

Pages 114–15
Mannerheim's first sight of Jiayuguan, the western end of the
Great Wall of China. Note the ears of Philip the horse.
National Board of Antiquities/Finno-Ugrian Society

Page 119
Climbing the Muzart Pass.
National Board of Antiquities/Finno-Ugrian Society

Pages 130–1
Viceroy Sheng's banquet in Lanzhou. In foreground from left:
Alphonse Splingaerd, Léon van Dijk, Viceroy Sheng at front,
Robert Geerst, Mannerheim.
National Board of Antiquities/Finno-Ugrian Society

Page 135
Mannerheim taking notes in Lanzhou.
National Board of Antiquities/Finno-Ugrian Society

Page 138
Climbing the stone staircase at Mount Hua.
National Board of Antiquities/Finno-Ugrian Society

Pages 148–9
From left: Lukanin the Cossack, Chang the cook, Joseph Zhao
and Mannerheim, at the end of their journey in Kalgan.
National Board of Antiquities/Finno-Ugrian Society

Pages 158–9
Mannerheim's reports and pictures of the Chinese army made it clear Russia had nothing to fear.
National Board of Antiquities/Finno-Ugrian Society

Pages 164–5
Russian horsemen of the 13th Uhlan Regiment in Poland.
National Board of Antiquities/Finno-Ugrian Society

Pages 176–7
Machine guns in action against revolutionaries in Petrograd (St Petersburg), 1917.
TopFoto

Pages 184–5
October 1917: Soldiers of the Keksgolm Regiment marching with banners in Petrograd (St Petersburg) during the Russian Revolution.
Getty Images

Page 194
Mannerheim observes the Battle of Tampere. Painting by Antti Favén.
Finnish Defence Forces

Page 201
The White General, 1918.
National Board of Antiquities

Pages 210–11
Mannerheim rides in triumph, 1918.
National Bureau of Antiquities

Page 214
Regent Mannerheim and King Gustaf V of Sweden in Stockholm.
National Bureau of Antiquities

Pages 220–1
An oriental-themed party at the House of the Four Winds, 1925.
Mannerheim's sister Marguerite ('Kissie') is on the far right,
Kissie's husband Georg Gripenberg on far left. Prince Henry of
the Netherlands in the centre, wearing a boater.
National Bureau of Antiquities

Pages 228–9
Hunting a man-eating tiger with the Maharajah of Nepal, 1937.
Mannerheim Museum

Page 233
Mannerheim's path is strewn with white flowers on his 70th
birthday, 4th June 1937.
Finnish Defence Forces

Pages 238–9
Ten Finnish soldiers demonstrate the effectiveness of snow
camouflage at close range.
Finnish Defence Forces

Page 250
Mannerheim observing the front.
Finnish Defence Forces

Pages 258–9
Mannerheim (2nd from left) attends a strategy meeting with
Hitler in Germany.
Finnish Defence Forces

Page 266
Mannerheim and Hitler, 1942.
Finnish Defence Forces

Page 270
Mannerheim and Hitler bid their last farewells in Germany.
Finnish Defence Forces

Pages 276–7
Mannerheim greets a crowd of schoolchildren in the Karelian
town of Äänislinna (Petrozavodsk). The town was abandoned
during the Finnish retreat, and fell into Soviet hands.
Finnish Defence Forces

Page 280
The last known picture of Mannerheim, in Montreux, December
1950.
Mannerheim Museum

Page 282
Mannerheim's medals are carried ahead of his coffin.
Finnish Defence Forces

Page 284
Mannerheim in silhouette by Eric Sundström, 1920.
National Board of Antiquities

Note on Dates

Tsarist Russia used the Julian calendar, which was 12 days behind the Gregorian calendar and in use in much of Europe during the 19th century. From 1 January 1901, the Julian calendar was 13 days behind the Gregorian. This can cause a few historical anomalies – modern Russians, for example, are obliged to mark the anniversary of the February Revolution on 8 March, and the October Revolution on 7 November. Mannerheim habitually used the Julian calendar until 1906, when he adopted the Gregorian calendar in his correspondence from China as part of his 'Swedish' cover. In some instances, particularly when dating correspondence between Sweden and Finland, I have given both Gregorian and Julian dates to avoid confusion. All dates after 1917 are Gregorian.

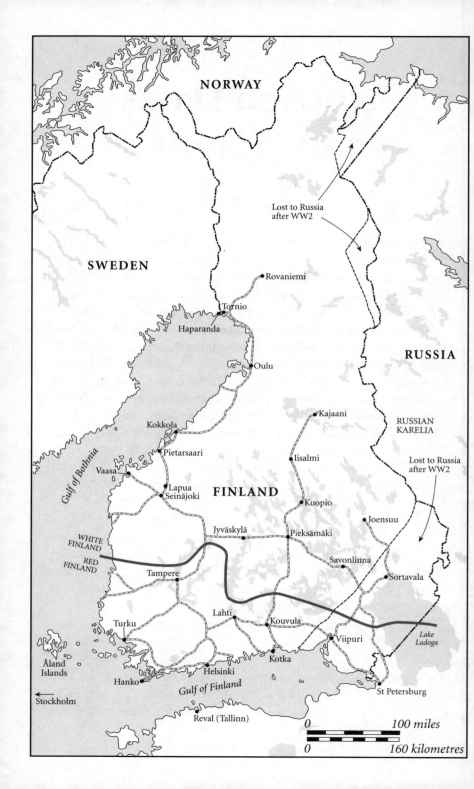

Cold Mountain

It was Friday 26 June 1908, a summer day, but the high slopes of the sacred Mount Wutai were still chilly. The Buddhist monks gave thanks even as they shivered – was this not further proof of Mount Wutai's great holiness? Was it not said that the spirit of the Buddhist deity Manjusri resided at a 'cold clear mountain'? Why not this mountain, even if it were in China?

Mount Wutai was not only a sacred site; it was also a refuge for the Thirteenth Incarnation of the Precious Victor, Wish-Fulfilling Jewel, Holder of the White Lotus, His Holiness the Dalai Lama. Forced to flee his Tibetan homeland after a British invasion in 1903, the Dalai Lama now enjoyed an uneasy residence in China, under the watchful eyes of soldiers of the Chinese Emperor of Glorious Succession.

The Chinese Emperor had 'invited' him to come to Beijing to discuss his situation, but for now he was suffered to stay at Mount Wutai. Chinese guards stood watch over the approaches to the mountain, and supposedly kept out troublemakers. Politically, the Dalai Lama was caught between the Chinese and the British, and hoped for a rescue by a third party.

Once every three days, he would venture out from his residence in the foothills, in order to wave at visiting worshippers – Chinese and Tibetans, Mongols and tribesmen from eastern Siberia. As was customary, each would present him with a ceremonial silk scarf, or *hatak*. He would give them one in return.

The Dalai Lama's residence was truly antique. Parts of the temple complex were more than a thousand years old, and it showed. Some buildings were in an awful state of disrepair, and strewn with junk and dirt. Others were incongruously well appointed, dotted with silver gilt idols and paintings of Buddhist saints. Horses quartered on the temple grounds added to the filth, and the stench of manure was overpowering. Regardless, the Dalai Lama donned a ceremonial robe of yellowish-gold and headed out into the daylight. He still had his entourage of monks, some of whom scurried before him as he descended the steps.

The monks remonstrated with the waiting crowd, pushing them back, urging them to make way for the spiritual leader, shouting in Tibetan, Mongol and Chinese. Suddenly, the Dalai Lama saw an unexpected figure. Standing among the worshippers was a towering European figure, a gaunt, moustached man staring right at him. The Dalai Lama paused for a moment in shock and surprise, before continuing his march to the next temple.

Who was the man? Not a British 'Yellow Head', but clearly one of the men of the distant regions beyond the ocean: a White Devil. The man had been spotted some time before in the distant central Chinese city of Xi'an, where he had been photographing the retinue of one of the Dalai Lama's lieutenants. He was, it was said, a Swedish explorer called Gustaf Mannerheim.

But there was more to this man than met the eye. The next day, the Dalai Lama sent a monk to summon Mannerheim into his presence. He waited in his chambers, but Mannerheim did not show up. Impatiently, the Dalai Lama sent a second monk, who was astounded to discover that Mannerheim had been changing his clothes and shaving before the audience – strangely gentlemanly behaviour. Eventually, Mannerheim arrived, blissfully unaware that he had kept a living god waiting, and unphased by the climb up the steep steps; he was accompanied by Joseph Zhao, his teenage Chinese interpreter.

Mannerheim bowed deeply before the Dalai Lama, who answered with the barest nod, still staring intently at the new arrival. The explorer took a blue silk *hatak* in both hands and offered it reverently to His Holiness. The Dalai Lama responded by offering him a similar scarf, of white silk.

Mannerheim spoke respectfully, in Russian. His interpreter converted the Russian into Mandarin Chinese, while one of the Dalai Lama's attendants, staring resolutely at the floor, hissed a re-translation into Tibetan.

There was some confusion as to where Mannerheim was from. Yes, Swedish was his native tongue, but he was actually born in a country called Finland. The Dalai Lama was disappointed. He had hoped that Mannerheim was a Russian. The Russian Tsar, Nicholas II, was believed by some Tibetans to be the White Tara, an incarnation of the Bodhisattva of Compassion, and the harbinger of peace in Asia. One of the Dalai Lama's advisers had even told him that the Russian Tsar was contemplating converting to Buddhism – if he did so, of course, the political situation in the Far East was sure to change forever.[1]

Quite unexpectedly, Mannerheim admitted that he had met the Tsar. Finland was an autonomous Grand Duchy, but the Grand Duke of Finland was the self-same Nicholas II.

Twice, the Dalai Lama ordered that his attendants check behind the curtains in the hall to make sure that nobody was listening – he was afraid both of Tibetan intrigues and his Chinese guardians. The Dalai Lama was very bad at hiding his excitement. His aloof, regal demeanour suddenly collapsed, and he began to twitch nervously. He asked if Mannerheim had a message for him from the Tsar.

Mannerheim was forced to admit that he did not, but offered to carry a message back to the Tsar on the Dalai Lama's behalf. The Dalai Lama hesitated, and asked Mannerheim his rank. Mannerheim revealed that he was a baron, which seemed to please His Holiness. The Dalai Lama presented Mannerheim with a silk *hatak* for the Tsar, and entreated the visitor to stay another day, so that the Tibetan ruler might 'ask for something'. Mannerheim told him that 'the sympathies of the Russian people were on his side, when he felt obliged to leave his own country ... These sympathies had not been weakened by the lapse of time, and wherever he might be, he could feel sure that Russians, both high and low, watched his footsteps with interest.'[2]

Before long, the throne room of the Thirteenth Incarnation of

the Precious Victor, Wish-Fulfilling Jewel, Holder of the White Lotus, His Holiness the Dalai Lama, resonated with peals of glee as Mannerheim showed him how to work a very unlikely gift: a Browning FN M1900 semi-automatic pistol. Mannerheim was mildly embarrassed at presenting a holy man with a weapon, but it was the most valuable item left to him after so many months of travel. 'The times were such,' he observed, 'that a gun might at times be of greater use, even to a holy man like himself, than a praying mill.'[3]

His Holiness seemed sure that they would meet again, and promised Mannerheim that on that occasion he would let him take his photograph. As they parted, the Dalai Lama invited Mannerheim to come and visit him in Lhasa on his next visit —clearly he was not planning on staying long in China. 'The Dalai Lama impressed me as a keen, intelligent man equipped with considerable reserves of physical and spiritual strength,' Mannerheim wrote. 'His sympathy with and faith in the Chinese were evidently not great.'[4]

But it was not to be. The meeting in the Mount Wutai temple was not a beginning, but an end. The two men never met again. The next day, the Dalai Lama was squirreled out of Mannerheim's sight, offering the mysterious demurral that he had not received an 'answer' that he had been expecting. Soon after, he received the long-feared summons to Beijing, possibly even *because* his wardens had been spooked by the arrival of Mannerheim.

For all Mannerheim's talk of Russian 'sympathies', there would be no aid for the Tibetans. The Russian love affair with the Far East, which had lasted two generations, had enjoyed its final reprieve, and Mannerheim was its last herald. His meeting with the Dalai Lama was a tail-end encounter on a two-year mission aimed at assessing the danger that China presented to Russia. Mannerheim had already realised that China presented little danger at all, which meant that the Dalai Lama would be abandoned to his fate.

On Wutai, the 'cold mountain', Mannerheim was present at a crucial turn of karma. He was there on the fateful day that something *didn't* happen. The Tsar's interest in Russian expansion in Asia, already wavering after his defeat in the Russo-Japanese War, was at an all-time low. The Dalai Lama would get no help in his struggle against a neighbouring empire – but neither would Mannerheim.

Mannerheim had staked his career on the Far East. He had fled his debts in St Petersburg to serve in a war against the Japanese. He had invested years of his life in a fact-finding mission that had already discovered an inconvenient truth – China was too weak to present any threat to Russia. Mannerheim was shortly due to return home to an uncertain future. On that Friday at Wutai, he had no idea that his greatest battles were still ahead of him, and would be fought not in Asia at all, but in his home country of Finland. After serving Russia faithfully for his adult life, Mannerheim would soon reinvent himself in a new incarnation, ready to spend an entire second career opposing a new enemy: Russia itself.

⇒⇐

Gustaf Mannerheim's career path in the Russian military had been unorthodox. He specialised in horsemanship, a discipline that was already fading before the unstoppable advance of the internal combustion engine. One of the masters of the dying days of cavalry, Mannerheim was a highly esteemed buyer of horses for regiments, and the leader of the imperial Russian cavalry demonstration team. His other area of expertise, through accidental family connections and an element of blind chance, was the Far East. Against the advice of his family and fellow officers, he volunteered for service in the Russo-Japanese War – a decision that would put him a critical few months ahead of his rivals on the promotional ladder. In peacetime, he returned to the East in a prolonged spying mission that was part of the 'Great Game' for mastery of Asia. He spent much of his forties preparing for a war that never came, a cataclysmic rematch between Russia and Japan that was postponed indefinitely by revolution in St Petersburg.

Mannerheim spent much of his life, as he put it, 'racing the storm', watching the political horizon for the signs of onrushing danger from the east. The battles that have made him truly famous, however, were not fought as he had expected against the Japanese, but against his own former masters, the Russians.

With the Russian Revolution of 1917, the Grand Duchy of Finland unilaterally put an end to its century under the Tsar's rule. Finland proclaimed its independence, and Mannerheim, a Finn in Russian service, returned to his homeland. He evaded capture and execution by Bolsheviks, and arrived in Finland to discover that he was the most experienced military man in the new realm. He became the leader of Finland's army of liberation, and fought a controversial, divisive war against Finland's own revolutionary elements. He marched in triumph through the streets of Helsinki, and then spent a decade in the political wilderness, shunned by the state he had helped to found. It was only then, ironically, that he found the time to master Finnish after a lifetime speaking Swedish, French and Russian.

Mannerheim's continually thwarted efforts to retire have an almost comedic pattern. He acccepted the position of head of state as regent of Finland at a time of national crisis, and then ran a coffee shop by the sea. He came out of retirement to fight an invading army with impossible odds, and in the Second World War would gain the remarkable distinction of being decorated not only by the Finns, but also by the Allies (the French Légion d'honneur), the Nazis (the Iron Cross) and neutral Sweden (Order of the Seraphim) among others. He was a lifelong enemy of Bolshevism, reviled by his enemies as a 'butcher-in-chief', but treasured a portrait of the Lion of Finland made for him by grateful Russian prisoners of war. He was a fierce defender of Finnish independence, but never forgot his oath of fealty to the last Tsar, Nicholas II, whose picture he kept on his wall, and whose medals he still wore with pride. The surprise guest at his 75th birthday party was Adolf Hitler. He ended his career by briefly becoming President of Finland.

Mannerheim was one of the greatest figures of the 20th century, an international celebrity at his finest hour, now largely forgotten outside his native land. Despite, or perhaps because of, his amazing life, he continues to enjoy incredible changes of fortune long after his death. He remains a figure of great national pride to the Finns, a general whose name has been purloined not only by a children's charity but also by a rock band, the hero of a comic about tiger hunting in India, and the target of a malicious puppet show. He was cursed, as he might have observed himself, to live in interesting times.

1

Mannerheim's World

On 14 September 1887, the 20-year-old Gustaf Mannerheim prepared to take the train from Helsinki to the Russian capital St Petersburg. He was fêted at a banquet by his old school class-mates, who were incredulous that he had lived up to his promise to secure a place at the Nikolayevskoye Cavalry School – many were probably unaware of the number of family favours that had been called in. Mannerheim also did his best to assure his friends that he knew what he was doing, climbing steadily to his feet, and raising his glass to the assembled crowd.

'I swear,' he proclaimed, 'that I shall never forget Finland.'

Then he tossed his glass over his shoulder, where it smashed into a hundred pieces against the wall.[1]

His friends' concern was not unfounded. In leaving for Russia, Mannerheim risked betraying his birthright. Finland had once been a border march of the Swedish Empire, only to be snatched away by Russia in 1809. Finland had been a Grand Duchy of Sweden, and was allowed this same status by Russia. The Russian Tsar was hence also the Grand Duke of Finland, who appointed a Russian governor-general to administer the country in his name. Almost a century on, Finland's inhabitants included native Finns, migrant Russians, and the remnants of the old Swedish nobility, among which the Mannerheims counted themselves. 'Swedish-speaking Finns' were hence a curious minority, a tenth of the population of Finland, largely concentrated in the south-west and on the Baltic coast.

At the time of the Russian acquisition, Mannerheim's grandfather had been one of the Finns who petitioned the Tsar for the territory to be afforded its own constitution and to be permitted to exist as an autonomous region within the Russian empire. When this request was granted, he served as one of the officials of the newly convened Finnish Senate, a body whose 'economic division' functioned as a cabinet, and whose 'judiciary division' functioned as Finland's supreme court. The Russian-appointed governor-general remained the ruler, but his cabinet was exclusively drawn from Finnish nationals. As the first vice-chairman of the economic division of the Finnish Senate, Mannerheim's grandfather enjoyed a position analogous to that of a modern prime minister. The head of the Mannerheim family was also entitled to membership of the Estate of Nobles, an exclusive council of the aristocracy. But despite such concessions to the old order, the Finns remained intensely wary of Russians.

A valedictory letter from Mannerheim to his siblings suggests that there was still suspicion about his decision to serve the Tsar. In a jocular but tense fashion, Mannerheim framed his goodbyes as a last will and testament, as if (except on vacations) he was never expecting to see his family again.

> This is my last farewell. I have today been admitted to the Cavalry School. In one hour I shall get into my uniform. Divide my estate accordingly: May Johan have my Nagaika riding whip. My shoes I can wear out myself during leave. My books can be freely stacked with the ones I left in Helsinki. And thank you for lending your tailcoat, Carl; I hope it isn't damaged in anyway. Fare thee well. Sincerely, Gustaf, the Traitor.[2]

Baron Carl Gustaf Emil Mannerheim, to give him his full name, was born on 4 June 1867 at Louhisaari Manor in south-west Finland. The Mannerheim family had wealthy relatives in Sweden, and his mother, Hélène von Julin, came from a huge family, thanks in large part to her father being a multiple widower who married four times. His last two brides were the Jägerskiöld sisters – one the mother of Hélène, and the other the mother of Hélène's

half-brother and cousin Albert von Julin. It was thanks to this massive set of relatives that the young Mannerheim was able to enjoy an indulgent support network, even when times were hard. Throughout his teens and twenties, he was able to call upon the connections of two powerful godmothers, as well as Albert von Julin, the long-suffering 'Uncle Albert' who would bankroll Mannerheim's early career, and refused every one of the older, richer Mannerheim's attempts to pay him back.

Mannerheim's childhood was entirely spent in the Swedish-speaking countryside of southern Finland, at the family seat of Louhisaari. There he grew up with his elder siblings Sophie and Carl, and the younger Johan, Eva and August. Another sister, Annika, died in childhood.

Beyond the stout, square mansion house with its steep roof, the sloping grounds rolled gently down towards the sea. A long avenue of trees separated the mansion from the nearest road, and the edges of the mansion grounds were thickly wooded. There was a playhouse for the children, and a coterie of servants to fuss over them. Until Mannerheim was sent to a boys' school in Helsinki, he and the other children were taught by a Swiss governess, Anna Lockert, whom they liked best for her dramatic descriptions of the far-flung regions of the world, particularly the bandit-infested wildernesses of distant China.[3]

Despite such an apparently idyllic existence, the young Mannerheim grew up in a country whose protected status was merely a whim of the Tsar. So far, every Tsar had honoured the promises of his predecessors to uphold Finland's autonomy – unlike the luckless Poles or Lithuanians, the Finns were still permitted to speak both their languages (Finnish and Swedish) and to run their own affairs. But it would only take one Tsar who lacked that attitude to overturn all the previous goodwill. And then what would happen?

Poland offered the most chilling omen. Commencing with protests from Poles unwilling to serve in the Russian army, an 1863 uprising had been ruthlessly suppressed. Hundreds of ringleaders were executed; thousands exiled to Siberia, still more forcibly relocated to other Russian provinces. Colluding churches were abolished, their lands seized and the price of the suppression exacted from the Poles themselves in the form of an additional war indemnity tax. Thereafter, the Poles were educated entirely in Russian, in a region that was partitioned into Russian provinces, staffed solely by Russian officers.

In Poland and many other Russian possessions – Ukraine, Lithuania, Moldova – the Tsar's government was intent on stamping out local ideas of nationhood. In those unfortunate realms, what the Russian bayonet started, the Russian school would finish. Russian was made the official language of education, and Cyrillic the only approved script. The Russian Orthodox variant of Christianity was given pre-eminence over other sects, and many civil service positions were barred to natives. This both encouraged Russian job seekers to come to the borderlands, while encouraging the natives to seek employment elsewhere in the Tsar's empire.

There were already those among the Finns who doubted that Russian goodwill would last forever, and there was occasional talk of how Finland might become an independent country in its own right. But such talk was liable to frighten the Russians. It was, after all, the Gulf of Finland, a long strip of coastline dotted with Finnish harbours, that formed the long approach to St Petersburg. Strategically, Finland was the guardian of the sea approach to Russia's capital, and Finnish pilots were the steersmen who guided in ships from every part of the empire.

The young Mannerheim had developed a great interest in the sea and in exploration, partly because far-flung exploration, particularly in the Far East, was the fashionable topic of discussion among the Tsar's subjects, but also because Mannerheim's own relatives were intimately involved with it. His distant cousin Leonard Jägerskiöld (1831–71) had sailed in the corvette *Griden* to the mouth of the Amur River in furthest Siberia. The Tsar had given up on the New World, selling Alaska to the Americans in the year of Mannerheim's birth. Instead, Russia was positioning itself as a power that straddled East and West, and the allure of the Orient was the talk of Russian society. Already, Russian explorers had reached the fabled land of China, not through the traditional sea route, but by walking there across the wilderness of Russia's Far East. The Russians hoped for trade with the newly opened Japanese market at the far end of the Amur River, and even with the Chinese Empire. In an age drunk on *chinoiserie* and *japonisme*, Europe was crazy for the decorative wares, porcelain, textiles and images of the exotic East, and the Tsar's own country residence, Tsarskoe Selo, even had a fake Chinese village in its grounds. This fad served to remind the subjects of the Russian Empire that their fate did not only lie with Europe, but also far towards the rising sun, where Russian domains met the sea.

On the Pacific coast, Leonard Jägerskiöld found a superb harbour near a place the Chinese called Sea Cucumber Cliffs. At the time, it was home to a scattering of local fisherman, but Jägerskiöld thought it would be an excellent place to spend the winter. The cluster of huts and workshops that sprang up at the bayside was first called Jägerskiöld's Town, although by the time Mannerheim was born it had gained a new name, Vladivostok. The town was Russia's first attempt at a port on the Pacific coast, and its name, 'Rule of the Orient', was a blatant statement of Russian attitudes towards the Far East.[4]

Jägerskiöld's part in history would be largely forgotten, unlike that of Mannerheim's uncle, Adolf Nordenskiöld. Nordenskiöld had been an old college classmate of Mannerheim's father Carl Robert, and had fallen in love with Carl's sister Anna during a social occasion at Louhisaari. The couple had been married there, and the eldest of the Nordenskiöld cousins was born at the manor.[5]

Out of favour with the Russians after he had been implicated in a student skit at the Tsar's expense, Nordenskiöld had taken Swedish nationality, and was finding fame as a 'Swedish' explorer. His wife, however, spent much time back at Louhisaari with her own relatives, and Gustaf Mannerheim grew up with an aunt and cousins who waited intently for news of Nordenskiöld's seafaring exploits.

In 1868, the year after Gustaf's birth, Nordenskiöld sailed further north than anyone had before in the eastern hemisphere. He would break his own record in 1872 and 1875, and in 1878 Nordenskiöld sailed in search of the fabled north-east passage, an Arctic sea route to the Far East. He was not heard of for several months. News of the continuing adventures of Nordenskiöld eventually drifted back to Louhisaari. After wintering amid the frozen Siberian ice,

Nordenskiöld had successfully reached the Bering Strait, and was even now sailing in the Pacific.

On the last day of August 1879, Anna Mannerheim Nordenskiöld received a curt telegram from her prodigal husband, transmitted at great expense from Yokohama, Japan: 'ALL WELL. ADOLF.' Nordenskiöld had squandered most of his money sending a much longer message to the King of Sweden, and those three little words were the best that he could manage.[6]

Writing at greater length as his vessel left Nagasaki for the long voyage home, Nordenskiöld offered his prediction for the role that the Far East would play in the coming decades. As he saw it, the region would dominate the lives of the next generation:

> It is difficult to foresee what new, hitherto undreamed blossoms and fruit this ground will yield. But those Europeans who believe that it is only a matter of putting modern European dress on an old feudal nation of Asia, are very much mistaken. Rather, it seems to me that the day is dawning on an age when the lands surrounding the East Asian [sea] will play a truly important part in the further development of the human race.[7]

But while the future looked bright for the Nordenskiölds, their Mannerheim relatives faced a series of disasters. Gustaf Mannerheim's mother Hélène died in 1881, shortly after her bankrupt husband ran away to Paris with his mistress. Although Mannerheim's father Carl Robert would soon return to Helsinki with his new wife and their infant daughter Marguerite, 'Kissie', they would not, could not mix in the same circles as the family of the late Hélène. The surviving Mannerheim children were split up and raised in the homes of relatives after their mother's death, scattered across Sweden and Finland, and staying in touch largely by letter.

It was Uncle Albert who inherited the wayward 13-year-old Gustaf Mannerheim, already nicknamed *Vildboken* ('Madcap') by his siblings and suspended from a Helsinki school for smashing the windows. It was Uncle Albert who had reluctantly carried out Hélène's wish to send Mannerheim to the Hamina cadet school, and who stoically endured his ward's rebellious teens. Mannerheim's name was rarely out of the Hamina logbook of student misdemeanours, with citations that include laughing during dance class, exiting a classroom by the window instead of the door, general laziness, not paying attention, talking in class, a series of unspecified 'misbehaviours', cheating in an exam, and fighting with a younger cadet.[8]

In 1886, after a far from illustrious career at Hamina, Mannerheim was apprehended in the countryside after having gone absent without leave on Good Friday. It was the final straw, and the boy was asked to leave before he could be expelled. At the end of his tether, Uncle Albert agreed to Mannerheim's latest scheme.

At first, Mannerheim was as glad to be rid of Hamina as Hamina surely was to be rid of him. However, any hopes he may have had of running off to sea for a life of adventure like Nordenskiöld were soon given short shrift – quite possibly by Nordenskiöld himself.

> As a matter of fact, I intended to become a sailor. It was only later, when a friend of my father persuaded me to complete my studies and get my school certificate and give up my ideas of the sea, that I began to seriously consider what I had said as a joke.[9]

When it became clear that he really had no choice, he boasted to his classmates that he was not being pushed out so much as choosing to leave, so that he might enrol at the prestigious Nikolayevskoye Cavalry School in St Petersburg.

This was news to Uncle Albert, but it had a certain appeal. Mannerheim's removal from Hamina had killed any chance of joining the Finnish army, but he might still win a chance to study in Russia, at a St Petersburg cavalry school. This would mean, however, a prolonged period in Russia, where Mannerheim's relatives feared he would go native. Nevertheless, after 18 months cramming, and two summers spent billeted at a Russian military camp through the connections of a family friend, Mannerheim took the entrance exams, passed even in Russian, and found himself at Nikolayevskoye.

The Cavalry School occupied three rectangular city blocks in St Petersburg, with a majestic stone façade, classical architecture and its own regimental chapel. Behind the outer buildings, there were extensive mews for the horses and three *manège* areas, training hangars for practising horsemanship. The living quarters for the first and second squadrons overlooked the central mews; those for the third and fourth squadrons were across the street.[10]

St Petersburg was a cosmopolitan city, an imperial hub that attracted residents from all over Eurasia. Mannerheim's Swedish-accented Russian was nothing unusual in a city where the upper classes preferred to speak French, and the markets were crowded with Eastern Europeans who, despite the efforts to stamp it out by the Tsar, still used German as a *lingua franca*. There were six other Finns in Mannerheim's class, but generally, the only time Finnish was heard in St Petersburg was below stairs – many poor Finns had flocked to the capital to work as servants.

The students in the Cavalry School's lower grades were described as 'vermin', and forbidden from using the same staircase as their superiors, a bizarre rule which the younger Mannerheim would have been sure to break as soon as possible. However, the old 'Madcap' had changed for good. Mannerheim soon demonstrated a natural aptitude for horse riding. He excelled at dressage, fell in love with polo, and was the first of his year to 'win spurs' for horsemanship. When the time came to make the announcements of the first term's grades, Gustaf Mannerheim's highest grade was for Good Conduct.[11]

That Christmas in 1887 several Mannerheims assembled at the von Julin home. Sophie Mannerheim reported that her brother was almost unrecognisable; he was tall and gaunt, and came across as alarmingly 'Russian' in his manner. In Helsinki, his father and elder brother also noted the change in his character, and did not wholly approve of his newfound condescension towards civilians.

Life at the school continued to drain his, or rather Uncle Albert's, finances. After seeing Mannerheim off, Albert had given him an allowance that was supposed to last an entire month. Instead, Mannerheim found the money leaking away with great speed. As the first to gain a commendation, he now had the 'honour' of buying celebratory cakes for all his classmates. Soon afterwards, all students were ordered to contribute 15 roubles each to aid in the decoration of their *manège*. 'After these expenses,' commented a rueful Mannerheim, 'my purse is empty.'[12]

In 1888, a bout of typhoid cost Mannerheim dearly in the exams, and would eventually lead to his graduation at the lower rank of second lieutenant. He did, however, make it back to the School in time for the annual field trip, a prolonged sojourn in the Russian countryside at Krasnoye Selo ('Beautiful Village'), a resort to the south of the capital close to Tsarskoe Selo ('Imperial Village') where the Tsar had his summer residence. There, the cadets studied subjects that were unfeasible in urban St Petersburg, including camp construction and gunnery, at which Mannerheim did not excel. However, he was to surprise himself and his teachers with a newfound aptitude for drawing maps, coming top of his class.[13]

Back in St Petersburg for their second year, the cadets gained extra privileges. They did their horse drills outdoors in all but the coldest weeks of winter, and made once-weekly rides through the centre of St Petersburg. Mannerheim continued to be plagued by ill health, and by family concerns that he was not eating well enough. Uncle Albert continued to grumble about the expense of maintaining a cavalry cadet, and was forced to spend over a thousand roubles on Mannerheim's upkeep during the two-year course. A basic uniform alone cost 200 roubles, and that was before allowances were made for wear and tear, and hidden extra payments.

For the hard-pressed guardian, Mannerheim's successes at the School were a mixed blessing. It was, Albert admitted, good news to hear that Mannerheim had found a deep-seated love for equestrian sports, winning great honours on the polo team, or had been awarded a silver tassel and shoulder sash for excellence in fencing. It was less agreeable to hear that Uncle Albert was now obliged to pay for such badges of honour.[14] Nor was he pleased to hear that officers were also responsible for contributions to the salaries of their grooms and stable boys. Mannerheim's letters tried to persuade his family that every decoration counted for something.

Getting through the School in Russia can be a matter of chance. You can never trust it to be a just affair. Because I have no lofty patron or wealth, I have to gain recommendations by serving in fine regiments, because uniform means so much more in Russia than you can imagine. I know some young officers who have been sent away on a whim from the School just before the final exams, simply because they were in the line regiment and it was not good enough for some professor.[15]

Uncle Albert's patience ran out in 1889. There were rumours that Mannerheim's old rebellious nature had reasserted itself, and that he ended his time at the School within a hair's breadth of expulsion, after a loud altercation with a superior officer on the train back to Krasnoye Selo from St Petersburg in July. Mannerheim, it transpired, had been at a favourite pub with fellow cadets all day, and then got into a drunken argument over the subject of Finnish autonomy. That, at least, is what he claimed to the fuming Uncle Albert, who might be expected to be mollified at least a little by the story that Mannerheim had been standing up to Russians on Finland's behalf.

Mannerheim swore that he would never drink to excess again. The damage, however, was done. He lost his previous top grades in Good Conduct, was stripped of his fencing honours, and fell in the class ranking from an impressive 2nd place to a mediocre 30th out of 84. Mannerheim volunteered for extra shifts of guard duty, and twice thwarted attempted robberies, which helped drag his grades back up again. But it was to no avail. Previously, Mannerheim had been so sure of graduating in the top section of his class that he had already ordered a commemorative plaque. But his fall from grace came far too close to the end of the academic year for him to reinstate himself. He was lucky to claw his way back to 10th place in the remaining time.[16]

Despite this setback, Mannerheim finished his cadet training by graduating at the rank of cornet: not a dishonourable end to his schooling. He had even managed to scrape back a first-class grade in Good Conduct. It was the hope of his family that he would return to Finland and a civil career, although they feared that he would desire to remain in Russia.

The prize commission for someone leaving the School was a post with the Chevalier Guards Regiment – a military posting at the heart of the Tsar's empire that brought with it a direct relationship with the Imperial Family and a fast-track into Russian high society. But Uncle Albert thought that Mannerheim had mixed up his sense of cause and effect. Chevalier Guards were part of the elite *because* they were rich. One had to be independently wealthy to become a Guard as they had to provide all their own equipment. Chevalier Guards wore white tunics with silver chasing, and white breeches made of the softest buckskin. It was considered improper for the breeches to be creased, and so the leggings were made deliberately skin-tight, and had to be soaped up and put on wet. The knee-high black boots were similarly troublesome, and most Chevalier Guards required a manservant merely to help them dress. For 'active' duty, the Chevalier Guards wore polished silver cuirasses and bright silver helmets topped by a Russian eagle, which they jocularly referred to as The Pigeon. At state occasions and balls, they substituted their armour for a scarlet waistcoat adorned with the star of the Order of Saint Andrew. Chevalier Guards might well cut an impressive dash through Russian parties in their ostentatious uniforms but, as Albert pointed out, *someone* had to pay for the seven different basic uniforms required. In fact, an officer's salary, even in an everyday regiment, was rarely enough to cover the costs of *being* an officer. Uncle Albert had agreed to support Mannerheim through cavalry school, but reminded Mannerheim that he had other wards to support, and that the Uncle Albert line of credit should now be regarded as at an end. Mannerheim was in his twenties, and it was about time he started supporting himself.[17]

When the day came for the passing-out parade, Mannerheim was not clad in the white tunic and silver cuirass of the Chevalier Guards. Instead, he wore the dress uniform of the 15th Alexandra Dragoon Regiment, widely known as the Hussars of Death for their jet-black uniforms with silver trim, and their gothic affectation for only riding black horses.

The Hussars of Death were billeted in Poland, near the German border in the town of Kalisz. Although Mannerheim came to develop a respect for the Poles, it was a sobering sight for him to see how his own country might be treated if the love affair with Russia ever soured. Mannerheim found Kalisz to be picturesque,

if remote at the furthest western reaches of the Russian empire, on the German border over a hundred miles west of Warsaw. He was less impressed with his regiment, particularly its commanding officer Fyodor Boborykin.

> The Commander of the Regiment is a complete failure, and the soldiers don't care for him in the slightest. There is one scandal after another, and confinement in the main guardhouse is the order of the day. There's no opportunity for socialising, and most of the ladies in the Regiment seem to be of common ancestry, dubious by both reputation and manner.[18]

At the time, Kalisz was 70 miles from the nearest train station, making it impossible for jaunts home like those Mannerheim had often made from St Petersburg. The town contained a large Jewish population that rarely mixed with the native Poles. Mannerheim was taken aback by the lack of Poles in business, a situation that only became apparent when he tried to buy supplies shortly after arriving, only to discover it was the week before Yom Kippur and all the Jewish-owned stores were closed.[19]

The only thing that the Poles and Jews could agree on was that they were wary of the Russians, forcing the cavalry officers to rely largely on each other's company. It was Mannerheim's first time in command of the normal Russian soldier, whom he found to be 'docile and easy to handle, and when treated fairly, he becomes devoted to his officers.' Since most chores at the Kalisz barracks could usually be accomplished by midday, this left the afternoons and evenings for endless rounds of vodka-fuelled card games.[20]

Mannerheim determined to make the best of the regiment's resources, proclaiming that 'there was no lack of work for those who took their duties seriously.'[21] He took part in military manoeuvres near Warsaw, determined to get as much experience as he could at defusing mines, bridge building and military road construction. He took his troops out on exercises, only to discover that his military readiness was causing difficulties for officers who wanted an easy life. His commander tried to talk the young Mannerheim out of excessive training, pleading that squadron leaders had a fixed budget for horse feed; if the horses rarely left the stables, their food intake remained low and the officers could pocket the budgetary surplus. But Mannerheim's unit, with its long rides and exhausting work-outs, was soon eating its way through a far larger food supply, making it difficult for anyone to cream off any profits.

All the while, Mannerheim's relatives intrigued to get him brought back from Poland to a commission in the Chevalier Guards in St Petersburg. The reluctant Uncle Albert had been won round with the assurances that Mannerheim's grandmother would write off his debts in her will. It was godmother Alfhild who pulled the necessary strings, using contacts among the Empress's ladies-in-waiting to suggest that Mannerheim was being wasted out on the frontier. Just over a year after Mannerheim had reported for duty in Poland, he received word that a place had been found for him in the Chevalier Guards.[22]

It was perhaps misleading to call the Chevalier Guards the 'best unit' in the Russian army. The Guards certainly had the best connections and the most ostentatious appointments, and they moved in high circles. However, beyond the ceremonial duties of guarding the Tsar's family, and the annual military exercises at Krasnoye Selo, a Guardsman did not expect much in the way of hazardous duty. The Guards' horses hardly left the stables during the winter months, when the officers busied themselves with fireside activities. For many of the officers, a career in the Guards was merely a means of having a place in Russian social circles, and they did everything they could to avoid the more strenuous aspects of military routine. Mannerheim, however, could not afford such a luxury. He remained a careerist even within the Guards, and volunteered to train the soldiers who had completed their first year.

Around the time that Mannerheim entered the Chevalier Guards in 1891, the Tsar began a grand project to link his capital with the furthest reaches of the empire, with the ultimate goal of a railway line that stretched all the way to Vladivostok on the Pacific coast. Transport connections were particularly important for St Petersburg, since the city had grown at such a pace that the surrounding farms were unable to support its vast population.

Mannerheim's famous uncle Nordenskiöld was now called upon

to put his knowledge of the Siberian coast to use in the service of the Tsar. Construction on what would become the Trans-Siberian Railway commenced in several places at once, and engineers were struggling to move resources to the farthest reaches of the line. With Nordenskiöld's advice, 6,000 steel rails were put on a ship in England, taken around the north of Russia, and then down the river Yenisei into the middle of Siberia.[23]

Work proceeded fast on the great railway. In 1891, Prince Nicholas, the 23-year-old heir to the Russian throne, was sent from St Petersburg to Vladivostok to mark the commencement of construction on the easternmost portion of the line that would eventually stretch all the way to Moscow. En route for his publicity stunt, it was decided that the prince would call in at Japan, in the hope that his presence would stir up amity and cooperation between the realm of the Tsar, and the realm of the Japanese Emperor, who now shared a common border. The trip, however, was a diplomatic disaster.

Expecting that the Russian prince would be devoutly observing the deprivations of a Russian Lent, his Japanese hosts did not arrange any entertainments for his first week in Japan. This was something of a misreading of the young prince's interests, as he had been painting towns red right across the world, and had been particularly looking forward to Japan after reading about the sexual availability of Japanese women in Pierre Loti's *Madame Chrysanthème*. Refusing to stay cooped up in Nagasaki harbour, Prince Nicholas sneaked off his ship when he was supposed to be praying and fasting. Instead, he hared around Nagasaki in a rickshaw, shopped madly for souvenirs and even got a tattoo.

Prince Nicholas continued his partying across Japan, writing excitedly in his diary of local colour, while Japanese secret police reports logged his excursions to geisha houses. There were, however, whispers abroad that Japanese radicals might be planning something far less welcoming for the prince. As his grand tour took him to Japan's former capital Kyoto and up to the shores of nearby Lake Biwa, the local authorities decided to double his police escort.

There is a certain irony in the fact that when someone did finally attempt to kill Prince Nicholas, the would-be assassin turned out to be one of his Japanese bodyguards. The crowd saw the man before Nicholas, whose first intimation of trouble was the glancing blow that sliced through the brim of his hat and left a gash on the right side of his head. Leaping from his rickshaw, clutching his bleeding wound, the prince fled from his sword-wielding pursuer, while his cousin Prince George of Greece struck the would-be assassin down with a bamboo cane. George was joined by the rickshaw drivers, who apprehended the man several conspicuous seconds before the tardy arrival of the police.[24]

The incident was a national embarrassment for Japan. In the immediate aftermath, the incumbent government resigned in shame, leaving the Meiji Emperor to offer his flustered apologies to the wounded foreign dignitary. Some 10,000 telegrams arrived wishing the prince a speedy recovery, and expressing the vain hope that he would not allow the incident to colour his opinion of Japan. There were genuine concerns in the Japanese government that Russia would use the incident as an excuse for war, and amid the desperate national attempts to atone for it, a woman in Kyoto slit her own throat.

The news was similarly shocking to the people of St Petersburg, particularly when early telegrams were misinterpreted as news of far graver wounds. The prince's mother ordered her son to leave Japan immediately; or rather, that was the excuse that a harassed Russian minister offered the Japanese when Prince Nicholas headed back to his ship instead of north to Tokyo as originally planned. Unsurprisingly, the wounded Nicholas left Japan under a cloud. He had arrived excited by what he saw as quaint traditions, erotic promise and imperial soul mates. He left describing the Japanese as baboons and conniving savages – an attitude that was to steer Russian policy in the Far East for the next twenty years.[25]

Talk in Russian military circles turned inexorably towards Russia's possessions in the Orient. Russia's steppe border extended for thousands of miles along the border with north China and was hotly contested in the area of Manchuria, the homeland of China's ruling dynasty. Beyond Manchuria, there was the tempting morsel of Korea, and the rich pickings of the Amur River valley. Vladivostok was Russia's port on the Pacific, but the harbour was iced over in the winter, and the Japan Sea, as the name implied, was entirely walled in by Japan. There remained those in the Russian service who hoped that Russia and Japan might cooperate in the exploitation of East Asian resources, but a growing majority began to suspect that war was inevitable.

As for Mannerheim, the last decade of the 19th century saw him become a family man. His *Memoirs* dismiss his family in a single sentence. 'As regards my personal life at that time, in 1892 I became married to Mademoiselle Anastasie Arapov, daughter of the late General Nikolai Arapov ... a former officer of the Chevalier Guards.' Despite Mannerheim's reticence, his nuptials were far more important to his career at the time, and lifted him temporarily from the penury under which he had struggled. [26]

It is unclear how Mannerheim and Anastasie first met. Family sources suspected, once again, the unseen schemes of his godmother Alfhild, who ensured that the 25-year-old officer bumped into the 20-year-old heiress at the right social functions. The Arapovs were a Moscow military family, but after the death of her parents, Anastasie and her sister were wards of their aunt, who lived in St Petersburg.

Anastasie had had the best education that her father's money could buy; she spoke Russian and French, and fancied herself as a musician and a painter. She was also, so her husband would later attest, notoriously indolent and impractical, raised in a rarefied environment that had left her unsuited for dealing with the real world. In one of her most notorious *faux pas*, she sent the cook out to the butchers with specific instructions to buy two pounds of liver, 'but make sure it has no bones in it.' [27]

Extant accounts of their courtship suggest that Mannerheim was far more attracted to Anastasie's younger sister, and that Anastasie had made her own interests so plain that Mannerheim felt ill at ease in her presence. If it is true that Mannerheim found Anastasie tiresome, he was soon dragged off for a talking-to from his godmother Alfhild. Perhaps Anastasie *was* starry-eyed at the thought of a tall, handsome baron from the Grand Duchy of Finland. But – Alfhild was blunt yet polite – Mannerheim should know that she was also very, *very* rich.

If Anastasie truly was a restless and effervescent spirit, entirely preoccupied with dances and music recitals, it is yet possible that she did not appreciate just how much money she had. Her father had left her substantial property in Moscow and the nearby countryside. Anastasie's personal fortune was valued at 800,000 roubles, with an additional income of 14,000 roubles a year from her investments and properties. Some of them, evidently, were in a state of disrepair, but all were valuable.

Extant photographs of Anastasie show an attractive, elegant, dark-haired Russian young woman, though the Mannerheim family disparaged her. Her in-laws unkindly described her striking features as 'pop-eyed' and 'matronly'. Nor did the Mannerheims approve of the wedding (or rather *weddings* – an Orthodox ceremony at the Chevalier Guards chapel, and a low-key Lutheran one at a relative's house later the same day), which was largely boycotted by the groom's side. Only the two Carls, the groom's father and brother, came to St Petersburg from among Mannerheim's close relatives. No money was forthcoming, not even from Uncle Albert, leading Mannerheim to lean on his bride's wealth for much of the cost of the nuptials. He supplanted part of the money himself with prizes he won in riding competitions and races at the Saint Michael *manège*.

Mannerheim's family soon paid a visit, however, in the form of his siblings Sophie and Johan, who were charmed by their new sister-in-law. Keen to impress people that she regarded as 'Swedes', Anastasie had decorated their house in blue and yellow, the colours of the Swedish flag. Before long, Mannerheim's father and elder brother could not resist the temptation to see for themselves. They returned distinctly unimpressed with Russia, but full of admiration for Anastasie, who chatted animatedly with her new in-laws in perfect French, and whose footmen had also been decked out in Swedish colours.[28]

The young couple soon travelled to meet the Mannerheims, von Julins and other relatives who had not graced them with their presence at the wedding. The couple chartered a steamer across the Baltic to Stockholm, where they called in for dinner with the many family members there, including Mannerheim's Aunt Anna and her husband, the famous explorer Nordenskiöld. Talk at the table turned to archaeology, as Nordenskiöld recounted his recent visit to Spain as part of the 400th anniversary celebrations of the discovery of the New World. Meanwhile, in America itself, Nordenskiöld's son was publishing a landmark archaeological study, *Cliff-Dwellers of the Mesa Verde*. Nordenskiöld, in particular, thought that Anastasie was a 'lovely bride', and Anastasie fell in love with Dalbyö, the country mansion that had been designed as a reminder of Aunt Anna's childhood at Louhisaari.

'Gustaf's wife,' wrote another aunt, 'looked healthy but plain.' She was also 'young and very alert, blue-eyed, with hair as blonde as ash, and a round face. Her appearance wasn't Russian, but European.'[29] Aunt Hanna, however, cannot have been paying too close attention — extant photographs clearly show Anastasie to have been a brunette.

Anastasie enjoyed less success with her in-laws in Finland, who remained deeply suspicious of the flighty Russian heiress, who was already eagerly styling herself Baroness Mannerheim. After a distinctly frosty reception at Louhisaari, Gustaf's grandmother Eva observed that 'Carl [Robert] seems to be happy with his ugly daughter-in-law. Indeed, the only way to make that girl look beautiful would be to paint her gold.'[30]

Anastasie loved aristocratic Sweden, but regarded Finland as something of a provincial anti-climax. She displayed little interest in returning there, and rarely accompanied Mannerheim on his subsequent visits. So it was, in Christmas 1892, when Mannerheim misled his relatives into believing that he would not be joining them at Louhisaari. He then sneaked into the manor and surprised them all, dressed as Santa Claus. They were delighted to see him and even happier to discover that he had not brought his wife.[31]

The couple's first daughter, named after her mother but nicknamed Stasie or Tasia, was born in April 1893. Anastasie was soon pregnant again, but the baby, a boy, was stillborn in late June 1894. Mother and father were both left heartbroken by the tragedy, and the boy was interred in St Petersburg's Smolensk Cemetery.[32] Mannerheim's father visited the family in St Petersburg shortly afterwards, and found the tension tangible. 'There is a tough atmosphere in their home,' he wrote, 'and no reason for it on the husband's part.' Cause and effect, of course, is all but impossible to assign in such cases, but if Mannerheim was not already seeking female company elsewhere, he was soon accused of doing so. On one occasion, Mannerheim supposedly went out to a charity event hosted by the society doyenne Countess 'Betsy' Shuvalova. He did not return until noon the following day, and went straight to bed, pleading exhaustion. It was one of many incidents that Anastasie would later cite as evidence of his infidelity.[33]

By the standards of his day, Mannerheim exhibited a stiff upper lip, a reaction that to modern readers might seem insensitive. He does not appear to have allowed the death of his unnamed son to have interfered with his work for the briefest moment, and reported for duty as usual with the rest of the Chevalier Guards at the annual Krasnoye Selo military manoeuvres. While he threw himself into his work, Anastasie was left grieving with an infant daughter. Starved of companionship and sympathy, she began attending séances in St Petersburg. Mannerheim deeply disapproved of such behaviour, despite Anastasie's claims to have communicated with the spirit of his late mother. Perhaps in a belated attempt to offer a distraction, he took his wife and the infant Tasia away on a long trip to Biarritz once the camp was over. The journey mended a few fences, at least for the time being. But new pressures would shortly come to bear.[34]

2

The Field of Vipers

At the turn of the 20th century, the Grand Duchy of Finland had its own stand at the Paris Exhibition. The event was used subtly to smuggle in some messages about the Finnish drive for independence from Russia, and the pavilion was decked out with murals by the artist Akseli Gallen-Kallela, depicting many famous moments from Finnish mythology.

Finnish mythology was, to a certain extent, a creation of the independence movement. The national myth, the *Kalevala*, had been assembled piecemeal by the author Elias Lönnrot through interviews and research conducted in the Finnish hinterland. It was an artificial construction, an idealistic evocation of what the myths of the native Finns might have been, had they not been stamped out by successive invasions of Vikings, Swedes and Russians. The poets, authors, composers and artists of the independence movement seized upon the *Kalevala* as a means of asserting Finnishness through the arts. Gallen-Kallela's images were loaded with symbolism, not the least the fresco *Ilmarinen Ploughs a Field of Vipers*, in which one of the evil snakes was later found to be wearing the crown of the Romanov Tsars.

The cause of the new-found bitterness that provoked the artists' promotion of the *Kalevala* was a process of 'Russification' – as had long been feared, the new Tsar would tire of the game of Finnish autonomy, and demand that Finland accept his rule without cavils or complaint. In the last decade of the 19th century, this new Tsar would demand 'Russia, one and indivisible'. Succeeding his father

in 1894, in answer to the rising nation-states in Europe, the new Tsar ordered his empire to present an outward face to the world of linguistic, military and institutional unity. Finland was pressured to embrace the Russian language, and to accept a new bill inducting Finnish men into the Russian army, not as volunteers like Mannerheim, but as conscripts. Nicholas II , the newest Tsar, would also be the last. If there was one thing he hated more than disobedient Finns, it was the Japanese.

The Mannerheims returned to a Russia in a sombre mood. Tsar Alexander III had died at his Crimean holiday home, unexpectedly propelling his wayward son, Prince Nicholas, onto the throne. The funeral took place in Moscow, with a silent procession of mourners that took two hours to pass, the only sound being the shuffling of feet on the cobblestones and the distant tolling of cathedral bells.

Nicholas was obliged to bring forward the date of his wedding to Princess Alexandra of Hesse, a favourite granddaughter of Queen Victoria, to 26 November, and encouraged to hold the ceremony in St Petersburg, before the largest number of subjects. It was, however, still a simple affair by Tsarist standards. Mannerheim, as a Chevalier Guard, spent the ceremony on watch duty at the Winter Palace. Since the country was still in mourning for the late Tsar, there was no reception, and the ceremony was over by the early afternoon.

Life went on, for the Russians and for the Mannerheims. On 7 July 1895, Anastasie gave birth at a St Petersburg maternity home to another daughter, Sophy – her name usually spelt thus to distinguish her from her aunt. Mannerheim makes only the briefest of comments about his children in his *Memoirs*, and even then only when they are fully-grown. In fact, he appears to have regarded them as, at best, a mild irritation. In old age, Tasia recalled that her childhood memories largely comprised being sent out of the room by a Mannerheim preoccupied with adult matters, and that they hardly got along any better when she was an adult.[1]

The new Tsar, now styled Nicholas II, was not crowned until May 1896. Mannerheim played a key role in the Moscow service, which he described as 'the most exhausting ceremony I have known'. Four officers of the Chevalier Guards stood before the amassed dignitaries on the steps of the cathedral, standing to attention for four and half hours 'with a heavy cavalry sabre in one hand and the helmet crowned with the imperial eagle in the other'.[2]

When the ceremony ended, Tsar Nicholas II walked in a procession to the imperial palace, resplendent in gold brocade and an ermine cape, and flanked by dozens of retainers who carried an ornate canopy above his head. Mannerheim can be seen in extant photographs, marching directly in front of the glowering Tsar, his eyes obscured by the visor of his helmet.

Mannerheim caught a glimpse of the banquet that awaited the Tsar and his consort at the palace, with the Chevalier Guard standing to attention with drawn sabres, while trembling, obsequious courtiers brought food to the table, leaving the chamber by walking backwards. A less sedate celebration was planned for the people four days later at Khodynka Field, a large open space in north-west Moscow. Entertainers, stalls and small stages for dances and skits, kiosks dispensing food, and 'buffets' dispensing gifts were arranged across the field, while crowds of eager commoners gathered beyond the fence.

By dawn on the morning of the appointed day, thousands of Russians had assembled at the edge of Khodynka Field. The numbers swelled to gargantuan proportions because of rumours that the Tsar's emissaries would be dispensing priceless treasures to the earliest arrivals. In fact, this was not true: the 'treasures' on offer were little more than a sausage in a roll, a piece of gingerbread and a kitsch coronation souvenir mug. This, however, was not what rumourmongers in the crowd had been mooting the previous evening, and the mob soon overwhelmed the 60 police officers sent to keep order.

The first Mannerheim heard of it was when a panicked call went up for the Chevalier Guards, still billeted in central Moscow for the coronation. 'We galloped through practically the whole of Moscow,' he wrote, 'and had scarcely drawn up at our destination on our lathering horses when we saw the Emperor and Empress, looking pale and serious ...'.[3]

Just as Mannerheim had been summoned to Khodynka, so had the Tsar, who heard at ten that morning that the crowd had reached such proportions that those at the front had been entirely unable to resist the pushing from the mob behind them. Many had fallen into the trenches, pits and wells that dotted Khodynka Field as the remnants of military manoeuvres. There, men, women and children were mashed into the dirt by the trampling of the crowd. Over a thousand people had been trampled to death in the rush for the mythical 'treasures' at the fair, and some 1,300 had been seriously injured. Even as Mannerheim and his fellow horsemen took in the scene of chaos, carts rolled past them.

'They were covered with tarpaulins,' Mannerheim remembered, 'from underneath which protruded a hand here, a lifeless foot there.'[4] The wagons were loaded with dead bodies, many of them crushed to a pulp, inert limbs protruding from the lumpen mass.

'At first,' observed the Tsar's sister, 'I thought the people were waving to us. Then my blood froze. I felt sick. Those carts carried the dead – mangled beyond recognition.'[5]

The grisly procession of death wagons was an attempt to clear the broken bodies from Khodynka Field before the Tsar's arrival. When the body count was found to be in the thousands, the marshals gave up and simply shovelled the dead under the imperial pavilion, in time for the Tsar's arrival.

Tsar Nicholas stayed for just twenty minutes before bolting from Khodynka. He reviewed a procession of soldiers that, if Mannerheim's memories are anything to go by, was in fact a hastily assembled march-past of military men who had arrived too late to prevent the tragedy. After a grim-faced rendition of 'God Save the Tsar' from the crowd, Nicholas and his wife clambered into an open carriage and fled the scene.

Many regarded it as a terrible omen. It was certainly remembered by many revolutionaries as an example of where the people stood in the Tsar's affections. When an Austrian archduke had died a month before, the Tsar had cancelled all festivities out of respect, but when over a thousand of his subjects were trampled to death in a fight for a free mug, he ordered business as usual.

With forced jollity, Nicholas led his bride that evening in the dancing of a quadrille with three aristocratic couples, while the new Empress did her best to hide a red face and eyes puffy from prolonged weeping. For the many thousands of people nursing their injuries or mourning their loved ones on the night of the Khodynka Field tragedy, the enduring memory of the day was that the Tsar spent the evening enjoying himself at a lavish ball.

Not long after the ill-starred coronation of the Tsar, Manner-heim's role in the Chevalier Guards began to change. His aptitude for appraising, buying and training horses had not gone unnoticed among his superiors, and he was seconded to the Court Stables Unit in 1897. He would eventually be promoted to *stallmeister*, deputy responsible for all the imperial stables. It was still a decade before the motor car began to make its presence felt in St Petersburg, and even then, automobiles would first be regarded as toys for the rich. An appointment to the imperial stables, then, was far more prestigious than it might appear to the modern reader. Mannerheim was technically a member of the Imperial Household, responsible directly for the transporting of the Imperial Family on any days that they were not using their train or sailing off on the imperial yacht. Whenever a member of the Imperial Family made a public appearance, it was Mannerheim who liased with the Tsar's security division, bringing him into close contact with the daily lives of the Tsar's family.[6] The commission brought with it a swish apartment near the court stables and another residence in the country, along with obligations to travel far and wide in search of good breeding stock and new mounts for the cavalry.

If Mannerheim thought of the position as a soft option, he would soon find out how wrong he was. In 1898 in Berlin, he was examining a potential mount when the horse lashed out and kicked him in the knee, breaking it in five places. The injury secured the sympathy of the Kaiser himself, who entertained the limping Mannerheim at a banquet, at which talk studiously avoided discussion of the long-term effects of the damage. The Kaiser's own doctor had examined Mannerheim's leg and informed him that the knee was likely to remain permanently stiff.

'He consoled me by saying that even if I should find it hard to command a squadron, I would be able to command a regiment,' wrote Mannerheim, 'and that nothing prevented me from becoming a distinguished general.'[7] In other words, if Mannerheim were

lucky, he might hope to be promoted far enough up the ranks that a stiff knee stopped being an issue. Until that point, he risked disqualifying himself from active service. Determined not to accept the diagnosis, he rested for two months, and followed the recuperation with extensive exercises that, as far as he was concerned, 'more or less' restored his knee to normal.

It was, ironically, the closest Mannerheim had then come to seeing action. He saw the dawn of the 20th century without ever having fought in a battle, and his sole 'war wounds' had been inflicted by horses. His family, both in St Petersburg and Finland, were eminently happy with such a state of affairs, but Mannerheim the career soldier knew that he had advanced as far as he was able without experience of the battlefield.

In previous years, Russia had been a conspicuous champion of Chinese sovereignty in Manchuria, not necessarily to benefit the Chinese, but to keep Japan from occupying the territory. At the end of the Sino-Japanese War in 1895, the victorious Japanese had hoped to occupy large areas of Chinese territory, only to be forced out by a Triple Intervention from Russia, France and Germany. The move had gained Russia concessions for the Trans-Siberian Railway, and also a lease on the coastal town of Port Arthur. Unlike frosty Vladivostok, Port Arthur was a warm water harbour, ideal for the Russian Pacific Fleet, and ominously close to Beijing.

In 1900, China was plunged into an international crisis over the Boxer Uprising, a rebellion orchestrated by a religious cult of anti-foreign agitators. The unrest in Beijing had an unforeseen consequence when some of the Boxer rebels destroyed a portion of the Tsar's precious Trans-Siberian Railway. Nicholas II wasted no time in ordering troops into Manchuria to protect Russian interests – a decision that annoyed both the Chinese and the Japanese.

The Tsar's relative Kaiser Wilhelm II summed up the mood of the time, when he proclaimed that he hoped the retaliation would ensure 'no Chinaman will ever dare to even squint at a German'. But the Kaiser had been spouting such rhetoric for many years, and had been stirring up the Tsar's anti-Japanese feelings since before Nicholas was even crowned. 'I shall certainly do all in my power to keep Europe quiet,' he had assured him, 'and also guard the rear of Russia so that nobody shall hamper your action towards the Far East! For that is clearly the great task of the future: for Russia to cultivate the Asian continent and to defend Europe from the great Yellow race.'[8]

Many in St Petersburg would have agreed with the Kaiser's inflammatory remarks. Popular feeling in the capital held that mastery of the Orient was Russia's manifest destiny, and that it was sure to come after skirmishes with the Chinese, whose territory they were on, and the Japanese, who coveted the same territory for themselves.

Caught up in the fervour for Russia's interests in the Far East, Anastasie Mannerheim volunteered to be a nurse at the far end of the Trans-Siberian Railway. Mannerheim was left in charge of the children, while Anastasie took the long route to Vladivostok, travelling by sea and stopping off en route at Singapore. A letter reached Mannerheim boasting that Anastasie was not seasick, and then nothing was heard for some time. Eventually news drifted back through the Red Cross that Anastasie had reached her destination, and had been posted to Khabarovsk, the 'second city' of the Russian Far East, on the banks of the Amur. It was, as Mannerheim commented to his family, a mercy that the town-loving Anastasie had been assigned to a place that had some semblance of city life. She was subsequently posted to the smaller city of Chita, where the genteel Russian lady was shocked and appalled by the treatment meted out to the local Chinese by the Russian soldiers.

After several months treating both Russian and Chinese patients, Anastasie suffered a carnival of disasters. A horse went wild, overturning Anastasie's sleigh, breaking her leg and trapping her beneath it in sub-zero temperatures. When rescuers eventually arrived, there was no doctor present, and Anastasie painfully set her own broken bones. Deciding to return home, she was unable to book a berth on a passenger train, and was forced to limp onto a goods train. As if her luck were not already bad enough, her carriage was derailed and then caught fire with her trapped inside. By the time she returned to St Petersburg, she had had enough of the Far East to last her a lifetime.[9]

Anastasie was back in St Petersburg for Christmas 1901. Despite the couple's differences, her adventures led to a brief thaw in the relationship between her and her husband. Mannerheim wrote that his daughters were overjoyed to see their mother again, although they were so used to seeing their father hobbling around the house on crutches after minor falls from horses that they were completely blasé at the sight of their injured mother.[10]

'The leg worries me,' Mannerheim wrote to his sister Eva, 'because her whole body is exhausted with the inhuman labours that she has endured.' But Anastasie had deeply impressed her husband, largely because she had done something that resonated with his own obsessions – she had volunteered for a form of military service. 'If someone had said a year and a half ago that she was capable of such feats, I would not have believed it. But she can be happy in the knowledge that she has brought aid and joy to some 600 ailing soldiers, and I believe that is a good thing to know.'[11]

But Anastasie's trip to Manchuria had not been for Mannerheim's benefit; it had been a symptom of a greater malaise, and while her leg eventually healed, their marriage did not. A year after her return from the Far East, she fled Russia for France, taking the girls with her and seeking asylum with Mannerheim's sister Eva in Cannes. At first it seemed like another temporary sojourn, but after intense negotiations, Eva wrote to Mannerheim with the news that Anastasie would not be coming back.

Mannerheim thanked his sister for her efforts, in a letter whose tone suggested that although he understood that Anastasie had left him for good, Anastasie had not told him so herself. 'Out of principle,' he added, 'I have given her as little information about myself as possible, so that her nerves might calm down and the children might not be caught in the crossfire.'[12] His choice of words seems strange – as if Anastasie believed that her husband had been unfaithful, but that although she was wrong on this occasion, she had been inadvertently right on others. One allegation, not published until almost a century later, was that Anastasie had returned from Manchuria to discover that her husband was having an affair with the famous Ekaterina Geltser, the newly appointed lead ballerina at the Bolshoi.[13]

Anastasie settled in Paris with the girls, and correspondence between husband and wife thereafter was usually indirect, through Mannerheim's father, Carl Robert, and revolved solely around financial matters and the girls' schooling. The true reason behind their break-up remains obscure, although in later life Mannerheim was prepared to concede that both sides were at fault, and had entered into their marriage with unrealistic expectations. The girls hated the 'English-style' boarding schools to which they were now subjected, and Mannerheim was dismayed in later life at their lack of command of Swedish. He made many efforts to influence Anastasie's choice of school and holiday destinations, but was forced to concede that the quarters of a Russian cavalry officer, now once more fallen on hard times, was no place to raise two young girls. Consequently, the daughters remained with their mother until their late teens, but flew that nest as soon as was humanly possible.

The Mannerheim girls had left behind an increasingly tense atmosphere in Russia. Tsar Nicholas II had no time for elected assemblies or constitutional reform, which he called a 'senseless dream'. He made it known that he had every intention of pursuing an autocratic regime very much in the style of his late father. Nicholas also seemed less willing to embrace his dual role as Tsar and Grand Duke of Finland. Previous Russian rulers had indulged Finland's peculiar situation as an autonomous region within the empire, but Nicholas initiated a series of schemes to hold Finland closer to Russia. The Finnish army was disbanded, the Finnish cadet schools shut down, and the Finnish parliament had most of its powers removed. From then on all correspondence between Finnish government offices was required to be in Russian, Russian language teaching was increased in schools, and Finns were subject to conscription into the Russian army. Governor-General Nikolai Bobrikov, who ruled Finland in the Tsar's name, was given new powers to fire unruly officials and ban newspapers. After decades of relatively benign co-existence with Russia, Finland was being transformed into a Russian province with alarming rapidity.

Many younger Finns saw the reforms as a betrayal of constitutional agreements between Russia and the Grand Duchy. The painter Eetu Isto allegorised the issue in his painting *Hyökkäys* (*The Attack*), which became a widely circulated print. In it, a white clad, blue-scarfed maid, representing Finland, is set upon by a vicious double-headed eagle, which tries to snatch a large book of law from her grasp. Less artistic protests also mounted, and a petition bearing half a million signatures was sent to the Tsar, who did not deign to look at it. Older Finns hoped to undo the damage through negotiation, but all could see that there was a renewed programme of Russification underway.

The Finnish opposition took many bizarre forms. When the Russian authorities refused to allow stamps bearing the Finnish lion to be used for mail within the empire, some Finns began refusing to put any stamps on their letters at all. They were then obliged to pay double the usual rate for an unstamped letter, but did so bloody-mindedly. Just to twist the knife, they then put their letters in envelopes that were decorated with large images of the self-same Finnish lion – a rampant, sword-wielding beast trampling on a distinctly oriental scimitar. The artist Akseli Gallen-Kallela, painter of the frescoes for the Finnish pavilion at the Paris Exhibition, joined in the fun by designing a fake 'stamp of mourning', which depicted the Finnish lion on a black background. Even though it was not legal tender, this design was used on some Finnish mail to make Finns' feelings clear.[14]

Mannerheim's own family were caught up in the growing independence movement. Aina Mannerheim, wife of his older brother Carl and a professional singer, gave several concerts designed to collect money for autonomous 'initiatives'. These soon attracted the attention of the authorities. The most notorious was scheduled for 9 May 1901, for which Carl attempted to place an advertisement in Helsinki's main Swedish and Finnish newspapers. Even though Carl already had police assent for the concert at the Helsinki University, the Tsar's censor refused to allow the newspapers to go to press while carrying the advert. Carl was then ordered to guarantee that proceeds from the concerts would not go to anti-Tsarist causes. When he refused to make any such promise, noting that his wife's money was hers to do with as she pleased, the concert permit was revoked.

Carl fought back with a new concert to be held at the fire department assembly hall on 14 May, with entrance by invitation only, albeit an invitation that anyone might secure by making a donation beforehand to Aina Mannerheim's 'Patriotic Fund'. Forced to switch venues yet again, the concert finally got under way at another public hall, only to be gatecrashed by the chief of police and the local governor Kaigodorov, the latter of whom had somehow obtained one of the 'private' invitations. Despite their threats, the concert went ahead – it seems that too many prominent Finns were present to risk an outright conflict. However, the thwarted police complained to Governor-General Bobrikov, and Carl's card was marked.[15]

In 1903, when Bobrikov gained further powers, Carl was among the first of the unruly elements who were ordered to leave Finland. Mannerheim was 'deeply hurt by this cruel and unjust blow' towards his brother, but even as he expressed his annoyance, his words hid family tensions. Mannerheim was unable to come to see Carl and Aina off as they sailed into exile because he was on duty, in St Petersburg, serving the very Tsar whose representatives had cast Carl out of the country.[16]

Mannerheim was the kind of Finn that the new Russian order admired, a man trained in Russia, speaking Russian, and directly serving the Russian throne. But back in Helsinki in the wake of Carl's exile, Mannerheim began to fear that he had advanced as far as he could in the Russian military. Even if Finns were not regarded as dangerous, he risked alienating many of his family unless he took a stand on the right side of the border. Despite all his years of long service in Russia, Mannerheim seriously considered resigning his commission. He discussed it in all seriousness with his father, Sophie and Johan, although pointedly not with Carl, as if he were sure already what his older brother's response would be. But, Mannerheim claimed, his younger brother, sister and father were all of the same mind – that he would accomplish nothing by resigning, and that it would be foolish for Mannerheim to throw away his career in Russia when he could conceiveably do more for Finland by remaining within the Russian system. Consequently, Mannerheim continued to serve in St Petersburg, even as his elder brother was cast out of Finland for anti-Tsarist agitation. Though he now hoped to help Finland's cause from inside the Russian establishment, he still hoped for a chance to rise swiftly through the ranks. Far in the east, an opportunity was just about to arise.[17]

Even though it had been several years since the Boxer Uprising, the Russian presence in Manchuria endured. The Japanese, still smarting from the Triple Intervention, had now entered an alliance with the British, part of the terms of which obliged the one to assist the other if conflict broke out with more than one foreign power. This was seen by the British as an attempt to cool down the situation in the Far East, but it had the opposite effect on the Japanese. As far as Japanese warmongers were concerned, the Anglo-Japanese Alliance made it possible for the Japanese to fight a small war against the Russians, sure in the knowledge that nobody would risk British involvement by coming to the Russians' aid.

The Japanese feared that Tsar Nicholas had his eye on Korea, a tempting parcel of land in the Pacific that sat in between Russian possessions at Port Arthur and Vladivostok. Military advisers to the Japanese Emperor warned that Korea would become a Russian colony within four years unless the Japanese acted. The concerns were entirely justified; the Kaiser, keen to keep the Tsar out of European affairs, had been stirring things up again, writing that, 'It is evident to every unbiased mind that Korea must be and will be Russian. When or how ... is nobody's affair and concerns only you and your country.'[18]

In August 1903, the Japanese minister in St Petersburg tried to calm things down. Kurino Shinichiro repeatedly asked to see the Russian foreign minister, with whom he wanted to arrange a conference, and for whom he had some proposals designed to establish who had proprietorial territory rights in the Far East. By the time Kurino was granted his audience, the Tsar had issued a proclamation guaranteed to rile the Japanese. Henceforth, all Russian interests east of Lake Baikal – military, economic and diplomatic – would be the purview of a newly created Viceroy of the Far East, Yevgeny Alexeiev. If the Japanese wanted to do any negotiating, they were welcome to set up a meeting in Tokyo with the Tsar's representative, a diplomat described by one of the Tsar's own ministers as a man with 'all the sly mentality of an Armenian rug dealer'.[19]

It was an outrageous loss of face. The Japanese were obliged to negotiate with a man whose very title implied a Russian sovereignty over East Asia. Nor did the viceroy even grace them with his own presence, sending a mere flunky to Tokyo. Russia proved implacable over terms in the Far East, and the Japanese were kept dangling for weeks waiting for the Tsar's tardy approvals of each clause. The Russians were banking on their belief that the Japanese would cave in rather than go to war. They were mistaken.

A meeting of the Japanese Emperor's highest officials, in the presence of the Emperor himself, had agreed that war was inevitable as early as January 1904. Thenceforth, any further negotiations were merely intended to keep the Russians busy while the Japanese military prepared for an attack. On 6 February, minister Kurino curtly notified the Russians in St Petersburg that negotiations were over, diplomatic relations were henceforth suspended, and the Japanese would take whatever actions they deemed necessary to preserve their position in the Far East.

Kurino's Russian counterpart in Tokyo was summoned to hear the same news. On returning to his legation, he heard that the Japanese navy had left port at dawn that morning, for an unknown destination. The minister was unable to warn St Petersburg, as all foreign telegraph messages had been suspended.

As far as the Japanese were concerned, 'whatever actions they deemed necessary' included military ones, and it should have come as no surprise to the Russians when, on 8 February 1904, the Japanese navy attacked them in several locations. The Russian reaction, particularly outside the Tsar's own court, was one of indignant affront, at what was seen as a violation of international law.

'Japan had decided on hostilities,' wrote Mannerheim, 'and ... without any previous declaration of war, the Russian squadron at Port Arthur was crippled by a Japanese attack. The transport of Japanese troops to the mainland could then proceed unmolested, and the Russian garrisons in Manchuria were too weak to resist the Japanese bridgehead in Korea.'[20]

The Japanese decision to attack had verged on the suicidal. Naval specialists had estimated that Japan might lose half of her ships in the conflict. Instead, the tactics of the Japanese Admiral

Tōgō Heihachirō, coupled with the lack of Russian preparation, led to an overwhelming Japanese victory. Matters were not helped by the fate of the Russian Pacific Fleet Admiral Stepan Makarov, who went down with his flagship when it struck a mine. Before long, Japanese land forces had swarmed across south Manchuria, seizing unprepared Russian forts. The Tsar's beloved Trans-Siberian Railway, while it linked east and west, did so only precariously and was not capable of immediately shipping thousands of soldiers with their equipment to fight a war. The Russian response consequently was slow, allowing Japanese advances to supersede even Japanese expectations.

With the outbreak of war, antipathy between Finland and Russia continued to grow, particularly since the war in Manchuria was an excuse for heavier censorship of Finnish newspapers. Finnish opinion about Manchuria was that it was a problem entirely of Russia's own making, and Finns were actively discouraged by their own countrymen from taking any part, even as ambulance drivers. The war was regarded as so inconsequential to the Finnish newspapers that some only reported its outbreak on their back pages, somewhere below the adverts for smelling salts and riding gear, an unpatriotic gesture for which Governor-General Bobrikov reprimanded them.

In 1904, Eugene Schaumann, a clerk at the Finnish Senate, shot the hated Governor-General Bobrikov three times before turning his gun on himself. Bobrikov briefly survived, and was rushed to a nearby hospital. According to Finnish popular myth, a nurse appeared at one of the windows and shouted to the anxious crowd outside that things were 'going in the right direction'. She meant, in typical Finnish bluntness, that Bobrikov was dying.[21]

Finns in Russia were developing a reputation as sneaky troublemakers, as servants with ideas above their station, and as unreliable subjects. At the time of the first call-up directly to the Russian army, fewer than half of the Finnish conscripts reported for duty. Such continued subtle agitation from the Finns had led to anguished strategic debates within the Russian government about whether Finns could be trusted in any sensitive posts at all. It was noted, for example, that Finns formed an uncomfortably

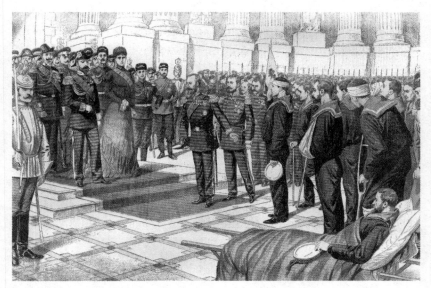

Flanked by a Chevalier Guard, the Tsar and his wife receive a party of wounded Russian sailors from the war in the east

large majority of the Baltic Sea pilots, on whose knowledge of shoals and shallows St Petersburg relied for safe shipping. If all the Finnish pilots were suddenly to go on strike, it would be as effective as a naval blockade against St Petersburg. Russian officials began swift measures to recruit and train Russian pilots, and hoped that none of their enemies had noticed the awful weakness. This, however, only showed up the difficulties of Finland's continued autonomous status. As Russian subjects, Finnish pilots and ship owners were free to dock (and, it was implied, cause mischief) all over the Russian empire. But the status was not reciprocal: Russian pilots were unable to work in Finland, and Russian ships had to pay higher docking fees as 'foreigners'.[22]

In June, Mannerheim decided to go to Manchuria himself – a resolution that threw his family into panic. His father travelled to St Petersburg in an attempt to change his mind, and Mannerheim was forced to justify himself in a letter to his exiled brother Carl. Carl and the younger Johan both strongly disapproved of Mannerheim's decision, and had made their feelings bluntly obvious in letters that Mannerheim found 'profoundly disturbing'. But, Mannerheim had made up his mind and, although he gravely regretted their opposition, he was determined to go.

'In war', he wrote, 'a man does not fight in support of a particular style of government, but for the army in which he serves. I don't think there is a great difference if he does it out of genuine loyalty or under duress, because he is merely doing an officer's duty.' Mannerheim stressed that, as in the case of Carl's exile, it would be futile for him to resign his commission. It was, in fact, better for Finland that there be Finns in the Russian army, the better to argue Finland's case and represent its interests. Mannerheim pleaded with Carl to understand that he was already 37 years old. He had spent half his lifetime training for a war that had not come, and before long, his operational usefulness as a regular soldier would be over. He implied that there would be plenty of time later for a desk job.

Mannerheim finished his letter to Carl with a grim change of subject. His finances were once again close to zero, and he was now obliged to support Anastasie and the girls in Paris. He was suffering from a deep depression, and had taken out two life insurance policies – one in German marks, the other in Swedish krona. 'Hence,' he wrote, 'I can with all conscience and purity of mind face the dangers of war. To my little girls in these sad circumstances, I am otherwise no use. I am so heavily in debt that I can barely survive by living with the utmost frugality ... If I remain in St Petersburg, my debts will only grow.' It would, Mannerheim seemed to be saying, almost be better for everyone if he died. [23]

3

The Baptism of Fire

Despite Mannerheim's bravado, it took a further three months for his transfer application to go through. As a Chevalier Guard, he required the approval of his superior officers, many of whom regarded the Manchurian conflict as a waste of time and resources, sure to be over with minimal fuss. Mannerheim's commanding officer even attempted to dissuade him from what he saw as a pointless transfer that could impede his chances of promotion within the Chevalier Guards; but Mannerheim stuck to his decision, arguing as he had done with his brother, that a military career without military action would be liable to stall his promotional opportunities in his forties anyway.

It was not until early October 1904 that he was assigned as a lieutenant-colonel to the 52nd Nezhin Hussars. Even then, he was initially assigned to the reserve, as there was no place for him at the front line.

Accustomed to buying his own equipment, Mannerheim went on a shopping spree on St Petersburg's main thoroughfare Nevsky Prospect, where he was a regular customer at the Nordenström winter wear emporium. Having been warned about the deprivations of the long Trans-Siberian journey, he stocked up on food, in addition to fur clothing and shoes designed to hold out a Manchurian winter. He also paid for three horses, including a charger he had been eyeing for some months. The six-year-old Talisman was the offspring of a famous racehorse, and had been the winner in a 7-furlong race in Tsarskoe Selo that summer. Talisman's owner

Bild Rtn Stefan. Nov. 1

had initially refused to sell him, but relented in October as Mannerheim made preparations to leave for the east.[1]

'He was a fantastic creature', Mannerheim wrote. 'From his sire, the derby winner, he had inherited a classical speed, and a high talent in racing and dressage, which I would bring to full vigour and ability on those wintry months in the Manchurian storms. Beside those rare qualities, there was a fine and fiery temperament, good pacing, flexible trotting, superb cantering and fantastic at the gallop ... If it hadn't been for his meanness to other horses, he would have been the perfect steed.'[2]

However, getting the horses to the Far East was no easy matter. The Trans-Siberian Railway, intended by the Tsar as the engine of his conquest and the lifeline of the Russian forces in the Far East, was still a single track for much of its length. The increased traffic of the war had stretched it to the limits of its capacity, and lesser cargoes were only transported when space was available. When it came to horses, this meant reserving a place in special equestrian carriages, each of which held eight animals. Unable to say for certain when he would be leaving, Mannerheim was unable to book passage for his mounts. Nor was he all that impressed with the furnishings – the equestrian carriages came with ventilation holes that he was sure would do more harm than good in a Siberian autumn.

Gaining little sympathy from over-stretched railway staff, Mannerheim leaned on his association with a conductor who had helped him transporting horses in the past. A regular cargo carriage was generously fitted out with blankets to stifle the noise and cold, and Mannerheim was told that his horses were likely to catch up with him in Harbin a few days later.

Mannerheim set off, first for Moscow, where, having missed a farewell from Betsy Shuvalova after she was held up by a broken wheel on her carriage, he climbed aboard the Trans-Siberian. The train's coaches were now augmented with steel shutters in case of attack by Japanese-sponsored bandits – the *Hong Huzi*, or 'Red Beards'. Four days later, his train reached a nondescript section of track beside a small white obelisk marking the boundary in the Ural mountain range between Europe and Asia.

As an officer, Mannerheim travelled in relative comfort, and became worn out merely by the monotony of spending day after day in the company of the same men in the restaurant car, there being nowhere else to go. The length of his journey served to impress upon him the difficulties of fighting a war at such a distance. The Russian newspapers were full of dismissive reports of Japanese military strength, convinced that it would only take the arrival of the properly-trained Russian army, with better luck and no duplicitous sneak attacks, for the war to be over before it could even start.

Mannerheim's train trundled for days through forests and empty plains. When it finally reached Lake Baikal, it had to stop. The Trans-Siberian Railway was not yet complete – in winter tracks were laid across the ice, but in summer train passengers were obliged to cross Baikal in boats, and then join a new train on the opposite shore. The carriages on the far side of Baikal were even less well appointed than those in the west. There was no longer a restaurant car, and prolonged military use had made the trains filthy.

In Chita, Mannerheim saw his first real-life Chinese, a thin, hunched officer accompanied by two lower ranks, smiling and bowing to the occupants of each carriage, in what Mannerheim guessed to be a cursory customs inspection – the train might technically be on Chinese soil, but the railway was under Russian jurisdiction, no matter what the Chinese may have claimed.[3]

The vital junction on the Trans-Siberian in China was the station of Harbin, 'the Moscow of the East'. From there, there was a line all the way down to Port Arthur itself, with connections to Beijing by land and sea. Arriving several days ahead of his horses, Mannerheim soon exhausted the delights of Harbin. The Russian town was built in imitation of a European city, and was new enough that its central areas had been planned to the nearest inch. Straight, bold boulevards radiated out from the station, although all too soon the buildings gave way to Chinese slums. It was also obvious that a war was close by – many buildings had been converted into hospital wards, and several mansions and public buildings had been commandeered for military use.

Rather than lurk in Harbin for a few more days, Mannerheim took advantage of an officer's discount on train fares and continued

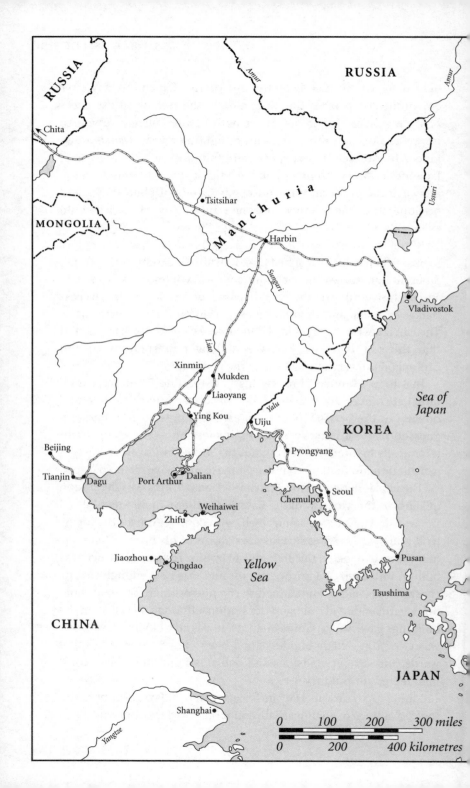

east to Vladivostok. His diary records two days of sightseeing, restaurants visited, ships seen in the harbour and the prices in the local shops, although he neglects to mention who accompanied him. Instead, the Vladivostok pages have three suspicious gaps where Mannerheim later excised material. 'In fact,' he confessed to Sophie, 'I have a lady friend to whom I am very attached, who works in a hospital not far from Vladivostok. She was kind enough to come and join me for two days, touring the city. It was so wonderful to see her as I sped off to the front. But let this just be between the two of us.'[4]

In the pages of his diary, which he knew would be seen by others, Mannerheim noted that he was a little taken aback by the number of Russian women in the area. Chinese girls were in short supply, and he reported that those few whom he did see were unattractive. Instead, Manchuria seemed to be crawling with attractive young Russian ladies, offering companionship to lonely soldiers. 'In the station of Tian Ling there are a lot of pretty women, whose profession is certainly without a doubt,' he wrote. 'I later discovered that they were "full service nurses" who worked for an institution called Miss Maud's Complete Nursing, originally established in Ying Kou, but soon diversifying its franchises as far afield as Mukden, Harbin and Tian Ling.'[5]

Not all the women were prostitutes. Others claimed, truthfully or otherwise, to be the recently widowed spouses of soldiers on the front, who had come out to the east to support their husbands, only to find themselves marooned far from home with dwindling finances. Newspapers of the time referred euphemistically to an 'Army of Women' from central Russia, which somehow managed to ship itself eastwards with better success than many of the regiments that were supposedly commandeering the trains. The incidental details of one story are particularly telling – a woman arrested for soliciting, who sobbed that she had been stranded in the Far East after travelling from St Petersburg to be at her 'husband's' deathbed. In fact, she was a soldier's long-term mistress, who had accompanied him to the East because she had no means of support in St Petersburg when he was not there. Sexually transmitted diseases were on the rise in the eastern regiments, forming a new front for the Russian army to resist. Mannerheim, however, had other battles to fight, initially against nothing so dangerous as boredom. [6]

By the time Mannerheim reached his post, the war had ground to a temporary standstill. Far to the south, the Russian harbour at Port Arthur was under siege. The Japanese, who had successfully taken the port once before, from the Chinese in 1894, had not expected the Russian defensive improvements to be quite so impregnable, a cause of great embarrassment when successive bloody assaults failed to take the town. With the Japanese under General Nogi Maresuke dug in all around Port Arthur, a second army pushed north to take the vital railway junction at Liaoyang. The Russian forces had fled north for Mukden, leaving the railway to Port Arthur in Japanese hands, and turning the next stage of the battle into a series of skirmishes over the rivers that formed natural boundaries in the area. Mannerheim's unit was some 15 miles south of Mukden, waiting for mobilisation orders, while the generals in Mukden bickered over their next step.

Mannerheim waited in vain for reinforcements and new supplies, over endless days of inactivity. He was billeted in the remains of a grimy Manchurian village with only a few buildings still standing. With very little sign that a war was going on, he and his fellow soldiers were expected to remain until further orders arrived. Nobody among the hussars expected orders any time soon, as there were few in the military command with any appreciation of what cavalry might be used for in Manchuria. Until such time as a cavalry supporter was appointed to the strategists on staff, none of the hussars expected to get any orders at all.

Mannerheim and his comrades were quartered in a huddle of nondescript clay sheds with thatched roofs. 'Our village has six huts in some sort of inhabitable condition,' he wrote to his brother Johan, 'and seven of us living in a room that is barely two-thirds the size of your lounge ... The weather during the day is lovely, but at night it gets rather cold. Big paper windows let in the air but do not spare us the freezing winds.' [7]

Their horses were stabled nearby in an even less accommodating hut made from a wattle of sorghum straw. Sorghum grass seems to have been the basic crop of the surrounding fields. Mannerheim reported that it was as tall as a horse and rider before harvesting, but that the fields looked bare and desolate without it.

'It's quite remarkable,' he wrote, 'that we are out here in a war zone and yet we are entirely unable to follow what is happening. We rarely see any newspapers, but if some do turn up, they are God-knows-how old, and tied up in a bundle that arrives all at once.'[8]

Mannerheim makes no mention of locals, but several Chinese terms creep into his letters, suggesting that he heard them being used. Someone, it seems, came around to sell the soldiers local produce. Apart from the ever-present mud, the only item available in large quantities was booze – sorghum being ideal for fermenting grain alcohol. By the time Mannerheim had arrived, his bunkmates had drunk their way through a significant quantity of *gaoliang* moonshine. However, he was soon able to report that, 'Drinking of hard liquor has, thank God, diminished and I think that's largely on my account ... I find it ridiculous that I should have become some sort of temperance activist and moral sermoniser, but you can guess how necessary it was if I tell you that our room amassed 82 bottles of alcohol in just 18 days.'[9]

Apart from the occasional cannon shot in the distance, there was little sign that Mannerheim's squadron was anywhere near a war zone. 'The ennui continues,' wrote Mannerheim to his father. 'We have come to believe that the Japanese are not planning to advance any farther, but will dig in until we can push them out of their fortifications.'[10]

While more men and provisions were moved across land on the Trans-Siberian, Russia sent its not-so-secret weapon by sea. A squadron was peeled away from the Baltic Fleet, and sent to replace the ships lost at Port Arthur. Sailing under the command of Admiral Zinovy Rozhestvensky, the squadron was ordered to keep as low a profile as possible so as to catch the Japanese unawares.

The Baltic Fleet's long journey got off to an ignominious start in the foggy North Sea on 21 October. A drunken Russian supply ship captain saw a Swedish trawler, mistook it however illogically for a Japanese torpedo boat, and signalled that he was under attack. The rest of the fleet was put on full alert, and soon sighted a number of indistinct shapes in the distance. As one might expect in the famous fishing waters of the Dogger Bank, the ships were a fleet of British trawlers. This possibility, however, eluded the Russians, who opened fire, successfully sinking one, damaging several others, and killing three British sailors. Although the British trawlers were unarmed, the Russians still lost two men in the 'cross-fire', as in the confusion some vessels ended up shooting at each other.

When he realised the magnitude of his mistake, the Admiral added insult to injury by ordering his squadron to ignore the survivors in the water and flee. It was a public relations disaster for the Russian navy, and brought Britain to the brink of actively entering the war on the side of Japan. Moreover, it helped ensure that world opinion, among the people, press and politicians, largely favoured the plucky Japanese underdogs in the Manchurian war, rather than the drunken, trigger-happy Russians, who had managed to incur casualties in an 'exchange' of fire with unarmed fishing boats.

The news, when it limped in on old newspapers, did not do much to boost morale in Mannerheim's Manchurian village. The stand-off between the Japanese and the Russians left them with perilously little to do. By digging in in their trenches and waiting orders, the two sides found themselves sharing more in common with their neighbours than they expected, and an impromptu spirit of camaraderie broke out between the supposed enemies.

At a place Mannerheim called Linshinbu, the enemy lines converged so close to each other that the two sides found themselves drawing water from opposite sides of the same river. Mannerheim reported that an unspoken agreement developed, by which any unarmed soldier was allowed to approach the water without drawing fire. However, anyone approaching the water with a sidearm or rifle was soon subjected to warning shots to send him scurrying back to cover.

In the quiet Manchurian nights, the rival soldiers became united by their common boredom. On one night, a drunken Russian officer treated his fellow soldiers to a song. When he finished, there were the sounds of applause from behind the Japanese lines, and shouts of 'Encore!'

Some Russians entertained themselves by making dummies

from stuffed sacks of sorghum straw. Although there were several designs, the most popular was a female dummy with large breasts. The soldiers then stuck their handiwork up on poles on the front line for the enemy to shoot at, and held up improvised scorecards for the Japanese marksmen.[11]

Such horseplay was only a temporary respite from more serious operations. Both sides mounted occasional night raids to snatch back prisoners of war, and Mannerheim's letters home make gloomy references to dwindling supplies. Firewood was in short supply, particularly with an army's worth of new arrivals to keep warm. Russian soldiers soon exhausted all the available timber from standing forests, and began breaking up boats on the Liao River to use in fires.[12] Mannerheim noted that foraging parties, which once only had to walk into a nearby field to gather up sorghum straw, were now taking all day to amass enough combustible materials to fire up the kitchen and keep the huts warm at night. Nearby villages had barns of firewood, but Mannerheim doubted that they alone would provide enough to last the winter. While out riding on Talisman, he saw some orderlies chopping down trees in a Chinese cemetery. Mannerheim felt a twinge of concern, as he had been told that such trees were planted over particular graves as part of a funeral service, and he feared that the Russians were desecrating a Chinese tradition. He was also worried about the effect the stay was having on his horses. There were no oats for them to eat, and sorghum straw was diminishing daily. Mannerheim subsidised their meagre fodder himself, doubling their daily allocation of straw.

Mannerheim's boredom reached its height in mid-December. He had complained before of cramped and noisy living conditions, but now observed that his bunkmates woke up so late that their quarters were not cleaned until midday, breakfast was often at lunchtime and the sun was setting by six, making it impossible for him to read or write letters. Mannerheim refused to play along, and would rise at seven in the morning and go for a walk, usually on his own. He would train one of his horses in the afternoon.

Around November time, Mannerheim travelled to Mukden, the capital of Manchuria, for what appears to have been a simple tourist trip. He visited the palace of Nurhaci, the ancestor of the incumbent Chinese emperor, and Beiling Park, the site of the grave of Nurhaci's son Aberhai. He reported his concern at the damage being done to Manchuria by the troops who were supposedly there to preserve it. 'I am sorry to see the ruined villages around here,' he wrote. 'Some [infantry] make sure that no rock is left atop another when they pass. Others want to hunt, or ransack places for materials or wood. The Chinese like our hussars because we respect them and their property. The Chinese say that cavalrymen are *zhen hao*, which means "good."' [13]

Horsemen like Mannerheim might have impressed the locals, but he was worried about his troops' readiness for combat. Captured Japanese prisoners were well fed, well equipped, and clad in khaki uniforms that rendered them almost invisible against the wintry Manchurian plains and hills. Mannerheim also noted that the Japanese had thick leather coats and even long johns, and were thus far more prepared for a Manchurian winter than the Russians.

Mannerheim began a regime to encourage his fellow horsemen to take a more active interest in their surroundings. His tactics, beyond haranguing other officers for their dereliction of duty, drew on his experiences as a horsemaster in St Petersburg. He discovered that the younger officers in particular were eager for orders, and soon kept them busy by organising a series of 'reconnaissance' missions, none of which had initially been ordered by his superiors. [14] He sent squadrons of hussars out into open territory, to exercise their horses and examine the local terrain.

The German military observer Richard Ullrich reported that Mannerheim and Talisman cut an impressive dash among the Russian soldiers. 'On my line there was a graceful and particularly well turned-out lieutenant colonel in the blue uniform of the 52nd Nezhin hussars. He looked surprisingly young for his rank, slender and was apparently [transferred] from the Tsar's own regiment, the Chevalier Guards. ... The fantastic horse is just like his master, from the Tsar's regiment in St Petersburg.' [15]

On one occasion, Mannerheim himself led a posse of riders all the way over to the Don Cossack division, which faced the frontline of the Japanese. His presence aroused suspicion among the other officers. One busybody was led to suspect that Mannerheim might be a spy with Japanese sympathies because of his immaculate uniform, which was still clean.[16] The easternmost outpost was half a mile or so from the Japanese trenches, and the Russians' trenches were guarded by the infantry. As an officer who had ridden out to the Japanese lines, Mannerheim walked among the trenches, talking to the infantrymen, and pointing out where the Japanese trenches were in direct relation to their current position.

Mannerheim's activity, however, aroused considerable suspicion in other trenches. One officer, snooping with his binoculars, simply saw an unknown figure gesticulating and pointing among the Don Cossacks, and called it in. As a result, Mannerheim wrote, 'my guide became my guard', and he was escorted away. Everything was soon settled with a call to headquarters, although the army rumour mill would carry the incident much further than expected. Before long, there was talk of a tall Japanese spy, who had supposedly been captured by the Don Cossacks in their trenches.

'That would be me,' confessed Mannerheim in a letter to his father. The Finns found it all mildly entertaining, although his family did note that it hardly augured well for Russian military intelligence.

'No wonder they mistake a bunch of trawlers for torpedo boats,' Carl Robert observed, 'when they think Gustaf looks Japanese.'[17]

The story might have remained a minor family anecdote, had it not been picked up by Hugo Backmansson, a Finnish officer in Manchuria who sent occasional letters and reports back to the Helsinki newspaper *Hufvudstadsbladet*. A somewhat caricatured account of events appeared in the newspaper on 19 February 1905, although Mannerheim failed to see the funny side when Backmansson tried to embellish the story by falsely claiming he had been out of uniform.

Although Mannerheim's family were amused by the suggestion, the Russians were not entirely wrong to suspect Japanese espionage. It was only after the war was long over that suspicions were raised, for example, about the fall of Port Arthur. The Japanese fleet had somehow been able to approach through a maze of mines and sandbanks, and appeared to have done so using stolen charts provided by a European agent, Sidney Reilly. Japanese intelligence operations comprised an invisible second front throughout the war, successfully misinforming the Russians about Japanese troop strengths in the region since even before the outbreak of hostilities. Through carefully arranged security breaches, the Japanese had steered the Russians into believing that Japanese intelligence was entirely incompetent and misinformed, when in fact the opposite was far closer to the truth. Meanwhile, Russian forces arrived in Manchuria believing that there were fewer Japanese in position than there really were, with less equipment and supplies than they actually had.

But the true triumph of Japanese espionage in the war was conducted thousands of miles away from Manchuria, in Europe itself. The main instigator was Colonel Akashi Motojirō (1864–1919). A former military attaché in St Petersburg, Akashi's value was seriously assessed by Japanese high command as worth more than ten divisions of troops. He was given a million yen budget from Tokyo, and used the money to encourage anti-Tsarist revolutionaries. In 1904, he convened a secret meeting in Paris with 30 sympathisers, with whom he arranged a plan of sabotage and corruption within the Russian empire, designed to divert resources from the war in Manchuria.

Many of the agitators who caused trouble in Russia and Finland did so with financial assistance from Akashi. His associates included a rich American widow who smuggled arms on her yacht, and journalists who helped foment revolution. Mannerheim's brother Carl was another of his associates, although relations frosted between them when war broke out in Manchuria. In his own account of his espionage activities, Akashi wrote:

> Count [Carl] Mannerheim, an exile friend of mine, heaved a sigh and said to me: 'My younger brother, now a Russian [Lieutenant-] Colonel, has gone with General Mishchenko to fight against your army.' He hoped that his brother would not be injured.[18]

Carl's devotion to Mannerheim transcended his personal interest in fighting the Tsar. Akashi, however, was later implicated in the voyage of the *John Grafton*, a ship from London that ran guns to northern Finland in 1905, only to be blown up off the coast of Pietarsaari in the Gulf of Bothnia – for Akashi, the scare caused by the scandal was almost as useful as the guns themselves. He found particularly willing accomplices in Stockholm among the community of Finnish exiles, and used them to funnel money to Finland in support of anti-Tsarist enterprises. Akashi was a firm believer in the power of propaganda, and was happy to fund journalists and newspapers that might encourage the Tsar's subjects to question their ruler. He was a secret backer of Konrad 'Konni' Zilliacus, a Finnish exile who smuggled his own anti-Tsarist newspaper into Finland and revolutionary literature into St Petersburg itself. He even appears to have bankrolled a new foray into publishing by another would-be journalist, Vladimir Lenin, who suddenly acquired financial backing for his own newspaper under mysterious circumstances.[19]

Anti-Russian agitation in Europe was not solely down to Japanese spies, but Akashi's projects helped put pressure on the Tsar, which in turn led to increased stress on the soldiers in the Far East. Such strains were to push soldiers on the line like Gustaf Mannerheim into ever more dangerous and hasty missions.

Mannerheim received what he would call his 'baptism of fire' on 23 December 1904, when his squadron was sent to investigate a village that was suspected of harbouring Japanese soldiers. Russian activities had been seriously compromised by what might be euphemistically termed lack of intelligence. In fact, it was more serious – after the under-estimation of initial numbers encouraged by Japanese misinformation, many commanders now deliberately *over*-estimated their assessments of Japanese numbers in their vicinity, in order to gain access to better supplies and more impressive success rates. By December, this meant that nobody in the Russian forces was entirely sure where their enemy actually was.

Four or five advance scouts made it to the outer wall of the silent village without any trouble, and Mannerheim was watching them through his binoculars when the bullets suddenly began to fly. The horsemen had agreed beforehand that the nature of their mission was to confirm a Japanese presence, not to engage the enemy. Accordingly, they wheeled and galloped for cover. Mannerheim estimated that it took him three minutes to reach the relative safety of a sandbank, although 'it felt like twice the time'. His horse was so frightened by the encounter that Mannerheim had to struggle to stay in the saddle. It was only after he had gained control of his mount that his attention turned elsewhere: two Russians and a horse had been seriously wounded. Mannerheim seemed more shocked by the pain of others than by his first brush with actual enemy fire. 'I am not sure what kind of effect this salvo of bullets had on me, but I can say it was not pleasant', he wrote. 'However, that did not shock me. I was shocked by the sight of the wounded men in such pain.'[20]

On Christmas Eve, Mannerheim's men ran into a far more serious encounter. Fifty horsemen literally ran straight into a series of trenches occupied by Japanese infantry. With several men already in the trenches, the others charged in after them. Mannerheim was impressed by the foolhardiness of riding one's horse into a trench full of enemy soldiers. After the vicious hand-to-hand fighting that ensued, the Cossacks returned with 7 men dead and another 6 wounded, leaving 30 dead Japanese behind them.

Mannerheim spent Christmas in a village called Eldhaisen.[21] Struggling to keep warm with a new pair of socks from his sister Eva, he wrote about his apprehension for the new year. General Kuropatkin had supposedly begun arranging facilities to receive 70,000 casualties, implying that the Russians were going to make their stand in Mukden against an inevitable Japanese assault.

The general had decided to send troops south to cut the line at Ying Kou, which would have seriously delayed Japanese troop movements, and caused the enemy to doubt the security of the entire stretch of line from Ying Kou to Liaoyang. However, Kuropatkin suddenly changed his mind, deciding instead that the prime objective of the mission would be to capture Ying Kou. The railway sabotage could wait.

Mannerheim was astonished at the mismanagement of the mission. With some 7,000 cavalry in action and 4 units of horse-drawn artillery, it was possible for much of the force to reach Ying Kou in record time, with the benefit of surprise. Indeed, Mannerheim fully expected to be given a prime role in the mission, and wrote a farewell elegy to his daughter Sophy in case he did not return.

Even before he received his full orders, Mannerheim had assumed that he would be asked, as one of the riders of the fastest horses, to head south as fast as possible, while the slower forces engaged the outposts to his rear. Instead, all the squadrons were ordered to stop at each and every fortified village to deal with the Japanese there. Rather than leaving a small detachment at each place to keep the Japanese busy, the task force dawdled across Manchuria at a pace little different to that of a column of infantry, and gave the Japanese plenty of time to warn the defenders of Ying Kou.

To make matters worse, neither Kuropatkin nor his troops knew that Port Arthur had already fallen in the first days of January 1905, and that consequently the majority of the Japanese soldiers who had been besieging it for a year were now free to head north, or indeed, west to Ying Kou. By the time Mannerheim's squadron was engaged with the defenders of Ying Kou, they had not only had the chance to prepare, but were visibly in the process of receiving trainloads of reinforcements from Port Arthur. 'During the ensuring battle,' wrote Mannerheim, 'we could see a troop-train coming from Port Arthur, and the Japanese waving their caps from the trucks, shouting "*banzai*".[22]

Mannerheim volunteered to lead a party to blow up the railway line – the original purpose of the mission and much more crucial now that Port Arthur was in enemy hands – but he was told that he was too high-ranking for such a minor task. Eventually, the cavalry were obliged to retreat before their exit route was cut off, and Ying Kou remained occupied by the Japanese. Mannerheim later discovered that a paltry force of only a few hundred men, drawn from disparate units and hence unaccustomed to each other's operating procedures, had been sent to blow up a bridge to cut the railway. 'The attempt,' he fumed, 'as might have been expected, failed.'[23]

Mannerheim was much more appreciative of the efforts of Oscar Grippenberg, the commander who would lead him in an engagement in late January. Grippenberg had been born in Finland, and Mannerheim's letters home describe him as 'one of us' – i.e. not a Russian.[24] Most of the generals, on both sides, had assumed that there would be no more action in Manchuria until the worst of the winter had passed. Grippenberg, like Mannerheim, however, thought the time was ideal to press on, particularly when he realised that the Japanese near the tiny village of Heikoutai were exposed and vulnerable. The result was the four-day engagement, often fought in a driving snowstorm, known as the Battle of Sandepu.[25]

It was widely believed, although never proved, that Russian forces were urged to attack Sandepu in an attempt to score a propaganda victory in the wake of a national tragedy back home. On 22 January, a demonstration had marched upon the Winter Palace in St Petersburg, intent on presenting the Tsar with a petition. The crowd was entirely peaceful, and determined to behave as loyal subjects. They sang hymns and patriotic songs, and treated the march as a day out, with entire families attending en masse. The protestors' aims included an end to the wasteful war in Manchuria, along with other demands that had a certain revolutionary taint. They asked for the liberation of political prisoners, the recognition that all were equal before the law, universal public education, and the accountability of government officials to the people. It was precisely the sort of democratic reform that the Tsar had been resisting during his reign, and he was unlikely to look favourably on it. Furthermore, the rhetoric of the petition, while polite and deferential, seemed to speak of 'workers' and their rights.[26]

The Tsar, in fact, was absent from the Winter Palace, but troops acting in his name dealt with the crowd savagely. Ordered to fire into the air, they fired into the crowd itself, killing dozens of people both in the gunfire and the resultant stampede to escape. It was another disaster for the beleaguered Nicholas II, and many believed that he tried to obscure the incident by calling for an immediate and decisive Russian resurgence in the war with Japan.[27]

Sandepu was a landmark battle in the history of warfare. At the time, it was regarded as merely an unpleasant, indecisive struggle over a forgotten village. It would be another decade before its participants realised that they had witnessed the future of armed conflict. With its trenches and its dug-in positions over a no man's land, Sandepu was a presentiment of a war that was to come.

'Nobody desired to believe', wrote one participant, 'that a time could ever arrive when armies would be so exhausted and bled that they would have no other course but to scrape themselves holes in the ground, wrap themselves round in barbed wire, and collect their strength in readiness for a new clinch.'[28]

Sandepu was a fortified village some 36 miles south of Mukden; its clay walls were 3 feet thick and frozen rock-hard by the cold. The Japanese within had the additional bonus of a stone temple building, which provided better than average cover from Russian gunfire. Russian artillery could have easily annihilated Sandepu with high explosives, but arrived in the area supplied with nothing but shrapnel rounds for use against personnel in open fields.

However, the only troops in the open were the Russians. Where they would have once been invisible amid fields of *gaoliang* grass, they were now easily spotted amid the post-harvest wide plains. The last remnant of the *gaoliang* was its sharp, tough stubble, which continually threatened to pierce the thin boots of the infantry, and prickled the legs of the warhorses.

On 26 January, the Russians threw themselves against the dug-in Japanese. A rain of artillery, exhausting what few high-explosive shells could be scrounged, fell upon the huddle of huts. The fighting was bitter but short, and Grippenberg's exhausted men seized the village. The victorious Grippenberg cheerfully sent his guns off to another position, told his men they could have the next day off, and signalled General Kuropatkin that Sandepu had fallen.

The Russians piled in to the small hamlet, observing their Japanese prisoners face-to-face. One officer handed a cigarette to a wounded Japanese soldier, who thanked him profusely. The Russians eyed the small pile of a dozen captured enemy rifles, and some even commented that it seemed like a remarkably small defensive force for such a supposedly important location. After midday, the Russians began the work of fortifying the village in case of an enemy counter-attack. Their shovels and picks had trouble breaking the frozen ground, but they worked with the satisfaction of soldiers who had finally done something right. Strangely, the captured village did not appear to have the stone temple that they had heard about.

There was still the noise of gunfire in the distance, growing steadily louder, although nobody could see anything through the pale grey mist. It was only when some of the artillerymen came fleeing back to the village that Grippenberg realised his mistake. He had stormed the wrong village.

Thanks largely to the vagaries of Russian maps, Grippenberg's men had wasted a day attacking, taking and fortifying an insignificant village guarded only by a token force of Japanese. Sandepu, a much larger enclave of some 100 houses, was over a mile away, and still merrily occupied by an entire division of the enemy. To make matters worse, Grippenberg's elated victory message to Kuropatkin had already been telegraphed back to the Tsar, who was now celebrating the Russian 'success'.

Grippenberg desperately tried to rectify his mistake before it was found out. He ordered his exhausted men into battle once more, against a far stronger force, without artillery support, and with their mortars. The real Sandepu proved to be much harder to capture. As night fell on 28 January 1905, the Russians took the outskirts of the town, only to be repelled by a Japanese bayonet charge. The Russians retreated, leaving many wounded to freeze to death overnight. An entire Russian rifle regiment, only recently arrived from the west, was reduced to a handful of men.

Any ground that Grippenberg might have gained was lost through interference from his own superiors. Kuropatkin eternally hoped for magical reinforcements from the Trans-Siberian, and trusted in the eventual arrival of the Baltic Fleet, whose whereabouts was still a mystery. Consequently, he strongly disapproved of any action that might provoke the Japanese into battle before the Russians were sure of winning. Claiming that many of Grippenberg's battalions were needed elsewhere, Kuropatkin pulled them off the line in mid-battle, and eventually ordered Grippenberg directly to break off. A furious Grippenberg returned to St Petersburg, ostensibly to account for his failings, but actually in a euphemistic resignation. Despite the demands of protocol, he did not pay his respects to Kuropatkin before leaving, and wasted no time back in the capital before complaining of his superior's timidity and incompetence.

Mannerheim similarly brushed off Grippenberg's casualties. Whereas the Japanese lost 9,000 dead, the Russians lost 1,781 dead, almost 10,000 wounded and another thousand missing in action. However, while certainly not minimal, such losses were only to be expected, and claims that Grippenberg had endangered his men's lives seemed disingenuous when applied to a general in a war zone. As Mannerheim put it, 'That shouldn't have scared the supreme commander [Kuropatkin], not when he has already been preparing to take care of 80,000 wounded.' Nor did Mannerheim think that many of the casualties could blamed on Grippenberg when the weather on its own was doing a good enough job of creating casualties. 'The sub-zero temperature has been harsh, and many men have frostbitten feet, despite wearing Chinese over-trousers and felt buskins.'[29]

In the aftermath of Sandepu, the Japanese were able to bring forward most of the men who had previously been tied up taking Port Arthur. Mannerheim was one of many cavalrymen sent out to gauge where the Japanese were. He was detached from his own unit and put in charge of two squadrons of scouts on the western side of Mukden. He was authorised to engage the enemy when he thought it appropriate, and otherwise to report troop movements to headquarters. This was not as easy as it sounded, as the act of identifying troops often required being within a sword's length of them. On one occasion, the first inkling that Mannerheim had that nearby soldiers were not Russians was when they began shooting at him. Instead of believing his flank to be protected, he realised too late that they had run into a rival squad of Japanese, whose heavy machine gun made short work of Mannerheim's hussars. Mannerheim charged directly into the enemy, scattering them, but not before ten of his own men were dead.

The pressure on the Russians was severe. The fall of Port Arthur had not only freed soldiers, but also artillery and machine guns from the south, and these were now liberally scattered among the enemies closing in on Mukden. Mannerheim's reconnaissance missions provided General Kuropatkin with precisely the information he did not want to hear. The Japanese were approaching Mukden on the west flank and would shortly close off the north exit to trap everyone within. Kuropatkin's options were to stand and fight or run for the north on the railway. He ran.

Throughout his time in Manchuria, Mannerheim remained spookily uninjured. He took great risks on the battlefield, such that Hugo Backmannson commented, 'What is the matter with Mannerheim? It is as if he is trying to get killed?' [30] Mannerheim himself noted his peculiar invulnerability. He had seen one of his own fellow officers, a count, shot in the heart as he turned to acknowledge a new order. And in the middle of one exchange of fire with the Japanese, Mannerheim had felt his horse Talisman suddenly shudder, struck by an enemy bullet.

'The bullet that hit Talisman did not kill him instantly,' wrote Mannerheim. 'Even when mortally wounded, this noble creature carried me to the end of the battle. And only when he had completed his mission, he collapsed to the ground and gave up his life, to my deep sorrow.' [31]

Mannerheim was disconsolate at the loss of Talisman, and devoted more space to it in his letters home than to the deaths of his human comrades. He lamented that his remaining mounts were jumpy and afraid of bullets, and was sure that he would now be a worse soldier for the absence of his beloved steed.

During the fighting over Mukden, rumours reached Finland that Mannerheim had been killed in the battle. His relatives anxiously scanned the regular issues of *Russki Invalidi*, a bulletin listing all known casualties, but the name Mannerheim failed to appear on it. Eventually, a new letter reached Finland from Mannerheim, in which he noted, 'Even I don't know how I managed to survive, but the fact is that not a hair has been harmed on my head.' [32]

Mannerheim may not have been shot or stabbed, but he had been laid low by a powerful fever that struck him with devastating force even as the Japanese troops moved in on Mukden. Despite a temperature of 104°F, leaving him 'so weary that I was ready to lie down under artillery fire', he led his horsemen out into the fray.

With Mukden falling to the Japanese, General Kuropatkin decided it was time to withdraw all Russian forces back to the next city north along the railway line. The departure of the Russians was a complete debacle, with the order to retreat reaching every unit at the same time. Instead of an organised withdrawal, with some regiments covering the departure of others, the Russian forces scrambled to quit Mukden. There was, of course, only one railroad out of town, and an extremely limited number of wagons. Mannerheim's own squadron was riding through the outskirts of the town when their passage was blocked by a group of Japanese soldiers. The Russians were obliged to charge their enemies and hack their way through Japanese lines at sword point. Mannerheim would not find out for many months, but the day when he kicked and slashed his way through lines of Japanese soldiers was the day on which he was promoted to colonel.

Mannerheim was sure he had left some men behind. 'Nobody knows what happened to them,' he wrote. 'I hope they were taken prisoner, although they were surely wounded in action, and I fear they were all killed. I lost 15 men and 25 horses.'[33] The station was already under attack when Mannerheim's hussars arrived, to the sound of a Finnish cavalry march, bringing much needed support to the tired infantry. One observer reported that the Japanese had been pursuing the infantry with such fervour that they had been throwing off their overcoats. Once Mannerheim's squadron arrived, the tables were turned, and the Japanese fled with such speed that they cast aside their rifles.[34]

Finally, an exhausted Mannerheim collapsed in a railway carriage heading out of Mukden for Gongzhuling. The carriage was a cargo truck, transformed into an improvised field hospital, with a stove burning in the middle and beds clustered around. It was impossible to move from one truck to another, as they has not been designed for human access, and the train ground its way along the tracks at a walking speed that took three days to reach safety. All the while, the overcrowded carriage was beset by other Russian soldiers, attempting to clamber aboard the lumbering train in an attempt to rest from the miserable business of walking to Harbin.

By the time Mannerheim reached Gongzhuling, he was in serious need of medical attention. His fever, which he had held back with strong medication, needed to run its course. He had picked up a urinary infection after days in the wilderness, and a dangerous ear infection. He found a friendly face in a distant

relative, Fanny von Julin, who was a nurse with the Finnish Red Cross in the area. A doctor, Richard Faltin (a childhood friend of Mannerheim's), was found to lance the boil on his left ear, but he was plagued by recurring aches and was left partially deaf. In the brief period he spent in the hospital, he discovered that the man in the next bed was Hugo Backmansson, the sometime correspondent of the Helsinki newspaper who had reported on Mannerheim being mistaken for a Japanese spy.[35]

Mannerheim's ailments required daily medical attention, but once the fever had passed he was mobile and relatively sprightly. Only half in jest, he and Backmansson purloined some spare crutches, just in case a visiting officer saw them walking around the ward and accused them of malingering. An extant photograph from the hospital shows Mannerheim and Backmansson, their hands shoved in their hospital cassock sleeves like mandarins, larking about to the bemusement of Fanny von Julin.

Mannerheim was grateful for the attention of the Finnish doctors, and his hearing had begun to return by the time the hospital was required to withdraw. When Mannerheim had arrived at Gongzhuling, it had been significantly behind Russian lines, but within a week the Japanese were approaching. Mannerheim stayed at Gongzhuling, considering himself fit enough to stay behind. The hospital and the more severely wounded patients were packed up into railway carriages and shipped north to Harbin and then home to the west. Mannerheim was put under the care of a new Red Cross unit, staffed largely by Baltic Germans. He got on well with the Germans – in fact, he had been reprimanded earlier in the conflict for conversing fluently with German military observers in their own language – but remained largely in the dark about the progress of the war. The whereabouts of the Baltic Fleet remained a mystery, although it was known that passage for much of it through the British-controlled Suez Canal had been denied, and that it would hence have to take the long route around Africa. In April, an Australian journalist broke the news worldwide that the vessels were assembling in Indochina's Cam Ranh Bay, still many weeks away.[36]

Spring was brisk and cold, and Mannerheim grumbled that he had to wear his overcoat indoors, even though he was now posted at the same latitude as Naples. Shortly before 1 May, a Finnish holiday, he noted that there was a snowstorm outside his hut.

Reunited with his unit, Mannerheim was given another reconnaissance mission, this time to the west. His instructions, officially, ordered him to head into 'Mongolia' to assess the level of Japanese penetration there. But, as he himself observed, Russian maps were unreliable. Russian intelligence falsely believed that the Liao River was the border of Mongolia, although in reality *Inner* Mongolia was another hundred miles to the west, and Outer Mongolia another 300 miles beyond that.

About 5 miles west of the Liao, Mannerheim and his three squadrons of horsemen came to an ancient, nondescript dike of rammed earth, falling down in some places and almost completely worn away in others. 'As far as the local people know,' he wrote, 'the border is a line of sand walls ... only then comes the Mongolian settlement and the change in language from the Manchurian tongue.' [37] Mannerheim never knew it, but the low 'sand wall' was an ancient tributary of the legendary Great Wall of China, which had been extended in an earthen rampart to encompass the Liao River valley. If he had been able to follow it all the way to the north, it would have taken him back to Mukden. Instead, by crossing over it to the north-west, he had effectively stepped out of 'Chinese' Manchuria and into Jehol, the homeland of the Manchu emperors. The area in which he found himself had been Chinese territory for hundreds of years.

Despite Chinese claims of ownership, it was still lawless, and Mannerheim was on the lookout for the *Hong Huzi*, the nomad bandits who rode across its hills and valleys. He split his squadrons into smaller groups in an attempt to bring them out of hiding – several groups were rumoured to have allied themselves with the Japanese, but none took the bait. Mannerheim was eager to find a tribe of *Hong Huzi*, partly because he yearned to see one of their legendary 1,000-strong herds of horses, but also because local Chinese had claimed to have seen Japanese 'advisers' riding with them – a prime target for interrogation. From a distance, all *Hong Huzi* looked the same. Mannerheim needed to get close enough to determine whether the long, braided queues down their backs, a mandatory hairstyle for all Chinese subjects, were real or simply false hairpieces stuck onto the hats of disguised Japanese officers.

Mannerheim was not authorised to engage any enemies. Instead, he led his squadron across the plains west of the Liao, occasionally running into local Chinese personnel riding on plucky steppe ponies. He was amused to find one of the Chinese lieutenants wearing a 'medallion' that, on closer inspection, was found to be an 1878 Russian belt-buckle commemorating the founding of modern Bulgaria.

Mannerheim made several further forays to the west, largely to improve the awful quality of Russian maps, but also in an attempt to lure the *Hong Huzi* into action. He exchanged fire with several groups of them, often at river crossings that he presumed them to be 'defending', but the bandits soon fled when the Russians approached.

In late May, as the snow turned to pounding rain, news arrived of another Russian setback. The Baltic Fleet, whose arrival had been awaited for months, had run into the Japanese navy off the coast of Japan, near the strategic island of Tsushima. There, Admiral Tōgō had inflicted a crushing defeat on the would-be saviour of the Russian land forces. Altogether 21 of the ships in the Baltic Fleet were sunk, while several others were captured, and still more scuttled, beached or otherwise abandoned. After a world cruise of some 18,000 miles, only three vessels of the Baltic Fleet limped into Vladivostok harbour. There would be no last-minute rescue; no marines landing to retake Port Arthur; no counter-attack against the Japanese home islands. The war was already over.

4

The Tournament of Shadows

All across Asia for years afterwards, Finns were renowned for their refusal to fight in the Tsar's war. This conception, whether held as insult or in admiration, was entirely untrue, as attested by Louis Seaman, a reporter for the British press who noted in the *Daily Mail* that many of the 'Russian' prisoners of war in Japanese custody were not Russian at all:

> The prisoners at Matsuyama were all from White Russia, mostly Finns and Poles, with a decided sprinkling of Jews. Pondering on … the woes of these people in their own unhappy land, the thought was forced upon us that his Imperial Majesty the [Tsar] of all the Russias was emulating with emphasis the illustrious example of David of old with Uriah, in sending these people as cannon fodder to the Orient, where the more killed the better for the safety of his throne at home.[1]

The Baltic Fleet, of course, had been largely staffed by men from the Baltic, forcing many Finns to be part of the Tsar's defeat after all.

Already, in distant offices, representatives of the American President Theodore Roosevelt were making overtures to the enemy, in the hope they could agree an armistice. The Russians knew that, with the Baltic Fleet gone, there was little chance of anything but a steady erosion of their position in the East, and the sooner a line was drawn, the better. The Japanese, meanwhile, had driven themselves into the verge of bankruptcy in fighting the war, and were grateful for the chance to save face by 'agreeing' to discuss peace.

While these machinations proceeded, Mannerheim was kept busy implementing some last-ditch Russian plans for a counter-attack. His unit maintained reconnaissance patrols in case the Japanese were sneaking up on their flank, but had no encounters with them. Then the Russian authorities decided to lean on a new source of potential recruits, and put Mannerheim in charge of an experimental company of local militia – in other words, *Hong Huzi*.

It is unclear how these *Hong Huzi* were different from the Japanese-controlled irregulars that Mannerheim and his men had been shooting at on the plains of Jehol for the previous month. The politics of the Manchurian locals is difficult to unravel, but possibly Mannerheim's superiors had found a group of local bandits who were prepared to stand up to other local bandits in order to supplant them.

From a distance, Mannerheim had a horseman's admiration for the *Hong Huzi*. He was impressed by the athletic ease with which they controlled their mounts and the breakneck speed by which they would gallop past his quarters at night. Up close, however, Mannerheim began to suspect that the swift and dashing night-riders were an entirely different breed from the dirty, listless 300 horsemen who were now assigned to him.

'Their horses were bad,' he wrote, 'untrained, with poor saddles. The new recruits were sloppy and nondescript, better suited as street-sweepers and shop-boys than riflemen. In a word, my troops were complete dregs, with no sense of discipline or unity.' They were also oddly idiosyncratic. Mannerheim's personal favourite insisted on wearing a stripy Panama hat with velvet flowers around its brim, and carried a large blue parasol with him at all times, even when on horseback. 'You can imagine,' Mannerheim wrote to his sister, 'how military that looked.'[2]

The *Hong Huzi* were a false economy. They were offered a basic salary of 45 roubles a month, but had to bring their own weapons, fodder and horses. These necessities they inevitably stole from local farmers, leading their recruitment to amount to little more than banditry sponsored by St Petersburg. Since they were intended to replace absent or wounded Russian hussars, they were often put under the control of young and inexperienced officers. Mannerheim himself noted that the only discipline they understood was 'a Russian rifle and some bullets'. Since Mannerheim spoke Russian and the bandits only spoke a dialect of Chinese, controlling them was also a nightmare. The simplest instruction needed to be repeated several times by the interpreter until it was understood by all concerned, and even then the *Hong Huzi* had an irritating habit of answering back.

'Once an order had been translated,' he wrote, 'there came a loud debate, such that you would think they were Jewish merchants dickering over who could influence a buyer the most. Everybody had to have his say.'

Regardless, Mannerheim set out on an eight-day long-range patrol with his 300 new recruits. In only a couple of days, the number had dropped to 140 through a series of made-up excuses, malingerers and disappearances. Mannerheim bid the lightweights good riddance and pressed on with his 'luxury' remnants. Eventually, the posse ran into Japanese-backed *Hong Huzi* in open country, and Mannerheim got to see his recruits in action. He was, unsurprisingly, disappointed.

'They really want to shoot even if there aren't any enemies around. They think war is about as much shooting as possible, no matter if you hit anything or not. When retreating, they sling their rifles over their shoulders and shoot behind them without looking back. In other words, they shoot all over the place, all the time.'[3]

Despite 'losing' half his men, Mannerheim's mission was a roaring success. He found himself outnumbered and almost surrounded by Japanese and enemy *Hong Huzi*, but successfully evaded them by slipping away at night. He had successfully mapped some 200 square miles of unknown territory, and established without a doubt that there was a heavy Japanese penetration into the area west of the Liao. Mannerheim was mildly disappointed, as he felt that with better prepared troops he would have been able to

engage and defeat the enemy scouts, but he was congratulated on his return to base for a mission well done.

The Russo-Japanese War officially came to a close on 5 September 1905, but Mannerheim was trapped in the Far East for several more weeks. The end of hostilities did not magically increase the capacity of the Trans-Siberian Railway to ship everyone home, and his squadron stayed where it was for some time. He estimated, correctly, that it would be months before all the Russian soldiers could be cleared out of the Far East, and worked on the assumption that his squadron would be moved to policing duties along a section of the Trans-Siberian until their turn came to head home. Resigned to a prolonged period in the Far East with even less to do, Mannerheim organised a show-jumping competition to stop the soldiers from returning to drink and indolence. However, he was able to leave the East behind in November, thanks to a loophole in his commission that only assigned him to the Nezhin Hussars for the duration of hostilities.[4]

By the time he was able to get on a train home, the embarrassment of the Japanese victory had caused new problems. In many of the stations Mannerheim passed, the walls were daubed with the word *SVOBODA* ('Freedom'). On the Black Sea, sailors had mutinied on the famous battleship *Potemkin*, and called for revolution. Demonstrators in St Petersburg were calling for a revolution against the regime that had plunged Russia into its ill-fated attempt at conquest of the Far East. A poem written at the time by Konstantin Balmont recounted the various disasters of the reign of Nicholas II, and noted that it was far from a Golden Age. Instead, it was a catalogue of humiliating defeats and desperate oppression, a reign that had begun with deadly disaster:

> Our Tsar? Mukden.
> Our Tsar? Tsushima.
> Our Tsar? A bloody stain.
> A stench of gunpowder and smoke.
> Black is his soul.
> Our Tsar? Sickly and blind,
> Is prison and the whip, shooting and hanging,

Tsar! You are the gallows-bird ...
The hour of retribution awaits you.
What began at Khodynka Field
Will end at the scaffold.[5]

The Russian love affair with the Far East was over, as was the Tsar's complete hold on his people. Already among the subject peoples of Siberia, there were the first whispers of a doomsday cult, which claimed that a new messiah would lead them in revolution. One of this mythical war leader's names was *Yapon-kan*, the Ruler of Japan.[6]

In the west, reformist ambitions were no less passionate, although the war with Japan was regarded as a symptom, not a cure. The European Russians favoured self-help: constitutional reform in the people's name, to drag Russia out of its outmoded monarchical system. If the Tsar wanted so much to be a European monarch, the argument went, then why did he not start acting like one?

At one of the Trans-Siberian stations Mannerheim's train stopped at, newspaper sellers were passing out copies of a constitutional manifesto that brought limited democratic reforms to Tsarist Russia. Drafted by two of the Tsar's ministers in reaction to the growing unrest, it promised freedom of religion, freedom of speech and freedom of assembly; these new ideas did not, however, apply to rebel sailors on the renamed battleship *Potemkin* on the Black Sea, nor to the rebels whose early agitation Mannerheim had witnessed as he headed west along the Trans-Siberian, and whose short-lived proclamation of a Chita Republic in December 1905 was crushed within a month by Tsarist troops. The manifesto also promised a consultative State Duma (or parliament), which would theoretically devolve some autonomy to the regions of the empire. Mannerheim thought it was a 'dangerous game' for all the players, but broadly welcomed the news that some parts of Russia, including the Grand Duchy of Finland, were to receive some limited return of their autonomy.

Mannerheim returned to Finland very briefly, to assure his relatives that rumours of his death were greatly exaggerated. Even after that myth had been scotched, stories of revolutionary lynchings on the eastern reaches of the Trans-Siberian had led them to wonder if he would survive the journey home.

His elder brother Carl had had his exile revoked as part of the reforms, but had elected to stay in Sweden. This left Mannerheim as the senior member of his family in Finland, and to him fell the task of representing his family at what would be the last meeting of the aristocratic council, the Estate of Nobles. But although he attended, he remained silent. Instead, he fretted privately that plans to introduce universal suffrage among the Finns would prove disastrous at such politically sensitive times. Mannerheim remained an avowed monarchist, and was wary of democracy for the opportunity it afforded to demagogues. He believed, with a sense of entitlement common to the Finnish aristocracy, that democracy would only flourish if the right sort of people were elected. Instead, his experiences on the way home on the Trans-Siberian had left him deeply suspicious of those on the left wing who styled themselves 'Social Democrats'.

A bill was passed, inaugurating a Finnish parliament (strictly speaking, a Diet) in 1906. Mannerheim fretted that the decision would return to haunt the aristocracy, and that the working men of Finland might all too easily be led into lynch mobs and strike gangs, preying upon the upper classes in the manner that Mannerheim had already seen along the Trans-Siberian in the nascent but still-born Chita Republic. Even if the new Finnish democracy proved to be entirely benign, and became a chamber of healthy debate between differing factions, Mannerheim remained concerned over the effect it would have on Finnish relations with Russia. The Grand Duchy of Finland would be bound to demand more from its Grand Duke the Tsar – a man who was already known for turning guns on Russian subjects who had asked for the same.[7]

Despite the Russian defeat in Manchuria, Mannerheim had returned to Europe a satisfied man. Although it took several months for the military bureaucracy to grind through the details, he was promoted to colonel in recognition of his performance. Mannerheim had worried that promotion would be slower in peacetime, but was overjoyed to hear that his new rank had been backdated to the harshest day of the fighting in Mukden. This not only gave him an unexpected salary bonus, it also put him a year ahead in the peacetime promotional ladder for his next rank. He received several medals, but was disappointed in his hopes of being decorated with the Sword of St George, a medal that carried with it a monthly stipend.[8]

Mannerheim's time in Finland was cut short by orders to report back to St Petersburg. He was summoned to the presence of General Feodor Palitsyn, chief of the general staff, who had a proposal for him. It was, specifically, not an order – Mannerheim was free to refuse.

It was the concern of the Tsar's general staff that Russia might be missing a trick in Central Asia. Were the Chinese border regions really strengthened and garrisoned with Chinese troops? If they were, did they pose a genuine threat to Russia itself? The border with China was thousands of miles long, and Russia had only recently lost a war with the Japanese. The Russians were still learning of the extent of the Japanese intelligence network – could it be that, even now, the Japanese were extending their influence south of Russia's long border? Were Japanese spies plotting a surprise attack through Chinese territory, to cut the Trans-Siberian Railway in a lightning strike north?

The Tsar needed a detailed report on military reforms in China, particularly in the dry, dusty, forbidding regions of Chinese Turkestan (*Xinjiang*: 'The New Frontier'). Someone, preferably a high-ranking officer with map-making expertise and little to lose, was required to embark upon a mission that might take up to two years, travelling right across Asia. Moreover, the officer should be undercover, preferably a man who was not actually a Russian national. A Finn, perhaps, who could speak Swedish like a native, and present a reasonable alibi that he was conducting ethnological or geographical surveys in the area. In short, the Russians needed someone to take part in the ongoing dance of espionage and surveillance in Central Asia that came to be known to the British as the Great Game, but to the Russians was 'the Tournament of Shadows'.

Mannerheim was taken completely by surprise. During the war

in Manchuria, he had once idly suggested that it might be fun to head home on horseback, across Mongolia, but this was an entire level of magnitude above his daydreams. His first thought, as demonstrated by his diplomatic request to think it over and read up on the area, was that it was career suicide. However, he soon came to realise that the opportunity might have the opposite effect. It was a special, unique mission, for which had been handpicked by General Palitsyn. He no longer had any dependents in St Petersburg, and with the anti-Finnish feeling in Russia, it might be healthy indeed for him to remove himself from local politics for a while. Far from destroying his career, it might be the best way of preserving it.

'I studied everything relating to similar missions in the archives of the General Staff,' Mannerheim wrote, 'and my interest grew day by day and ended with my acceptance. ... I began with the writings of Marco Polo in the thirteenth century, which I read with absorbed interest.' [9] His researches reacquainted him with the voyages of his uncle Adolf Nordenskiöld, remembering in the process his childhood ambition of becoming an explorer. He read about a Captain Höök, a Finn who had explored the seas of Kamchatka and married a Manchu princess; Dmitri Klementz, who had brought back Buddhist manuscripts from lost cities in the desert, and Nikolai Przhevalsky, who had explored the Gobi, the mountains of China and the upper reaches of the Yangtze. But it was the man who had translated Przhevalsky into Swedish that had the greatest impact on Mannerheim. His name was Sven Hedin.

Hedin had grown up in Stockholm. Unlike Mannerheim, whose elder he was by just two years, Hedin had never had a rebellious youth. 'Happy is the boy', he once wrote, 'who discovers the bent of his life-work during childhood. That, indeed was my good fortune.'[10] At the age of twelve, when Mannerheim was still having snowball fights in Kaisaniemi Park, Hedin had already decided on his career. 'My closest friends were Fenimore Cooper and Jules Verne, Livingstone and Stanley, Franklin, Payer, and Nordenskiöld, particularly the long line of heroes and martyrs of Arctic exploration.'

Like Mannerheim, Hedin had followed Nordenskiöld's adventures with bated breath. Hedin had been fifteen years old when the *Vega* returned triumphant to Stockholm – one of the lucky people

Mannerheim had envied, who had been able to watch first-hand from the southern heights as Nordenskiöld's ship edged through the harbour, towards a city aflame with celebratory gaslights. 'And I thought,' wrote Hedin, 'I, too, would like to return home that way.'[11]

While Mannerheim had stumbled from school to cadet academy, Hedin enjoyed a much more sedate career. A brilliant scholar, he seized the chance to be the tutor to a rich man's son in the oil-fields of Baku. Instead of coming home by train, he squandered his wages on a journey through the Caucasus, Persia and Turkey, learning Persian and Tatar en route. Back home in Europe, Hedin enrolled in universities in Sweden and Germany, and discovered that instead of costing him money, his travels were generating it:

> In a volume illustrated by my own sketches, I told the story of my Persian journey. As I had never before written for publication, I hardly trusted my ears when a kind old publisher came to my home and offered me six hundred dollars for the right to publish my travel-experiences. I had only hoped to get the book published without having to pay for it myself and here was an amiable old gentleman, willing to buy my manuscript for a sum which, in my circumstances, seemed enormous.[12]

The effect of Hedin's adventures on Mannerheim should not be underestimated. Mannerheim faced pressure from both Finns and Russians to pick a side, and had lost Anastasie's financial support. Some officers in St Petersburg might have regarded the mission as an awful exile, tantamount to expulsion from the service, but for Mannerheim it was a golden opportunity. It was, for him, the perfect way of hedging his bets for two years while the political situation in Russia settled down. He could return as a hero and a Russian officer, or as a noble Swedish-Finnish explorer: either way he was determined to treat the mission as a welcome sabbatical. The prospect of actually being paid to recount his adventures cannot have escaped him, either.

Mannerheim embraced his cover with gusto. General Palitsyn may well have hoped that Mannerheim would keep an outward pretence of scientific interest, but Mannerheim went all the way.

He went to consult with members of the Finno-Ugrian Society, a scientific body with an avowed interest in researching the peoples of Central Asia and asked them what would interest them. He met with representatives from Helsinki Museum, and asked them what gaps they thought might need filling in their collection. The result, when he eventually returned from his spying mission, would be several academic papers on the peoples of Central Asia.

If we read Mannerheim's diaries alongside Hedin's, it is plain to see how keenly Mannerheim wanted to emulate Hedin's achievements. Mannerheim's early route through Asia closely matched that which Hedin had followed in 1891. Mannerheim put himself in similar situations and often used similar vocabulary in describing local colour and customs. Although Mannerheim never stated so outright, he seems to have intended that his account of his travels, *Across Asia*, would be a work in the tradition and style of Hedin's *Through Asia* (1898) – it was no accident that, in addition to his reports for St Petersburg, Mannerheim kept extensive personal notes. But Mannerheim's close study of Hedin was not merely hero worship; Mannerheim was also determined not to make the same mistakes.

Hedin's diaries recount his failures alongside his achievements. Mannerheim was determined not to find himself crawling on his hands and knees across a desert, mere hours from death, all thanks to inadequate water provision or loss of horses or pack animals. He would use Hedin's writings, particularly *Through Asia*, as a map and guide and thus was prepared to avoid many of the problems that beset other travellers in the region.

Mannerheim's cover was complete. He was authorised to discuss his mission with Russian officers at legations en route, but was otherwise to maintain the facade at all times of being a Swedish geographer. He could write letters home, but only in Swedish – they were to be sent to his father in Helsinki, and would then be forwarded to St Petersburg. General Palitsyn was never to be named in correspondence, but would instead be referred to as 'Uncle Feda'. Even Mannerheim's dates were to be in Swedish – his diary employed the Gregorian calendar, not the Julian calendar that remained in use in Russia for another decade.

Part of Mannerheim's cover involved placing him in the company of a scholarly expedition that was already heading towards Central Asia. Chinese Turkestan was not merely a 'new frontier', but it was also the bulk of the legendary 'Silk Road'. For centuries, caravans of traders had picked their way across the forbidding deserts and the chilly highlands, staggering in perilous journeys from remote oasis to remote oasis. At the far eastern end of the Silk Road was Xi'an, once a Chinese capital, now a lowly provincial centre. Silk and other goods from Xi'an and places east would be loaded on ponies and camels for the long trip west, crawling across the desolate sands of Turkestan, skirting the edges of the Gobi and Taklamakan deserts, leaving China proper for the 'barbarian' cultures on its periphery. The Silk Road – a route rather than a specific road – left Chinese territory west of Kashgar, continuing through Bukhara (now in Tajikistan), Samarkand (now in Uzbekistan) and Merv (now in Turkmenistan). From there, it meandered through the Middle East before reaching its western terminus – Damascus, whence the silk and other goods might find European markets.

The Central Asian part of the Silk Road was, and to some extent still is, a mystery to European scholars. The sands famously hide the ruins of dry oases, the remnants of an entire society that flourished when the desert was not so inhospitable. Even in the days of Marco Polo, the Silk Road was a place of hauntings and legends, where travellers confused mirages and ruins, and swapped stories of lost treasures in dead cities beneath the sands. It was a lure to several prominent scholars of the period, who arrived in Chinese Turkestan determined to unearth pre-Islamic relics. To do so, a European scholar approaching from the west would require the necessary documentation from one of the states at the western end. For the young French academic Paul Pelliot, this meant Russian visa approval for his own archaeological expedition in 1906. When Pelliot applied for his visa, he discovered that it came with a taxing condition – he must accept a man called Mannerheim into his expedition and ask no questions.

Pelliot was used to getting his own way. When he was only 21 years of age, he had been among the besieged Europeans in Beijing during the Boxer Uprising, and had infamously crossed over to

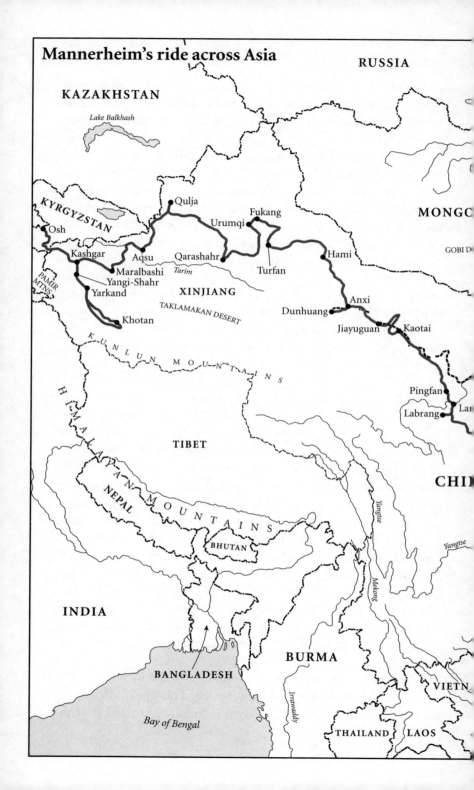

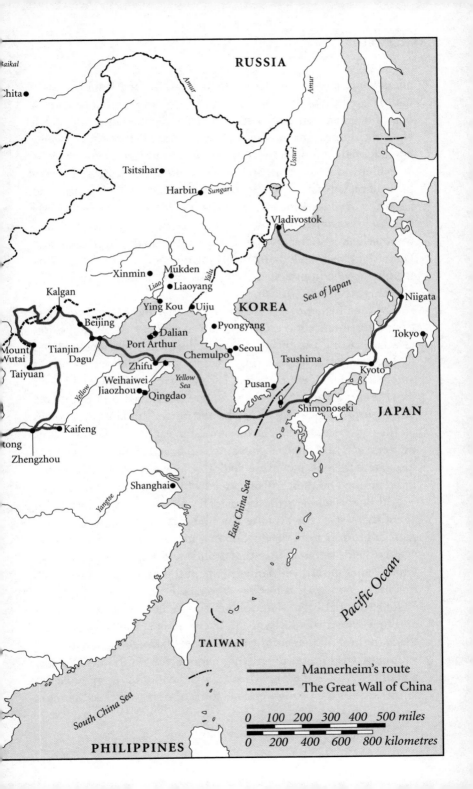

enemy lines in search of food. Surrounded by fanatical Boxers, he had dazzled them with his mastery of Chinese, joined them in a cup of tea, and then returned to his own people laden with fresh fruit. Becoming a professor of Chinese at 22, Pelliot spoke twelve languages, including better Russian than Mannerheim himself.[13]

Pelliot was an extremely reluctant accomplice. He hated Russian bureaucracy, bristled at the conditions attached to his visa, and regarded Mannerheim as an unwelcome interloper who was likely to bring disaster if his true nature were ever discovered. When Mannerheim caught up with the French expedition in Bukhara, Pelliot had been kicking his heels for two entire months, waiting for his heavy equipment to arrive. To keep himself occupied, he had taught himself Turkish.

The men had apparently met briefly once before, and renewed their acquaintance in a crowded train en route to Tashkent. Pelliot, as was his wont, was busily charming the awe-struck locals, elated to discover that he was sharing his carriage with the large family of an ousted Afghan emir. He had barely begun to insinuate himself into the entourage of the wealthy émigré, dazzling the party with his linguistic prowess, when an apparent stranger suddenly muscled in on the conversation and blurted something at him in French. Mannerheim was in civilian clothes and had shaved off his moustache, a disguise sufficient to confuse Pelliot, who was first irritated by the interruption and then embarrassed by his memory lapse.

Although Pelliot wrote in his diary that he and Mannerheim spent the rest of the evening chatting into the small hours, both men came away from the encounter with premonitions of trouble. Mannerheim noted sourly that Pelliot had not recognised him, while Pelliot described Mannerheim, in the subtlest of Gallic put-downs, as '*un voyageur d'allure américaine*'.[14]

Relations between Mannerheim and Pelliot had begun frostily and they would steadily worsen. In the early stages, the two men made the best of their enforced company. Mannerheim did his best to impart wisdom on the buying and stocking of horses. Pelliot, still only 27, offered Mannerheim the benefit of his encyclopaedic knowledge of the peoples and customs of Asia, whether Mannerheim wanted it or not.

In Andizhan, the two men struck up a friendship with a friendly local merchant, who invited them to dinner at his home and served an almost inedible dish of *pilaff* – rice and mutton. Pelliot sternly hissed at Mannerheim that they needed to finish it all. Pelliot's diary describes a sumptuous feast, whereas Mannerheim's account likens the meal to a form of torture, in which the Frenchman was a disapproving accomplice who wielded his ethnological knowledge like a weapon. 'Pelliot claimed that it would have been a grave insult to leave anything on the dishes,' wrote a resentful Mannerheim. 'After a great deal of sighing and eating the dishes were emptied and we hastened to bid our host goodbye in fear and trembling lest there should be any more mutton fat.' [15]

Their newfound merchant friend, however, was a godsend. With his help, they were able to cable ahead for other assistance, and were even directed miles out of town to a prime horse market. Mannerheim seems to have realised early on that their initial plans to travel with a large baggage train of carts would not be wholly practical. The carts would have to keep to the main track, while any archaeologist (or spy) was sure to want to head off-road. Mannerheim decided to buy extra horses, while Pelliot frowned and dickered over what he regarded to be outrageous local prices.

Pelliot protested that he had read in the books of Sven Hedin that a horse in the region should cost 8 roubles. But this was not a cue for Mannerheim to note his shared love of the writings of the famous explorer – Pelliot was making another subtle dig at his companion. Pelliot had discovered the inflated local prices were the result of a Russian trade tariff, and regarded the expense as another unwelcome imposition forced upon him by Mannerheim's masters. [16]

Once the trip began in earnest on horseback in August 1906, the French travellers got on Mannerheim's nerves. Travelling in the height of summer required diligent timekeeping. For Mannerheim, it was vital that everyone be up at dawn, the tents packed and horses checked, ready to get underway while the day was still cool. He was soon frustrated by the constant fussing of Pelliot's photographer Charles Nouette, as well as the frequent over-sleeping of the doctor Louis Vaillant, and the general French habit of dithering over breakfast and ablutions.

Mannerheim's concerns were purely logistic – it was bad for the horses to walk too long in the summer heat, and always preferable to complete each day's allotted travelling with daylight to spare. Travelling was rarely a matter of walking in a straight line; the ground could become rough or uneven, and there were local encounters that could not be predicted. On one occasion, Mannerheim's horse stumbled while crossing an irrigation channel, plunging Mannerheim and his mount into the water. They retrieved most of his possessions, including his soggy notebook, but had to wait a while for one of the men to retrieve a lost stirrup 'which at that moment was far more valuable to me than many more expensive things a month ago'.[17]

Mannerheim had been assigned several Cossacks from the 2nd Ural Cossack regiment in Samarkand. All were fully aware of the length of the mission awaiting them, and yet had embraced it with enthusiasm. General Palitsyn had put three of them under Mannerheim's direct command – if Pelliot wanted them to do something, he had to ask Mannerheim to order it.[18] To make matters worse, one of the Cossacks fell ill only two weeks after they were underway, forcing the travellers to pitch camp for a couple of days while the sick man suffered nosebleeds and vomiting fits. Determined to make the best of it, Mannerheim, Nouette and Pelliot left the camp and went hunting for partridges. This alone was exciting enough for Pelliot, although Mannerheim's diary lodges another complaint about the Frenchman, who fired too soon at a flock of 15 birds, putting them to flight and causing the hunters to return empty-handed after three wasted hours on the hillside.[19]

Mannerheim was also dissatisfied with the joint mission's incompetent cook. While the main party pressed on at the slow pace of the pack animals, the cook was routinely sent ahead to a predetermined camping spot, where he was ordered to get to work preparing food for the rest of the group. Neither cookery nor geography appeared to be in the man's skillset, and he regularly set up his kitchen in the wrong place. On one occasion, the expedition had barely travelled 8 miles before they found the cook cheerfully preparing dinner over a campfire. Only two days later, the weary travellers stumbled into their next campsite after a hard day on a dusty track, but the cook was nowhere to be seen. Instead, he had ridden far beyond the appointed spot, forcing the expedition to stay in the saddle far longer than planned.

But it was Pelliot who annoyed Mannerheim the most. As the expedition climbed the foothills towards high mountain passes, the temperatures at night edged below zero – it may have been summer, but conditions in the highlands were wintry. A similar coolness began to affect the relations between the Finn and the French. Unkindly, but not unfairly, Pelliot openly doubted whether Mannerheim would be able to carry out any part of his mission, lacking as he did any knowledge of Asian languages. Mannerheim had inadvisably told Pelliot of his lack of confidence in spoken Russian, and the Frenchman confided to his journal that 'in Russia, his Russian does not permit him access to as much information as me. How does he think this will improve in China?' [20]

While at first he had appreciated the idea of travelling with a sinologist and polyglot, Mannerheim soon tired of Pelliot's endless pedantry, and complained in his diary that Pelliot the great Asia expert was entirely ignorant of the basic truths of horsemanship – that 30 miles a day was not impossible for horses on flat ground, but unduly taxing on uneven terrain. Pelliot was so keen to exert his authority that he even tried to eke out the expedition's supply of sugar lumps, and when it came to Mannerheim's tasks of survey-ing, often displayed no consideration, brashly pressing on while Mannerheim was still setting up his instruments. Pelliot refused to accord Mannerheim an official place in his expedition, treating him at all times like an unwelcome gatecrasher imposed upon him by incompetent Russian officials. When the expedition called in at towns along the route, Pelliot was quick to schmooze the locals and accept their hospitality, leaving Mannerheim outside with the porters. While Mannerheim saw this as French snobbery, Pelliot's own diary pleaded private concern about Mannerheim's dismiss-ive attitude towards local potentates. As part of his collecting, Mannerheim had bought a loom and a woman's headdress from Kirghiz tribesmen, but, according to Pelliot, vocally complained to their chief when the articles were not delivered that same evening. The following day, Mannerheim grumpily rode past the Kirghiz

horsemen without bidding them good day. Pelliot was keen to establish among the locals that Mannerheim was riding *with* his expedition, but was not part of it. He was particularly bothered that Mannerheim might behave in this way among less forgiving Chinese officials over the border. 'I shall not be able to allow on Chinese ground', wrote Pelliot, 'this attitude most different to ours that Mannerheim has towards the natives.'

And yet, while Pelliot fretted over Mannerheim's behaviour, Mannerheim's own version of events is somewhat different. He was indeed in a foul mood that day, as his own journal attests, but not with the tribesmen. Instead, it was Pelliot who had annoyed him, by occupying so much of the chief's time that evening that Mannerheim had no opportunity to attempt any further purchases.[21]

Pelliot also rarely seemed to shut up about the matter of what he called his 'subvention' – he had inferred that he would be paid several thousand francs for tolerating Mannerheim, and had mistakenly believed that Mannerheim would arrive with the cash in his saddlebags. Mannerheim eventually told him that the nature of Pelliot's reward would be heavily contingent on how well the pair of them got along, although he doubted that he made his point.

Nothing clarifies the difference between the two men better than their reactions to a local custom. The travellers had happened upon a Kirghiz wedding, and were witnesses to a horse race (in the local language, *baiga*), for which Pelliot donated a prize. Mannerheim was in his element watching the horses, particularly when the *baiga* was followed by a game of *tomocha* – a scrum of horsemen fighting over the carcass of a goat. Mannerheim, who had already read about the sport in Hedin's writings, noted the origins of the sport in ancient folktales of bride-theft, and gamely entered into the proceedings. For him, it was a more visceral, primitive version of his beloved polo, although he regarded it more like 'wrestling on horseback'. An exhilarated Mannerheim once managed to get the goat onto his saddle, and briefly fought off his opponents with his whip and horsemanship, before losing hold of the goat once more. He reported that it was lighter than he was expecting, and that had he been riding one of the good quality horses of his army days, Talisman perhaps, he might have even successfully galloped ahead of the crowd to the finish line, where a winner was expected to throw the dead goat at the feet of the crowd to receive a monetary award from the local lord.

Pelliot, in contrast, seems to have remained aloof and timid throughout. He eventually asked the Kirghiz tribesmen to give him the goat, and then paraded in front of Charles Nouette's camera with it – the dramatic effect somewhat ruined by the polite refusal of his Kirghiz opponents to chase after him, and the concerned attention of a nearby tribesman who could see that Pelliot was no horseman, and protectively rode at his side, steering the reins of his horse so that the Frenchman was practically led to the finish line. There, amid half-hearted cheers from the crowd, he received a single rouble from one of the onlookers, while Mannerheim watched with head-shaking exasperation.[22]

The two men continued to feud over their specialist fields. On 22 August, Mannerheim arrived on schedule at the village of Irkeshtam, while the majority of the French did not limp into town until after dark, having wasted most of the morning chasing after escaped horses. Since the next day was lost anyway while they waited for the baggage train, Mannerheim was archly disapproving of the Frenchman's decision to press on in the dark across hazardous terrain. 'I'll wager', Mannerheim said to Vaillant, 'that Pelliot would be mad to come here without a guide.'

Needless to say, his comment soon made it back to Pelliot, who angrily wrote that 'there is no-one among us who doesn't know the route, and Mannerheim was merely sulking over the loss of a single day.'[23]

On 23 August 1906, the expedition reached the nondescript Russian frontier with China, a windswept customs hut in the mountains, whipped by flurries of snow. The only sign of civilisation came in the form of the telegraph poles that led back into the Tsar's empire. Pelliot seized the opportunity to send a cable to Russia, only to be sternly told that the telegraph was solely for Russian use.

A small stone pillar marked the boundary between the empires of Russia and China, and also a change in attitudes. The Chinese border was the official commencement of Mannerheim's spying mission, but it was also the tail end of Pelliot's Russian visa. The French no longer travelled under Russian sufferance. Ironically, now was the time they needed Mannerheim the most, as he offered genuinely useful advice about stocking up on provisions for the horses. Instead, Pelliot dismissed Mannerheim's suggestions with even greater regularity.

'He considers himself entirely independent from us,' noted Pelliot, 'keeping our company solely for bed and breakfast. But all the while he continues to profit from communal items, in which he never shares. He came to watch the *baiga*, but it was I alone who donated the [prizes].'[24]

Two could play at that game. Within the week, Pelliot was actively excluding Mannerheim from meetings with local dignitaries, on the pretext that the expedition's Chinese visa only allowed for Pelliot, Nouette and Vaillant, and the unexpected presence of a 'Swedish ethnographer' was sure to invite suspicion, particularly if he were actively poking around fortifications and barracks. Mannerheim clearly was – no sooner had the party reached Chinese soil, than his diary springs into action with discussions of military structures and the conditions of local soldiers.

Nervous at the sight of Mannerheim's mission properly under way, and still irked at his treatment at the border, Pelliot fought back. The big blow-up finally occurred on 26 August, when Pelliot implied it would be better for Mannerheim to abandon any pretence of travelling with the French.

Mannerheim felt that he was being punished for misgivings that Pelliot was having with the Russian government. It was not his fault, he contended, that the much-discussed 'subvention' had not turned up. Furthermore, the Russians had kept their side of the bargain, allowing Pelliot passage through the Tsar's territory. It was, thought Mannerheim, the height of bad manners for Pelliot to change the rules as soon as he was on Chinese soil, and if Mannerheim were not part of the French expedition, at least in name, his ability to observe the Chinese was sure to suffer. It was clear to both men that Pelliot had the upper hand, and could end Mannerheim's mission with a single word to the Chinese authorities. Mannerheim feebly offered to write to General Palitsyn for clarification of their mutual obligations, while Pelliot stormed off to write in his journal of the irony – it was, he crowed, formerly Mannerheim who had been so keen to disassociate himself from the French, and now their positions were reversed.[25]

Two days later, Pelliot's unrealistically punishing pace left four of Mannerheim's horses with sprains, saddle sores, or generally in need of rest. Pointedly, Mannerheim announced that he was going to let them recuperate, whether Pelliot liked it or not. Although still technically travelling together, the parties began to follow different itineraries. Ironically, Mannerheim's better-treated horses, despite taking things slower, often matched the pace of the increasingly inefficient Pelliot party. Even when the two groups shared a campsite, Mannerheim and his men would unfailingly rise with the dawn and head out before many of Pelliot's men had even woken up.

The two groups were reunited in Kashgar in the furthest western reaches of China, where they were to spend over a month recuperating, waiting out the end of the summer heat, and preparing their first batch of notes and materials to send home. The centre of town lay behind a mud wall the height of several men, encircled by many suburbs. Mannerheim found the local people to be indolent and work-shy, happy to live hand-to-mouth in an endless cycle of squandering their savings, working fiendishly to recoup the losses, and then squandering once again. For most of the week, much of the town was sleepy and shuttered, only truly coming alive each Thursday when the market came to town.

Relenting a little when they were billeted in a large town, Pelliot took Mannerheim along to meetings with both the Chinese prefect and trading liaison, but then spoke to each in Mandarin for a full hour on each occasion, while the uncomprehending Mannerheim fumed and sipped at a succession of cups of tea.[26]

Left to his own devices, Mannerheim wandered around town to observe the locals. He was deeply disparaging about Chinese business practices, noting that local merchants threw themselves deep into debt to set up enterprises that could not possibly work, trading with each other in unrealistic credit terms that would never come to fruition. 'The date of maturity', Mannerheim archly noted,

'simply means the time at which you begin to postpone payment on every imaginable pretext.' [27]

In October 1906, Mannerheim abandoned Pelliot, setting out on a mission to the south of Kashgar. For the explorer in him, it was a chance to see the little-visited southern reaches of the Tak-lamakan desert. For the military observer, it was an opportunity to see if rumours were true that Japanese agents were at work in the area. For part of the way, he tailed a caravan of traders from oasis to oasis, making careful note of the resources available at each. He was unsurprised to discover that Chinese language signs promising shade and sweet water often only led to 'a dirty pool full of weeds and, no doubt, swarming with microbes.' [28]

Mannerheim spent a month in Yarkand, in part because he was struck down with an attack of rheumatism that made it impossible for him to get back in the saddle. Unspecified aches and pains, which had begun as mere twinges during his time in Manchuria, soon swelled to painful proportions during the ride across Asia, and never quite left Mannerheim in later life. He referred to these outbreaks, as in Finnish folklore, as 'witches' arrows' (as if being attacked by invisible archers) and did his best to keep them out of public discussion.

Despite his poor health in Yarkand, Mannerheim was keen to make use of the expertise of a Swedish missionary, Gustaf Raquette, who offered much information about local life. Mannerheim met several European missionaries on his trip, and many of them annoyed him: 'It seems like the Bible and the New Testament are the only books they have ever opened.' [29] Raquette, however, was a different case, and Mannerheim's diary explodes with local colour in Yarkand. He reports on the poor medical condition of the population, the ubiquitous goitres and leprosy among the people, the timing of Muslim feasts and the organisa-tion of almshouses.

By now, however, Mannerheim was becoming increasingly frus-trated with his interpreter, Liu, who was remarkably bad at his job. Liu was from Manchuria, and hence presumably spoke a northern dialect of Mandarin away from the Turkic and Persian-accented language of Chinese Turkestan. He also insisted on addressing

Mannerheim at all times in Russian, a language which Liu had only just begun to learn. Liu is mentioned seventeen times in Mannerheim's diary, and on almost every occasion it is a negative comment about his failure actually to interpret. In Mannerheim's later *Memoirs*, he also notes that Liu was 'of little use' and 'with typical Chinese courtesy ... refrained from correcting me, which only added to my difficulties.'[30]

Mannerheim tired of missing out on what could well be vital local intelligence, and decided to make a stab at learning Mandarin himself. He commissioned an old man from Henan to teach him Chinese, and added the man and his servant, with their horses, to the growing numbers of his party. However, no mention is made of the Chinese teacher again, so presumably they parted company soon afterwards, quite possibly during one of Mannerheim's bedridden relapses with rheumatism. He later alludes to a new Chinese teacher called Guo, 'a rascal of 23, demoralised by opium smoking', so plainly made several attempts to learn.[31]

Mannerheim does not seem to have noticed, but the appointment of a Chinese teacher to the party was a considerable loss of face to Liu the interpreter, who was surely struggling daily to understand the thick accents of the natives. Liu soon began to muse that he wished to return to Kashgar and thence to Russia to get a train back home.[32]

Mannerheim's irritation with him reached new heights in Yarkand when he failed to gain him a long audience with a local mandarin. In Raquette's company, Mannerheim was invited to feasts with dignitaries, where he was obliged to struggle manfully through Chinese dishes that he plainly found revolting. Table talk, however, stayed on superficial matters, and when Mannerheim attempted to talk over more important geographical or strategic matters, he found Liu's Russian not up to the task of explaining what the mandarin was telling him.

Making virtue out of necessity, Mannerheim began to treat Yarkand as an example of all Chinese outposts in the region. He noted that the locals regarded the visit of a prefect from far Urumqi more as an imposition than an honour. The man's arrival was purportedly to dispense justice in answer to some local complaints,

but Mannerheim saw little justice forthcoming, merely some exchanges of bribes and pleasantries.

Late in November, Mannerheim was finally able to meet with the local *xiedai*, a rank that might be reasonably translated as the same as his own – colonel. With an element of glee, Mannerheim reported that he was a typical example of the hidebound Chinese army. The man was in his seventies, deaf and frightfully stupid. He bragged ceaselessly about the superiority of the 'invincible' Chinese army, and seemed to have a position, rank, and attitude all based on the claim that some thirty years earlier as a younger man he had led a regiment that had 'defeated' a group of attacking Tatars that outnumbered him ten to one. Mannerheim did not even bother to question this boast, but noted instead that the man's prime interest was in lining his own pockets with the grants he received to maintain his regiment. The regiment, however, only existed on paper. What pitiful troops there were, Mannerheim observed, seemed to comprise a huddle of opium addicts, who were forced to supplement their meagre stipends by working as farmers.

Unwilling to let a single man speak for an entire empire's soldiers, Mannerheim called on several other officers, and found them to be similarly obtuse. He even obtained permission to visit a local school, and found that the children there were only being taught how to read Chinese. The mandarin defended this with a paraphrase of Confucius: that having learned how to read, they would be able to teach themselves anything else that they desired. Mannerheim, however, had already noted that there were few books in Yarkand besides copies of the Koran, and that, with even newspapers in short supply, 'education' in Yarkand amounted to little more than marketplace gossip.[33]

Finally, Mannerheim moved on from Yarkand. With great discomfort, as he was still in too much pain to ride, he was forced to proceed for the next part of his journey by cart. He was a bad passenger, and berated his men for their failure to get a move on. In his diary, he fulminates about the failure of the Chinese to make an early start, even when they were travelling with a supply of 17 alarm clocks, donated by Pelliot as high-tech gifts for local potentates. When Mannerheim made the men take two clocks for their

Mannerheim taking hypsometer readings at the Chapchal pass, 8th May 1907

own use, one was found to be broken, and the other did not have a key to wind it up.[34]

In December 1906, Mannerheim arrived in Khotan, the furthest point south of his mission. Although Russian maps already existed for the area, he began making his own, partly to get used to the process once again. In Khotan, the 'Swedish explorer' Mannerheim asked to see the local brigade commander or *tongling*, and received an enthusiastic welcome.

Flattered by Mannerheim's request to take his photograph, the *tongling* treated Mannerheim to a demonstration of some of his military drills. Mannerheim tried to stifle his chuckles while a platoon of soldiers fought imaginary enemies with bamboo poles. For the man who had once charged Japanese machine gun positions in Manchuria, it was yet another sign that the Chinese army presented no threat to Russian power.[35]

5

The Horse Reaches China

Mannerheim was to spend only a few days in Khotan before returning to Kashgar where he hoped to catch up with Pelliot again and continue their trip together. Khotan in the south had merely been a diversion – the true focus of Mannerheim's observations would still be the pathways around the north of the desert, heading to the east. On the road back, the locals' generosity towards him led him to regard them much more warmly. When not thinking in purely military terms, Mannerheim was far more forgiving of the Chinese. He was often overwhelmed and humbled by their hospitality, and was keen to note in his diary the many small kindnesses, favours and gifts bestowed upon him by people who could barely afford to eat. He also discovered, to his genuine embarrassment, that his arrival in the outlying towns was such an excitement that many locals went out of their way to make him feel welcome. When he deliberately chose to take a different route back to Yarkand, in order to map new areas, he left a string of broken-hearted officials on the old road, one of whom had even set aside a room for him in his mansion in the expectation that Mannerheim would pass through again.

Back in Kashgar, Mannerheim was elated to be riding a horse again instead of being dragged behind one in a cart. He was reunited with some of his equipment, received some long-delayed letters from his family, and was even able to have his broken camera repaired. He also made some efforts to mend fences with the Pelliot group, since he still believed that it was in his best interests to catch up with Pelliot and travel with him. In making his reports back to General Palitsyn, he tried unsuccessfully to steer 'Uncle Feda' into clarifying who had command of the Cossacks. Nor, did it seem, was there any sign of the 'subvention' that Pelliot was still awaiting.

While Mannerheim plainly wanted to bury the hatchet, he was soon angered by the discovery that Pelliot had been less than kind to him in his absence. Pelliot appeared to have revealed Mannerheim's secret mission to the other Frenchmen in his party, in direct contravention of his orders. Furthermore, in Kashgar, Mannerheim finally received his Chinese passport, a vital document for the rest of his trip, to find it unhelpfully described him as 'the Russian subject, the Finn Baron Mannerheim'. Mannerheim was deeply suspicious as to why the passport should be so exact, particularly when it was issued by a Chinese official who had not even heard of Finland a few weeks earlier. Though he feared the worst, that the British were onto him, he thought it more likely that Pelliot had interfered in the passport's wording. In fact, although Mannerheim could never have known, the British had been entirely taken in by his Swedish disguise – Swedish was, after all, Mannerheim's native tongue. Rather, the description in the passport has all the hallmarks of Pelliot's linguistic precision, carefully establishing that Mannerheim was a Finn, and adding the distinctly unhelpful qualification that this made him a Russian subject of sorts. This seems, however, to have been the sum total of Pelliot's meddling; the Frenchman could have easily made Mannerheim's life considerably more difficult, but limited his efforts simply to disassociating himself from Mannerheim. This was, it seems, largely because Pelliot fully expected Mannerheim to hoist himself with his own petard if he continued to nose around military installations in such an overt manner. Pelliot feared that the Chinese would have the opportunity to compare Mannerheim's behaviour with *real* archaeologists in the region, such as himself and Aurel Stein, and would then find Mannerheim's activities suspicious. Pelliot would later note that among the Chinese there had been '... much talk of Mannerheim accompanied by a small Chinese who spoke fluent Russian, and who, instead of digging in old ruins like Stein, only enquired after geographical matters and the state of extant populations.'[1]

As the Chinese were entirely unable to pronounce European names, Mannerheim also received a Chinese identity. As was traditional, it was a rough approximation of the sound of his real name, but an unknown individual with a certain poetic leaning had chosen it. The name was *Ma Da-Han*, translated literally as 'A Horse Reaches China'.[2]

After intense negotiations with the sulking Liu, Mannerheim retained the services of his awful interpreter as far as Qulja. He remained thoroughly dissatisfied with Liu's performance, noting in his diary that he would be happily rid of him as soon as he could find a Chinese who spoke any foreign language. He even wrote a note back to his father, wondering if General Palitsyn could send someone appropriate from Russia, but to no avail. Mannerheim also got a new cook, although he was not holding out much hope of decent food. 'In the past three months,' he wrote to his father, 'I have had to change cooks five times, and at the moment I am nearly dying of hunger. ... One of my cooks was so messy that all of Europe's dirtiness would not have compared with his fumbling in the kitchen.'[3]

Mannerheim now gave up on Pelliot. There was no official break in their arrangements, but the parties split into two groups and were not reunited again. The decision was made easier, for both participants and any observers, by the fact that the Pelliot expedition often bifurcated and reformed en route, with heavy materials travelling with the porters at a slow pace on better roads and tracks, while the Frenchmen sallied out to remote spots and sites. If the Chinese authorities were to stop Mannerheim on the road, he might easily claim that he was simply a few miles ahead of the rest of his 'fellow' travellers. Before long, he had left them far behind, and was able to proceed at his own pace, mapping and observing.

Mannerheim and his men set out once more along the north side of the Taklamakan desert – the long, winding road that should eventually take them to the eastern terminus of the Silk Road.

Grateful to be riding again, Mannerheim trotted far ahead or to the side of his group on small hunting expeditions. Occasionally, he brought down a goat. He once shot a wild boar, only to discover that none of his Muslim bearers would carry it for him.[4]

Mannerheim continued to write of the crushing poverty of the people he encountered, and the resignation with which they endured bullying. Only a few days out of Kashgar, his supply wagon lost an axle, leading Mannerheim's men to cannibalise a replacement from the next luckless merchant to pass in the opposite direction. Mannerheim, who witnessed the incident, handed the man monetary compensation, but observed that if he had not done so, the victim would have simply trudged onwards on foot, and possibly lodged a complaint with a mandarin, in the expectation that justice was unlikely to be forthcoming.

At Maralbashi, Mannerheim went to pay his respects to the local mandarin, only to discover that the man was pretending to be away on business. Liu explained that Chinese New Year was approaching, and that no official wanted to get bogged down in protocol with only a few days to go. Mannerheim entertained himself instead by writing a detailed report on the town's military preparedness. It was, it seemed, ready to resist invaders, except at weekends, on national holidays or during pre-arranged vacations.[5]

Sending the bulk of his expedition supplies ahead on the main road, along with the useless Liu, Mannerheim deliberately took a little-used caravan track, both to evade local officials, and to scout unmapped territory. He never tired of gazing at the mountains towering above him (in years to come, the sight of the Austrian or Swiss Alps would make him yearn for China), and stared in wonder at the many ruined towns he passed.

He did not need to be an archaeologist to read the evidence before him. Hundreds of years before, parts of this desert realm had been lush and green. Low walls had held back the sand, and long-dead rivers watered carefully irrigated crops. The desert, true enough, had always been there, but the oases had been much more plentiful. People had carved out lives for themselves in this inhospitable region, but now most of the wells were dry and the towns were empty.

On some occasions, Mannerheim was in two minds whether he was looking at ruined towers or strange geological features in the rock. Nor were his fellow men much use; his Cossacks lived only for the ride and the hunt, his porters were Muslims who had no interest in the ancient Buddhist civilisation that had flourished in the region. Indeed, many Muslims in the region considered it their sacred duty to burn Buddhist manuscripts and deface ancient frescoes.

A few of the villages remained occupied. Regardless of the precise tribal ethnicity of the locals – Kirghiz, Sarts, Kalmuks – the local bigwig was usually Chinese. In one village, Mannerheim playfully noted that the Chinese governor's mansion still observed the daily firing of a signal cannon to mark the opening and closing of the town gates, even though the pitiful little cluster of huts no longer had any.[6]

In remote gorges and strategic points on the road, Mannerheim found that even the Chinese guard posts had been deserted for some years. Although the region was nominally part of China, it was so unwelcoming that not even the Chinese wanted to linger there. In days gone by, the desert regions had been regarded as a natural barrier to protect China proper. It was surely far better, ancient sages had argued, to let an enemy die of thirst trying to cross it, than to establish permanent bases in China's far west.[7]

In Aqsu, Mannerheim heard of plans underway to link the remote region to China proper by rail. He was, of course, deeply interested in the strategic implications. Despite the Russian defeat in the recent war against Japan, the presence of a railway would significantly improve military mobility in Central Asia for whoever controlled it. He was, however, unable to get more details from the local prefect. Though he was temporarily able to replace the incompetent Liu with a local telegraph operator, the man's English proved to be as impenetrable as Liu's Russian, and Mannerheim left with little more information.[8]

Mannerheim kept a soldier's eye open for the tiniest details about the local infrastructure. He noted that the telegraph poles on the Aqsu road were placed dangerously far apart, such that the wires sagged almost to ground level. In Aqsu, for the first time, he met troops whose skills with firearms matched his own – he noted at a military demonstration that every soldier he saw was able to put five rounds into a target at 200 paces. Mannerheim was even more impressed by the family of the local prefect, whose wives were similarly able to hit a target at 180 paces.

The next stage of the journey took Mannerheim over a mountain range towards Qulja. The spring weather soon turned wintry again as the men and horses climbed into the foothills. The path was fraught with treacherous bends, and Mannerheim noted that his horse Philip took an undue interest in the precipitous drops from the path. 'Philip ... was equally fascinated by the view,' wrote Mannerheim, 'and kept going along the extreme edge, so that I began to suspect him of contemplating suicide.'[9]

Most dangerous of all was the Muzart glacier, a series of monstrous, jagged hills of ice, tumbling down into the desert in geological slow motion. One of Mannerheim's Cossacks was running a high fever, but Mannerheim pressed on, determined to reach the summit before a storm closed the pass off for days. The horses sank girth-deep in the snow if they strayed off the path, and risked falling into a crevasse if they slipped on the ice. At the top of the glacier, a group of men were permanently stationed in a small hut. It was their job, every day, to climb down the glacier to its steepest point, hacking steps into the ice in order to keep the road open.

After the icy wilderness of the Muzart glacier, Mannerheim was thrilled to reach Qulja, a region that had been briefly Russian territory until only a generation before, and a town where he observed the difficult coexistence of Russian and Chinese laws. Qulja enjoyed strong contacts with Russia, but Mannerheim was galled at the number of criminals, charlatans and ne'er-do-wells who basked in the glow of extraterritoriality. He noted that Russian subjects could, at least in theory, get away with murder, and was unsurprised that the local Chinese bore so many grudges against them. He saw, for the first time, a local antipathy towards Russians that extended to a desire to raze Vladivostok and push the invaders back over the Amur River.

At Qulja, Mannerheim bid farewell to one of his Cossacks, who was still feverish after the crossing of the Muzart glacier. He was also finally able to rid himself of the troublesome interpreter Liu,

Climbing the Muzart Pass

'whose caprices were beginning to disturb me'. Instead, he hired a 16-year-old boy, Joseph Zhao, the son of a local man who spoke Russian well. Mannerheim deposited six months of Joseph's salary in advance with a local missionary as a gesture of good faith, and prepared to set off the following day, ahead of the onset of an Orthodox Easter. Liu, who had grudgingly agreed to accompany Mannerheim only as far as Qulja, was plainly surprised to discover that he had taken him at his word.[10] Mannerheim was soon left wondering if he had made the right decision. Joseph showed up for duty a day late, which was hardly a encouraging sign of his likely punctuality or mastery of Russian.

The next stage of Mannerheim's journey found his party making a strangely random series of trips. Mannerheim sent some horsemen ahead to Qarashahr, where he had sent some of his baggage, in order to bring back more gifts he could give to locals on the route. He sent another man back to Qulja to pick up rusks. Mannerheim enjoyed supplanting the party's provisions with freshly shot game, but seems to have come to rely on his ability to shoot goats, deer and other animals en route. Troubled by aching limbs and an inflammation of his bad knee, he now left incidental hunting to one of his Cossacks, but found the man's aim wanting.

Mannerheim now took a route across open terrain that may have been deliberately to keep him away from population centres, not to deter potential enemies, but to avoid an unwelcome ally. He knew from correspondence left at earlier post houses that Pelliot was camped in nearby Kucha, but seems to have made no effort to rendezvous with him.[11] Instead, he forged on ahead towards Urumqi, leaving Pelliot several weeks behind him. In the days that followed, Mannerheim's men became increasingly jumpy at the presence of unknown tribesmen nearby, and Mannerheim felt obliged to post a watch at their campsites. His cook, Ismail, who was tasked with the first shift, enjoyed this duty the most, and strode purposefully around the tents, a sword in hand, looking for non-existent bandits.[12]

Mannerheim busied himself making anthropological measurements of local tribesmen, in order to keep up his cover, while also quizzing them about their salaries and training. He travelled among the Torguts, a people whose ancestors had once relocated to the banks of the Volga in Russia, before fleeing back east into China before Russian armies. Some of the Torguts had dim recollections of old legends about their sojourn in Europe, but few were able to supply any further details. Like many of the other peoples in the region, they were barely able to subsist, and would wait for hours by a rat hole in the chance of killing a rodent for supper.

On the long road, Mannerheim's men would try to entertain themselves. The Muslim cook, Ismail, was prevailed upon to sing something every now and then. Joseph Zhao tried to get into the spirit of things by whistling a badly remembered snatch of 'La donna è mobile' from *Rigoletto*, which he had picked up from a gramophone record.

The party reached Urumqi in July. Mannerheim was grateful once more to be in civilisation, although his surroundings and even his own party were now overwhelmingly Chinese. Of Mannerheim's entire party, only Lukanin, the single Cossack now left, and he himself were not Chinese.

In Urumqi, Mannerheim was obliged to explain the strange

presence of two names on his passport. It was a bizarre situation – surely the Chinese, even in 1907, were more than used to the confusion arising from writing foreigners' names in Chinese and would have been easily able to see that the Mannerheim of the St Petersburg visa and the Mannerheim of the Finnish passport were one and the same? Mannerheim fretted, once again, that someone in China was suspicious of the true nature of his mission, and very carefully explained to the local consul that Finland was a Grand Duchy, and not 'part of' Russia per se.

In fact, although there certainly were occasional speculations among the Chinese about Mannerheim's habit of photographing military sites, the explanation for his treatment in Urumqi was much simpler. A local dignitary, Mannerheim was told, 'had a very old mother', a mealy-mouthed circumlocution that implied he might soon be obliged to enter the compulsory three-year mourning period demanded by Chinese tradition. The official was, we may assume, determined to line his pockets with as much bribe money as possible before his involuntary sabbatical, and seems to have manufactured the local suspicions about Mannerheim on a thin pretext. Mannerheim, however, was a plainspoken Finn and hence entirely immune to such subtleties – if the mandarin wanted a bribe, he was doomed to be disappointed.[13]

Mannerheim's mission changed slightly as he headed east. For the first part of his trip, he had been expected to examine troops and terrain, military installations and the attitudes of the local people towards their Chinese masters. For the second part, as he neared central China, Mannerheim had been instructed to find out as much as he could about educational and social reforms in China. The Tsar was worried that, like the Japanese, the Chinese might suddenly be able to leap ahead technologically and socially, changing in only a few years from a quasi-medieval, 'backward' society into a nation that might threaten Russia itself. Mannerheim was expected to poke around within Chinese institutions, in order to determine just how likely this was. He was also to make careful note of who was doing the teaching – he rightly suspected that much of the education was being provided by the Japanese, and had a pan-Asian, anti-Russian angle to it.

It should not have come as a surprise that Urumqi had corrupt officials. Many of the Chinese had been sent there against their will, including Prince Lan, a cousin of the Chinese Emperor, who had been exiled to Urumqi for the part he played in the Boxer Uprising. Mannerheim also received a mind-boggling presentation of Chinese etiquette when he asked his local interpreter Gui Yu (Joseph was ill) if there was anyone else he should call upon. Gui Yu told him that, as the president of the Russo-Chinese Commission, the last but by no means least important dignitary in Urumqi was a man called Gui Yu. Mannerheim obligingly went through the farce of making a courtesy call on his own interpreter, who had been at his side for the last two days.

Gui Yu taught Russian in the local school, and invited Mannerheim to see the building. A Mr Hayashida, who taught Japanese, suspiciously made himself absent while Mannerheim was in town. In the geography classroom, Mannerheim was amused to see that the map of Europe showed a railway in Finland that reached up to Tornio on the Swedish border. The Oulu-Tornio railway had been approved for construction in 1897, but had become the subject of heated debate as part of the late Governor-General Bobrikov's efforts to keep Finland within a Russian orbit, and not to afford it unwelcome connections to the Swedes. For Mannerheim, it was a distant reminder of the political wrangling that still continued in his native land.[14]

Eight local mandarins called on Mannerheim with conspicuous creases in their robes, as if they had been newly donned straight out of their boxes. The Urumqi authorities were certainly keen to impress Mannerheim with the quality of life in their town, although a degree of face was lost when a knife-wielding local tried to kill the governor while Mannerheim was staying there. The mandarins were very talkative, but Mannerheim was limited as ever by his interpreter in getting information out of them. He had far greater success in talking to a Mr Bauer, an Austrian ex-soldier who filled him in on the Chinese arms trade. By Bauer's estimation, all orders went through Beijing, and were subject to such inevitable squeezes and rake-offs on their long journey to the western provinces that the Chinese invariably ended up with the cheapest and most unreliable arms. Bauer regarded China as a dump for the outmoded weapons of all the other nations; an observation which Mannerheim thought very apt. Bauer had been commissioned to run an ammunition factory in Urumqi that could, in theory, make 500 cartridges a day. But the factory lacked important components, and even if it had been operational, the locals were so used to eking out their ammunition that Bauer doubted he would be expected to run at full capacity.[15]

Although Mannerheim was still in Xinjiang or 'Chinese Turke-stan,' the culture became progressively more Chinese as his party neared the Gansu Corridor, a long passage between mountains and desert that led all the way to China proper. In Turfan, Mannerheim conceded that the Chinese military drills he saw were far more impressive than the theatrical displays he had witnessed elsewhere.

The Chinese, however, remained quaintly hidebound. In the snows of a mountain range near Hami, two officers told him that they were wary of military or educational reforms, as it was tanta-mount to genuflecting to foreign pressure. To many of the Chinese Mannerheim encountered, railways and firearms, medicines and factories, plumbing and hygiene were not examples of progress but of an unwelcome threat to a local order that had endured for centuries. It was, Mannerheim thought, an excellent example of how unlikely the Chinese were to present a threat to the Russians along the shared border. As far as Mannerheim could see, it would take another generation of education before many Chinese people could even be persuaded to regard new technology as anything but an evil, pernicious foreign influence.

Ironically, Mannerheim was practically out of the 'lawless' western region before he was in any danger. He took a great interest in the town of Hami, which was divided on racial and religious lines. The Chinese authorities were clustered on one side in the 'Old Town'; the Muslim locals had their own district on the opposite bank, encircled by a high but crumbling wall, with dilapidated houses within. A huge mosque and mausoleum sat outside the town, where the Muslim princes of Hami were buried. The current 'prince' of Hami, Shah Mahmut, was nothing of the sort; instead he was a mere shepherd boy who had married the daughter of the last rightful ruler, and assumed the status of his late father-in-law.

Mannerheim found Mahmut to be a creepy and obsequious individual, living in a shabby mansion surrounded by tasteless knick-knacks. Mahmut had only recently suppressed a peasant uprising, in which his troops had dispersed a demonstration by firing their guns into the crowd. The situation intrigued Mannerheim for its division on racial lines – Mahmut was still nominally the ruler of Hami, but was forced to share his domain with a prefect who had been installed by Chinese troops sent to prevent further bloodshed. Consequently, Hami was an uneasy mixture of races, with the local population, mainly Sarts, still smarting from the atrocities committed by the Muslim prince, while the Chinese authorities warily hoped that the mere presence of an appointed official would keep matters calm.

Inadvertently, Mannerheim was able to put local law enforcement directly to the test. The streets of Hami were crawling with toughs determined to demonstrate that nobody could order them around. Eight such men waylaid Mannerheim's latest cook, Chang, demanded that he hand over the cartridges on his belt, and beat him up when he refused. Mannerheim was concerned about the precedent that this might set, and immediately went to the local prefect. The prefect, however, refused to get involved, as the muggers were technically 'soldiers' in the employ of Shah Mahmut. When Mannerheim demanded that Mahmut do something about it, the Shah tried to fob him off by telling him that two of the eight men would be punished. Mannerheim refused to accept this, and announced that unless all eight muggers received their due, he would telegraph Urumqi with an official complaint – precisely the sort of cross-jurisdictional issue that Mahmut would do well to avoid in the wake of the recent demonstrations. Eventually, Mannerheim allowed Mahmut to talk him around into agreeing to an apology from the muggers. Chang the cook, who had tried to keep the news of the incident secret from Mannerheim in the first place, readily accepted the mumbled contrition of his assailants, and a diplomatic incident was avoided.[16]

As winter closed in, Mannerheim became more eager to reach

central China. He was now approaching the western reaches of the Great Wall, whose easternmost extent he had once inadvertently stumbled across in Manchuria. Mannerheim did not know it, but he was already tracing a path along a ghost wall. He was still many days away from the Great Wall itself, but he was already passing between towns that were built as extensions from it, around forts which ancient emperors might have planned eventually to link by walls if they had the time or inclination.

On several occasions, Mannerheim berated his associates for their tardiness and stupidity. In one incident that would forever shame him, he even beat the wrong man for turning up late.[17] However, he himself was not immune to mistakes – one might even suggest that he was becoming sloppy. He had stood up for his Chinese cook in Hami only as a matter of principle – he was heartily sick of Chang's cuisine, and was relying more often on whatever wild game he could shoot and roast for himself en route. This epicurean fancy would cost him dearly in Dunhuang, a dilapidated town dwarfed by the nearby sand dunes.

Only a few miles outside Dunhuang was the ruin of a massive Buddhist temple complex, once comprising a thousand shrines, intricately decorated and richly appointed. Now it was largely deserted, but one of the few remaining denizens had recently uncovered a hidden room full of ancient scrolls. It would prove to be one of the most important archaeological discoveries of the 20th century, containing priceless manuscripts from the forgotten peoples of the Silk Road. There were complete copies of books that only existed in fragments elsewhere, ancient texts that nobody had even heard of, and even intriguing documents, such as the *Jesus Sutras* relating to the lost Christians of the Far East. At the time that Mannerheim arrived in Dunhuang, however, the true value of the find was unknown. A few of the scrolls had been carried off a few months earlier by the archaeologist Aurel Stein, but in November 1907, the Dunhuang Scrolls were there for the taking, assuming that one could reach a financial agreement with their self-appointed guardian, a Mr Wang.

Mannerheim set out in the general direction of the caves, but was soon diverted by the prospect of hunting local deer. In search of what he called a 'welcome change' to his diet, he chased after pheasants and other game, and put all thought of the cave behind him. The next day, he continued on his route east, and did not think of Dunhuang again.[18]

Six weeks after Mannerheim left Dunhuang, his erstwhile associate Pelliot rode into town and did not make the same mistake. Pelliot spent many days sorting through the manuscripts in search of the real treasures. He then shipped the ancient manuscripts by the crateful back to Paris, where they would eventually make his name.[19]

It would be many years before Mannerheim realised the magnitude of his lost opportunity. When he wrote his *Memoirs* in the 1950s, he carefully inserted the claim that he had known of the Dunhuang find, but that he excused himself through lack of qualifications:

> During my visit to this place my attention was drawn to a unique collection of documents discovered a year before by a Chinese priest in a passage through a cliff, the entrance of which was walled in. To examine this find exceeded my competence and even otherwise I would by no means have undertaken it as I heard that a French scientific expedition was on its way to examine it.[20]

Mannerheim's supposedly gracious decision to leave it all to Pelliot was concocted long after the fact. His professed 'lack of competence' in other areas of Central Asian studies had not prevented him from buying cratefuls of artefacts and shipping them back to Helsinki for more qualified individuals to study. Entire academic papers would later be written about small fragments of old scrolls he had already sent home from other locations. But the diary he wrote at the time has him shrugging his shoulders and going nowhere near the Dunhuang caves at all. In the 1910s, when Pelliot was pilloried by a doubting Parisian establishment, Mannerheim had nothing to say about the scrolls. It was only after 1912, when the publication of Aurel Stein's *Ruins of Desert Cathay* exonerated Pelliot that the magnitude of the Dunhuang find was truly realised.

But Mannerheim's lack of interest in Dunhuang was one facet of a general malaise that seems to have gripped him as he neared the eastern end of the Silk Road. A day out of Dunhuang, he rose early in the morning, as was his habit, oversaw the packing of the tents and provisions, and inspected the horses. 'The weather was grey and cold,' he wrote, 'and an unpleasant wind buffeted our faces.'[21] With sand in the breeze that forced them all to squint at the path ahead, Mannerheim then led his men onward ... back the way they had already come.

Mannerheim tramped for an hour and a half through the feature-less dunes before he sensed that there was something familiar about the terrain. When he asked his men why they had not said anything, they replied that they assumed he knew what he was doing.

The icy sand dunes of the Gansu Corridor were not a place for mistakes. Mannerheim's party came across a Chinese monk shiv-ering in the sands, his bare feet covered in ice. Mannerheim tried to coerce the man onto one of his spare ponies to accompany them to shelter, but the monk refused. A horseman tailing Mannerheim later reported that he had found the monk where they had left him, already dead.[22]

On 29 November 1907, Mannerheim and his travelling com-panions crossed a dried-up riverbed to see a veritable castle in the distance. Crenellated walls rose up from the iced-over ground, topped by three triple-storey watchtowers. Visible from a distance of 3 miles, it was an imposing sight after the huts and shacks of the Silk Road. As the horsemen drew nearer, they passed a stone carved with a portentous message: *Diyi Xiong Guan*, 'The First and Greatest Gate'. Mannerheim had reached Jiayuguan, the western-most end of the Great Wall of China. His luggage, however, was still a day or so behind him on a slow cart, and he was obliged to wait in the fortress.[23]

Jiayuguan is an important site in Chinese folklore. As the ter-minus of the Great Wall, it was also the edge of the traditional Chinese world. Mannerheim's wanderings in 'Chinese' Turkestan had been a journey through a place regarded for long periods of Chinese history as a distant, savage wilderness. Convicted crimi-nals and other undesirables were sentenced in former dynasties to banishment 'beyond the gate', meaning a one-way trip to the lands beyond Jiayuguan. Consequently, Mannerheim expected a considerably stronger military presence at the famous fort. Instead, he found soldiers whose matchlock musket practice was conducted solely with blank ammunition.

In Jiayuguan Mannerheim explored the temple of the Chinese war god, Guan Yu, and gazed in incomprehension at murals depicting the deity's great battles. Guan Yu was actually a deified mortal who had lived in the third century AD. The sight of the god's statue and depictions of his 'many brothers-in-law' inspired Mannerheim to conduct further research into the mystifyingly large pantheon of Chinese folk religion. On a cold November day in 1907, he began to formulate a plan to chart and catalogue Chinese deities.

Mannerheim maintained his interest in Chinese temples as he rode onwards towards the east. In the Temple of the Great Bell in the nearby walled town of Suzhou, he was amazed by the grotesque image of the twelve gods of hell, tormenting sinners in the Chinese afterlife:

> You see intestines being pulled out with long tongs, whole bodies being flayed, skulls being sawn asunder, eyes being gouged out or being pecked out by a cock, women being hanged by their breasts, tongues being cut off ... Such horrors should surely suffice to rid the inhabitants ... of any desire to sin.[24]

Mannerheim added, however, that he suspected most of the people in Suzhou would do anything they were asked if given a couple of copper coins, divine retribution or not. There were a number of soldiers at Suzhou on their way out to a new posting on the Russian border, many of them under the false impression that they were already at war with Russia. Mannerheim lingered for a few days, observing the behaviour of the troops in the streets and in the tavern where he stayed, which was cramped with extra beds. He also paid a visit on the *zhentai*, the local brigadier, a fat old man with a narrow beard that reached to his belt. He had once been posted to the Chinese embassy in St Petersburg, and when Mannerheim the 'Swedish explorer' feigned ignorance of the Russian capital, he insisted on regaling him with stories of its grandeur. Mannerheim, homesick for the glittering city on the river Neva, let the brigadier ramble on, and suppressed a smile as the old man tried to re-enact some of the dances he had witnessed at diplomatic parties, shambling through parodies of the quadrille and the waltz.

Mannerheim wandered through the wintry wastes for another month, before reaching the city of Lanzhou, the capital of Gansu and seat of the local viceroy, on 29 January 1908. He had always intended a long sojourn in such a major metropolis, but his visit was made much more agreeable by a local Catholic missionary, Léon van Dijk. Mannerheim was dragged to a better inn by van Dijk, and soon met members of the city's relatively large European community.

Mannerheim had arrived in the city three days ahead of Chinese New Year.[25] Having spent Christmas and New Year trudging across the wilderness, he greatly appreciated the chance to celebrate the beginning of the Year of the Monkey with a civilised banquet, champagne and evening dress. He was less pleased with the Chinese penchant for celebratory firecrackers, and commented that it often felt as if he was under enemy fire.

As one so often finds in the Far East, his European expatriate hosts were a mixed bunch. There were many missionaries, whom Mannerheim liked much more than most, and Alphonse Splingaerd, a chemical engineer and interpreter. Splingaerd had learned long ago that the way to impress the Chinese was simply to lie, and had gained a reputation as a man who could evaluate the mineral content of a mountain simply by looking at it. 'It is hard to imagine', observed Mannerheim, 'how such *bluffing* should succeed for any length of time, but after all, this is China.'[26]

Perhaps succumbing to exhaustion long suppressed, Mannerheim and four of his men came down with a flu-like bug soon after they arrived, which left them incapable of getting out of bed for several days. Mannerheim's torment was exacerbated by a group of itinerant acrobats and musicians, who insisted on striking up an 'unmusical' tune outside his window every day, finishing with a grand finale that included fireworks. While Mannerheim lay

helpless on the stone bed, he noted that his feelings 'went through the scale from fury to despair'. The New Year's celebrations, however, lasted for a full fortnight, long enough for Mannerheim to recover in time for the military parade that closed them – a sight close to his heart.

Once recovered, Mannerheim went to call on Viceroy Sheng Yun, the nominal ruler of the region he had spent an entire year traversing. Sheng, like so many Chinese officials of Mannerheim's acquaintance, was a smiling, portly gentleman who offered little hard information about his responsibilities. Whether it was the usual interpreting issues, Chinese humility or as a result of the mandarin's straightforward stupidity, Mannerheim reported that Viceroy Sheng seemed to possess no greater understanding of the disposition of the region than many lowlier officials. Mannerheim did note, however, that the viceroy had also once served in the Chinese embassy in St Petersburg, and had hence seen more of the world than most. Sheng also enjoyed a local reputation as something of a reformer, largely because he had told his underlings that he did not require any of the prescribed New Year's gifts. However, Mannerheim noted that the 'reformer' Sheng was still living far beyond the means that his salary would allow, and suspected that he was on the take.

Mannerheim had much more fun squeezing information out of one of Sheng's minions, a local prefect called Peng Yingjia. Peng had formerly been posted to Mukden in the years preceding the Russo-Japanese War, and hence had plenty to say about the Russians and the Japanese. To the 'Swede' Mannerheim, Peng confessed that the Russians had largely been welcomed by the Chinese, who enjoyed their tips and custom, whereas the Japanese were regarded as incorrigible, unpleasant sneaks. Peng was particularly surprised at the extent of Japanese spy networks there had been in Mukden, and related an incident of soon after the fall of the city in 1905, mere hours after Mannerheim himself had been evacuated to the north.

According to Peng, a Japanese general and his retinue had ridden into his mansion, presumably to announce officially that Mukden was now under Japanese authority. Peng had commented that the general seemed very familiar, and he asked if they had met before. The general replied that it was very possible, as he had lived in Mukden for many years, and had formerly run one of the city's most famous brothels.[27]

Mannerheim got to see Japanese espionage at work for himself in a nearby military school, the Lujun Xiaotang. Unlike many other schools in the region, it was large and well supplied with books, charts and maps. But it did not take Mannerheim long to notice how pro-Japanese the materials were. The refectory was decorated entirely with images of the Russo-Japanese War, all presenting the victorious Japanese in an heroic light. A series of pictures of world leaders on a classroom wall showed the Emperors of China and Japan regally seated, while the Tsar, the King of England and other royals attended on them like footmen. A long wall chart of important figures from world history ranked three Japanese figures at the top, alongside Napoleon, Confucius and Jesus Christ. Mannerheim was heartened to see the cadets made to perform rigorous callisthenics in order to fight off the indolence and apathy he perceived as common to Chinese academia, but he was also troubled by the wall charts demonstrating the various moves required, as all of them were performed by gymnasts in Japanese military uniforms.[28]

Mannerheim did not need to read Japanese himself to consider the implications of such superficial evidence for the rest of the curriculum. Japanese agents did not need to be present to steer Chinese policy if teachers were trained in Japan, and students were steered by Japanese materials. Japan's victory in Manchuria had not only beaten away the Tsar from East Asia, it had established Japan in Chinese eyes as a worthwhile nation for the Chinese to emulate. It was also, as one of Mannerheim's interviewees noted, cheaper for teachers to train in Japan and use Japanese teaching materials than to make the long journey to Europe or America for similar training. As for languages, teaching in Japanese, English or Russian was 'at the discretion of the masters', but if all the masters had studied in Japan, the implications for their students' curriculum was clear.

Mannerheim stayed longer in Lanzhou that he had planned, in

part because of a bout of neuralgia bought on by his attendance at a draughty banquet hosted by Viceroy Sheng. An extant photograph shows the diners at Sheng's feast, with Mannerheim in the place of honour, but conspicuously wearing his greatcoat indoors. Mannerheim also spent much time in conversation with van Dijk, with whom he would remain in touch for many years. It was with van Dijk that he confided his plans to compile a guide to the deities and demigods of Chinese mythology, an enterprise in which van Dijk would become a willing accomplice.

Mannerheim finally left Lanzhou on the next stage of his trip in early spring, a detour towards the Labrang temples. He left under a slight cloud when his last thermometer was stolen from the inn where he was staying. Mannerheim secured its return by first threatening to shoot the innkeeper and, when that ultimatum failed, by threatening not to pay his bill. Mystifyingly, the innkeeper feared loss of business higher than his own demise, and swiftly procured the missing thermometer from a light-fingered fellow guest.[29]

Perhaps because his Chinese was improving, Mannerheim started to appreciate how unwelcome foreigners often were in China. He became used to hearing the term *yang guizi*, 'Ocean Ghost' or 'White Devil', blurted by unwary children, and hissed with greater subtlety by their parents. Chinese often used the term in front of him, either assuming he would not understand, or expecting him to accept it as a reasonable classification.

Thieves were not the only danger in the western reaches of China. Mannerheim had been warned that the mountainous region was thick with murderers and bandits, and warned to be on his guard. With mounting irritation, he suspected that he had crossed the same river on multiple occasions, as it bent and twisted around the steep hills. Mannerheim's party pressed on through the steep forests of fir, up the sharp hills and down again through yet another torrent of fast, cold waters.

His men were armed with ancient rifles, in case of mountain bandits. The sight of them was worth more than their military effect; one of the guns only had ten rounds, another barely half a dozen more. Occasionally, they would see scraps of bright red in

the distance, starkly visible against the grey mountains. The scarlet figures were Buddhist monks in full regalia, walking across the hills towards the Labrang monastery; beyond the Chinese hills would eventually rise to become Tibetan mountains. Intermittently, the silver chasing on the monks' hats would flash in the cold sunlight, sparkling in the distance. It was said that a living Buddha was on his way to Labrang, and the monks were determined to pay him homage. Mannerheim was also hoping to meet the living Buddha, whom he rightly regarded as a figure of some temporal power, to whom it was worth paying the respects of the Russian Tsar. As the day came to an end, he saw 'the gilded roofs and spires of Labrang gleaming in the light of the dying sun'. The complex, which Mannerheim regarded less as a monastery and more as a city with 3,000 holy inhabitants, contained 18 huge temples, and 40 lesser chapels, and was sure to be a treasure trove for his newfound interest in Asian deities.[30]

Mannerheim sent one of his Chinese porters ahead with a calling card, to ask a senior lama at the monastery to put him up for the night. The card, however, fell into the hands of a local merchant, who called himself Uncle Ma. The weary handful of travellers arrived in Labrang in the afternoon of 25 March, to find a crowd of staring locals awaiting them. Brandishing the card, Uncle Ma directed Mannerheim to a grimy, unpleasant-looking guesthouse, claiming that the monastery would not see him. Angry that his orders had been ignored, Mannerheim gave Uncle Ma a piece of his mind.

He soon had cause to regret it. Uncle Ma was the undisputed fixer of Labrang, and nothing was accomplished there without him. Mannerheim soon discovered that his transit papers had failed to arrive from the last town – he was without a passport, in a politically sensitive area of China. The guardsmen he had been assigned in a previous town were openly afraid of the large crowd that had gathered, and told him that they would not make it far without Uncle Ma's approval. The following day, Mannerheim only got his men to follow him by saddling his own horse and threatening to ride up to the monastery on his own.

Despite the smiles of the elder monks, Mannerheim was not

permitted to see the living Buddha, who was apparently ill. He presented some gifts to an intermediary, and was taken aback when the priest returned with a bag of money in lieu of an audience with the living Buddha. Mannerheim declined the offer of money, but asked that he be allowed to look at some of the temples the following day. This request was, supposedly, granted, although Mannerheim was trailed throughout his explorations by a growing crowd of red-robed Buddhist monks.

At first, Mannerheim experienced little trouble. He gazed in awe at the long cloisters of giant prayer wheels, along which an endless line of pilgrims would march, turning each great mill in succession to crank out prayers to heaven. He noted with amusement that monks also walked among the lay pilgrims, but that they wisely each wore a single glove to protect themselves from the inevitable grime accruing from thousands of grubby hands on the prayer wheels. Used to gawkers after over a year in China, Mannerheim first thought nothing of it, but soon grew concerned at the monks' attitude. While he was in one temple, three elderly monks circled the building constantly chanting a prayer to ward off evil. Members of the crowd began to hiss, clap their hands, or even laugh. All of these acts, Mannerheim later found out, were supposed to dispel malicious spirits. Mannerheim came to realise that he was not being regarded as a welcome guest at all, but as a White Devil. He saw two monks picking up stones, and then narrowly ducked a rock thrown at his head. At the next temple, the door was rudely slammed in his face. He reached another plaza in the temple complex, but was beset on all sides by a crowd of monks and novices, yelling abuse at him and hurling stones. His guide dragged Mannerheim into a nearby house for an apparently pre-arranged visit with an elderly monk who collected Russian memorabilia. This, at least, shook off the growing mob, and Mannerheim passed a pleasant afternoon. Soon, however, he realised that the diversion was simply intended to keep him out of any further temples. When he asked if his tour could continue, he received such a non-committal reply that he angrily decided to give up on Labrang.[31]

Writing his account of his time in Labrang, Mannerheim recorded a story he had heard that Labrang monastery had ideas

above its station. Its leader, in fact, had once received a gentle rebuke from the Dalai Lama for addressing him as an equal. There was only one true authority in Buddhism, Mannerheim concluded as he departed the monastery complex, practically shaking the dust from his shoes as he left, and that was the Dalai Lama himself, on whom he hoped to call later in his journey. Labrang could keep its temples.[32]

That night, Mannerheim had an inadvertent lesson in karma, when he found his party far from their intended destination as night fell. Despite the increasingly strident protestations of his porters, he insisted on finding a bed for the night in the small village where they had ended up. One of his guards banged on doors and gates, but received no reply. Eventually, he scaled the walls of one of the compounds, and from within Mannerheim heard the sound of a heated argument. Eventually, the door opened, and the exhausted Mannerheim was told that a bed had been found for him.

As he stomped into the house, he caught a look of the bed's ousted owner, a leper whose face was almost entirely eaten away, riddled with scabs and putrescent flesh. Mannerheim and his men spent the night in a barn with two cows and a horse, and for many months afterwards Mannerheim fretted that he might have contracted leprosy from his hellish host.

On 21 April 1908, Mannerheim officially set down his orienteering equipment. He was now approaching a region of China that was already well covered in foreign maps, and regarded the mapping part of his mission as over. He was, at that point, only a few days outside the metropolis of Xi'an, a large city with stout medieval walls and a bustling population of over a hundred thousand. Mannerheim rode into town and pretended not to notice the crowds of soldiers from the military camp outside the city walls, who forgot their training and thronged to the roadside to witness the arrival of the White Devil.[33]

Mannerheim spent more time exploring schools and temples in the Xi'an area. He visited the Forest of Steles, a veritable maze of ancient stone tablets, containing, among other things, the entire works of Confucius and the 8th-century Nestorian Tablet recording the arrival of Christianity in China. He dropped in on the Temple of the Eight Immortals. He spent a day climbing Mount Hua, a holy site in the hinterland with such steep slopes that he was forced to clamber on all fours on steps cut into stone between the ridges, with metal chains for railings. On Mount Hua, he reached the Cave of the Sun and Moon, a shrine built inside a cave, surmounted by a perilous, cracked archway, before turning back for the long descent back to the plains. Mannerheim also visited the Famen temple, an ancient monastery favoured by the emperors of the Tang dynasty, where the founder of the Tang had enjoyed a brief contemplative retirement. Finally, Mannerheim approached the outskirts of Xi'an itself.

Xi'an had been the capital of China for several centuries, and was still a large city. However, this very civilised nature made it much harder for Mannerheim to practise the kind of archaeology and ethnology he had become used to in Central Asia. There were, it seems, far fewer unscrupulous locals around prepared to sell the foreigner whatever he wanted. Unlike many of the paupers of the interior, the people of Xi'an often knew the value of the artefacts around them, and were more than used to tourists. When Mannerheim visited the city's Great Mosque in its thriving Muslim quarter, the head imam even tried to sell him a guidebook.

'The sights are far less interesting than one might expect,' wrote a disappointed Mannerheim, referring not to their intrinsic value, but to their use to his academic mission. Xi'an was already well known to foreign historians, and Mannerheim doubted that he could bring anything back from the town that would add to the sum total of human knowledge. 'Possibly an archaeologist ... might discover hidden treasures that escape the inexperienced eye of a tourist. I doubt this, however, unless excavations were made in the vicinity.'[34] Mannerheim was more right than he knew. As in Dunhuang, he was close to two of the most incredible archaeological finds in 20th-century China, although neither would be discovered until long after his death. In 1975, farmers digging a well in a village outside Xi'an would stumble across the Terracotta Army, and in 1987, restorers at the Famen temple uncovered a hidden chamber containing finger-bone relics of the Buddha. Mannerheim had inadvertently camped within sight of both finds.[35]

Mannerheim wrote that life became progressively 'civilised' as he continued eastwards and northwards. This was, however, a mixed blessing. He was able to speed up his travels by train for several stops. The taverns were cleaner, but also more expensive, and he was sure that he was being overcharged simply for being a White Devil. He paid a sum for a night in Taiyuan that would have been 'robbery' further to the west, and in Zhengzhou he spent a 'far from pleasant' night listening to the 'caterwauling' of a prostitute in the next room, entertaining a drunken party of Chinese rail-waymen. At first, his complaints were met with promises to keep the noise down, but when he remonstrated with his neighbours a second time, they became aggressive.

Mannerheim had been in the wilderness for long enough, and the explorer's life had long since lost its allure. Now he was keen merely to press onto Beijing and file his report for St Petersburg, ready to return home.

6

The Paper Dragons

After just over 800 pages in its modern edition, Mannerheim's mammoth diary of his ride across Asia comes to an end in Kalgan, a few days' travel from Beijing, a month after his audience with the Dalai Lama, and just over two years after he left on his epic journey. 'This last picturesque and easy distance of my journey is all too familiar to the readers for bothering their attention with a description of it,' he claimed.[1] Most accounts of his life similarly gloss over what happened next, reporting that soon afterwards he was back in St Petersburg. In fact, he did not reach home until October, three months later.

In Kalgan, Mannerheim paid off his servants and associates, bidding farewell to most of his travelling companions. Joseph Zhao the interpreter and Chang the cook from Lanzhou stayed with Mannerheim, as they wanted to see the legendary Beijing for themselves.

After an uneventful couple of days, Mannerheim reached the city, the home of the ruling Qing dynasty. Although he may not have realised it, he arrived in town at roughly the same time as the Dalai Lama, who had come to pay his respects to the Chinese Emperor.[2] Their paths, however, did not cross again. The Russian legation building was a block away from the Tiananmen Gate that led into the Emperor's citadel, the Forbidden City. The Emperor, however, was not in. Beijing in July was unbearably hot, and anyone with any sense got out of the city to high ground or the far north. The Russian ambassador had found a different way to escape the inclement weather – by dying. Instead, Mannerheim was welcomed by Boris Arseniev, the temporary chargé d'affaires and the Councillor of the Embassy.

Arseniev had been expecting the traveller, and gave him a plush apartment at the legation building, overlooking a beautiful garden. The men spent the next two months preparing the first draft of Mannerheim's report to St Petersburg, which had to be written in Russian with the aid of an interpreter. Mannerheim sorted through his photographs, checked his maps, and sent the first of several crates home to St Petersburg, containing not only materials for the Tsar, but souvenirs of his own.[3]

Mannerheim finally said his farewells to the remnants of his party. The Cossack Lukanin was put on a train for Harbin and home. Chang, the last of many lacklustre cooks, presented Mannerheim with a parting gift, which turned out to be a fake Chinese queue. In a prank, Chang had tucked his real queue under his cap, and let Mannerheim believe that he had lopped off his own hair as a flamboyant oriental gesture. Since queues were still mandatory under Chinese law, it would also have been a punishable offence. Eventually, Chang confessed his deception, and revealed that his pigtail was still intact. 'As a matter of fact,' Chang added, 'there is quite a lot of silk in that, too.'[4]

Mannerheim was again not well – he would be plagued by back pain for the rest of his life, and often needed the relief of a soak in a sulphur bath. The embassy doctor disapproved even of the mild labours of assembling his report, and ordered him to rest, drugged if necessary. However, Mannerheim wrote like a thing possessed.

Mannerheim got on well with Arseniev and with Lavr Kornilov, a military attaché who spoke Turkish, Persian and Chinese. It was Kornilov who helped Mannerheim shape his report beyond the requirements of a mere military document, teasing out details that would be of vital significance to spies and intelligence officers in China if Russia ever needed to send them there. By the time the report was finished, it was 130 pages of typewritten Russian, which would be augmented back in St Petersburg with another 43 pages of additions.

The oppressive heat of the Beijing summer finally began to

ease off in September, and Mannerheim spent more time out of the office. He sometimes worked in the legation garden, and even took short walks out of the legation into the streets, alleys and boulevards. The legation quarter was like a small European city in miniature, stretching to the south-east of the Forbidden City. Mannerheim could stare up at the red-brown walls of the Forbidden City, and turn to the south to wander through the streets of hawkers, teahouses and rickshaws. At over 6 feet tall, he was a conspicuous presence, and often stopped the traffic.

In early September, he sent a telegram to General Palitsyn in St Petersburg, asking for permission to delay his scheduled return. He then wrote to his father explaining that the railway line between Mukden and Harbin was flooded, and that he would be obliged to find a different route home. He proposed to travel the short distance down to the coast at Tianjin, and get a ship from there to Port Arthur or perhaps even out to Japan, and then back again to Vladivostok.

Either Mannerheim was very forgetful, or he was writing a letter to his father in the full knowledge that other eyes would see it. Shipping himself to Port Arthur would have made no difference, as the line from Port Arthur would require him to use the same Mukden-Harbin section that he had just reported as impassable. Mannerheim had lived in Manchuria for an entire year, fighting a war that centred on the railways; he was not the kind of man to forget major details such as the route of the Harbin trains. The supposed choice was merely an illusion – Mannerheim already knew that he was going to Japan, but wanted to leave a paper trail that made it appear as if he was ending up there after a plausible effort to find a different route.

After weeks working on Mannerheim's report, Boris Arseniev had suggested that the two of them embark on a joint mission against a new enemy – Japan. His plan was to scout harbours and assess military readiness, and Mannerheim was unable to resist the opportunity for adventure – a chance both to see the Japan of the famous Nordenskiöld's writings, and the home of his enemies from the war in Manchuria. There may have been other reasons. Although Mannerheim makes no mention of it in extant letters of the time, his thoughts must have returned to the next step in his military career. If Russia really were expecting war in the East, first-hand experience of Japan might be vital in gaining a new commission. It would have been clear to Mannerheim by now, weeks ahead of his report reaching St Petersburg, that China was unlikely to be much of a threat. In 1908, particularly after two years' research, the Russian officer would surely have assumed that the next war would be with Japan, not China.

Arseniev secured visas for himself and his 'Swedish assistant' Mannerheim, and in the second week of September the two men made the short trip down the Shandong peninsula to the harbour town of Zhifu.[5] Zhifu, wrote Mannerheim to his father, was 'a small town between a grey-yellow mountain and a mighty sea'. The mountain had been a sacred site for over 2,000 years, and had been visited three times by the First Emperor of China. Mannerheim, however, was more interested in the modern view. 'The harbour is decorated with the ships of the American Philippines squadron, painted white. It is as beautiful as Biarritz, and this could be a paradise on earth were it not for the crowding of our vessel with bandy-legged, rude Japanese. The women are absent, which is very typical for the Far East.'[6]

Mannerheim's vessel, the *Eikō Maru*, sailed past Tsushima, the site of the Baltic Fleet's destruction, and onto the Japanese mainland. Ships from Zhifu put in at the strategically crucial Shimonoseki, a narrow strait between Japan's main islands of Honshū and Kyūshū. Shimonoseki was the gateway to Japan's 'Inland Sea', and was the domain of a powerful clan that had been instrumental in Japan's government since the fall of the Shōgun in the 1860s.

Mannerheim's mission seems to have been inspired, at least in part, by his reading of Marco Polo. The section on Japan in Polo's *Travels* is largely devoted to the attempted Mongol invasion of Japan in the 13th century, a massive assault by a huge fleet from the Asian mainland, which was only thwarted by unfavourable weather conditions and a freak storm. It would have made interesting reading for a Russian military strategist considering an attack on Japan, and it seems that, following his reading of the account, Mannerheim had decided to scout suitable harbours for himself, just in case such knowledge would prove useful in future. However, unfortunately for Mannerheim, Polo did not name the actual site of the Mongol attack, Hakata Bay. Instead, Mannerheim and Arseniev went to scout *modern* harbours that had supplanted Hakata in the region: Arseniev went to Nagasaki, and Mannerheim to Shimonoseki.[7]

Mannerheim appears to have fallen in with a group of Chinese travellers in Shimonoseki, and willingly accompanied them to a nondescript hotel. There were many better places to stay, but Arseniev had encouraged him to find somewhere that would not require any detailed records of its guests. The following day, Mannerheim toured the harbour, diligently looking out for anything of strategic importance. He was not a navy man, but Arseniev had carefully instructed him on what he should look for. He had also given Mannerheim a supply of invisible ink, with which Mannerheim marked the relevant details on a Japanese newspaper. Before long, Mannerheim had picked up some unwelcome attention. On several occasions, he spotted burly Japanese men, smoking cigarettes and loitering too close for comfort, alert and ready for action, looking to the nervous Mannerheim like 'black dachshunds'.[8]

Deciding that it was best to cut his losses, Mannerheim threw himself into benign and, he hoped, unobtrusive tourism for the rest of his stay. He took conspicuous delight in street entertainers and local colour, observed barbers and newspaper sellers, and did everything he could to look like a man who was not interested in wharfs, battleships or docking facilities.

For a 'Swedish' tourist, there was much to admire, although a Russian might have been irritated by much of the materials on sale. Pictures of Admiral Tōgō, the cunning annihilator of the Baltic Fleet, hung in every building. Among the woodblock prints of mountains and fishermen were newer examples of reportage, images of the Japanese navy sinking the Russians, and heroic depictions of the fall of Mukden. Japanese martial fervour even extended to women's fashions – Mannerheim saw hairpins and clasps fashioned in the shape of warships. The 'black dachshunds', however, stayed on his trail until the time of his scheduled departure from Shimonoseki.

There were two railway lines going out of Shimonoseki to the north. Mannerheim bought tickets for both of them, and made a great show of boarding the train for Iwakuni. As the train began to move, he leapt out of the carriage and crossed the platform for another train, heading along the other line to Yamaguchi. If the men tailing him had followed him on board, they would have been well on the way to Iwakuni before realising they had lost their target. The train for Kyoto thundered through the shimmering summer fields, past tightly packed squares of rice-paddies that stretched away towards tree-covered hills in the distant haze. The stops were frequent, but brief. The train ground to a halt at remote stations that were little more than a gravel platform with a place name neatly painted on a white board. The Japanese travellers, always organised, were up before the carriage stopped, and disembarked swiftly and silently. New travellers clambered aboard with similar speed, and the train was under way again after less than a minute – there were none of the great delays that could hold up Russian trains for hours on end.[9]

Mannerheim again attracted attention, but only from a distance. For a while, it seemed as if he might have his bench to himself. But as Mannerheim watched the scenery go past, he found himself sharing his carriage with a Japanese military officer. Much to Mannerheim's chagrin, the man turned out to speak excellent English, and was unable to resist quizzing the tall 'Swede' about his impressions of Japan. Mannerheim resolved to answer as truthfully as possible without giving away his secrets: he opined that Japanese women were elegant and beautiful, and the conversation turned to harmless topics. Inevitably, however, the Russo-Japanese War came up.

It was the worst possible temptation for Mannerheim. The officer was a cavalryman, a soldier after Mannerheim's own heart, and even implied he was a veteran of Mukden. If ever there were a man with whom Mannerheim could discuss technicalities, strategies and war memories, it was the nameless cavalry officer, but Mannerheim was obliged to maintain his Swedish disguise.

With jocular, facetious racism, the cavalryman offered asinine explanations for Japan's victory. 'We Japanese drink beer, but the

Russians drink champagne,' he said, as if this was important. 'Beer makes you stronger, but champagne destroys you.' [10]

The officer bragged about the peculiar qualities of the Japanese army, seemingly unaware that they were common to soldiers all over the world. Japanese soldiers trained and exercised. Japanese soldiers were recruited young, before they had time to miss home or gain family responsibilities. The Japanese army thought itself to be unbeatable.

He asked the 'Swede' what he thought of the Russian army. In two years of undercover travel, it was perhaps the moment when Mannerheim's mask stood the greatest chance of slipping. Mannerheim replied that he was a Swede, and did not know anything about such things.

Luckily, the cavalryman was not actually interested in hearing Mannerheim's opinion, as he had formed one of his own already. A Russian soldier, he commented, was good in battle, but lacked initiative. As for the officers, he said, 'they while away their lives happily appraising women and drinking champagne.'[11]

It was at this point that Mannerheim realised how much Japanese military intelligence had been gathered, misleadingly as it turned out, in St Petersburg. Japanese military men had had little opportunity to appraise Russian soldiers at rest, except in the capital, where presumably ministers and ambassadors would have run into members of the Chevalier Guard at public occasions. There had been a Japanese presence at the coronation of Tsar Nicholas II, and the Japanese ambassador had often seen the inside of the Russian government buildings. In most cases, the assessment of the Russian military seemed to have been based on this – in other words, on extended observation of the Chevalier Guard. Surely that was the only possible explanation for the ludicrous champagne lifestyle that the Japanese appeared to think was common to Russian officers? It was a long way removed from cabbage soup.

Unable to resist, Mannerheim stole some facts from the life story of his brother Johan, and claimed that although he was a Swede, he owned a stable in his home country, and was hence very interested in the Russian cavalry. The Japanese officer, however, dismissed the idea of cavalry in modern war, noting that horsemen were good for little beyond moving guns swiftly to important positions. Mannerheim tried to suggest that cavalry might have other uses, but was unable to cite examples without completely destroying his cover. He was thus obliged to listen to a prolonged lecture on the future of warfare, and the increasing importance of artillery and other machinery.

It was already dark when the train pulled into Kyoto station. As they prepared to disembark, the officer offered a final parting comment. 'We officers are well aware that, in a few years' time, Russia will avenge its defeat. We are preparing already for the coming war.' [12]

Mannerheim was too tired to search for an unobtrusive hotel. A rickshaw deposited him not far from Kyoto station, in a traditional inn, where he was swiftly relieved of his shoes and shown to a room with no furniture except a futon. Mannerheim was more than used to sleeping on the floor, but was unable to sleep for the noise of the street outside. When the rickshaw bells and clanking trams finally abated after midnight, he managed a fitful doze before the first of the pre-dawn temple bells began to ring out.

Maids transformed his room from a sleeping chamber to a dining area, and Mannerheim painfully folded his stiff knees under a low Japanese table. The proprietor seems to have gone out of his way to please his giant foreign guest – instead of the usual rice, fish and *miso* soup for breakfast, Mannerheim was offered a selection of Chinese foods, including black tea with milk in the European style.

Kyoto in September was still oppressively hot. Mannerheim had previously agreed to meet Arseniev at a temple on the opposite side of the river, but what appeared to be a short walk soon found him flagging in the heat. He stopped twice for refreshment, buying lemonade from a vendor, and later buying fruit juice drizzled on ice. [13]

He met Arseniev, as pre-arranged, at what is still one of Japan's most famous tourist spots, the *Sanjūsangendō* or Hall of Thirty-three Alcoves, whose claims to fame include a 'thousand-armed' Buddha. The two men strode quietly along a long hall containing hundreds of gilded statues of Kannon, the goddess of mercy, her gold haloes and multiple arms gleaming in the shadows. Mannerheim told Arseniev of his close brush with the talkative cavalryman on the train, and handed him the newspaper with the invisible-ink notations on it – Arseniev would take it back to Beijing and transmit the information in safety to Russia. Arseniev handed Mannerheim a train ticket to the northern port of Niigata, and the two men left the temple separately.[14]

Mannerheim's long spying mission was finally at an end, here on a balmy September day, surrounded by golden idols. He no longer had any compromising information on him, his baggage train was already en route for St Petersburg; his mission now was simply to head north to Niigata and board a ferry for home. Seemingly at a loss, he dawdled on the banks of the river. He wandered up to the bulky, towering gates of the Chion-in temple – the furthest point east that he reached in his career – and stared up at the stone steps to a mountainside shrine.

Mannerheim felt he could easily have enjoyed several more days in Kyoto, but he feared he was still being followed. Determined not to end his mission with the ignominy of a police interrogation, he returned to his hotel and took the first available train north.

At the windy coastal city of Niigata, Mannerheim climbed aboard the *Simbirsk*, an overnight steamer that took him out of Japan and back towards Vladivostok. There, the station commandant, who must surely have been warned of his arrival, handed him a first-class ticket for the Trans-Siberian Railway. Mannerheim's journey took him across the Amur River and back towards Harbin.

As if finally giving in after the stress of the previous year, Mannerheim suffered a relapse of his 'witch's arrows', his rheumatism and lumbago. Further aggravated by the lack of facilities on the train, even in first class, by the time he arrived in St Petersburg in early October, he was surviving on cocktails of nine aspirin at a time, crushed into his drinks.[15]

His reputation, in the form of his typewritten report, had preceded him in St Petersburg. He was fêted by his fellow officers, and General Palitsyn assured him that his long absence would do no damage to his chances of promotion. Far from it, in fact; Mannerheim's name had been added to a list of officers from which the next set of regimental commanders was due to be selected.

Mannerheim's trip had earned him an audience with Tsar

Nicholas himself. 'On Sunday I have the pleasure of a meeting with His Majesty,' he wrote to his sister. 'I'm a little anxious because I have been through a lot in the last few years and I would like my labours to be appreciated. Condensing two years' work into an audience of 15 or 20 minutes will not be easy, and I suspect it may involve skills I do not possess.' [16] In the few days before the meeting, Mannerheim put most thoughts of the Far East out of his mind, instead doing everything within his power to acquaint himself with the political situation in Finland. If the Tsar brought up the subject of Mannerheim's homeland, he wanted to have the facts at his command.

Mannerheim was ushered into the Tsar's office late in the day, to find Nicholas almost standing to attention, expectant and deeply interested. Neither Mannerheim nor the Tsar was expecting the meeting to take longer than a quarter of an hour – the Tsar did not even sit down to listen as Mannerheim began his account – but both men soon became unaware of the passing of time. As Mannerheim recounted his adventures, Nicholas frowned in concentration, a thin scar stretching across his right temple – a permanent reminder of his personal experience of Japan. When Mannerheim's narrative reached his meeting with the Dalai Lama, he presented the Tsar with the gift. Much to Mannerheim's surprise, the Tsar received it with oriental courtesy: 'he even accepted the *hatak* of the Dalai Lama in the manner prescribed by tradition, that is, by extending both hands.' [17]

Eventually, after some 80 minutes, Mannerheim realised how long he had been speaking, and apologised to the Tsar, who demurred that the information was so interesting that he, too, had lost all track of time. The meeting was called to a close, with the Tsar's assurance that Mannerheim would receive his just rewards for his efforts on behalf of Russia. The subject of Finland never came up.

Mannerheim was called to other meetings in St Petersburg, but pleaded with Palitsyn to allow him to return to Finland. Palitsyn agreed, even asking him to thank Carl Robert for his sterling duties as a mail drop during the mission, and Mannerheim was finally able to see his family.

Although Mannerheim's ride across Asia is known today through his hundreds of photographs, the oddities and artefacts that are on display in Helsinki museums, and the published version of his diary, his standing at the Tsar's court in late 1908 and early 1909 was based almost entirely on his Russian-language military report. This document, long since declassified, is thick with charts and plans, lists of prominent personnel and numbered assessments of military preparedness. Despite his own misgivings about the quality of interpreting during his journey, Mannerheim's report shows an incredible grasp of his surroundings and the mood of the Chinese of the period. He outlined the vaguely hostile feelings of the Central Asians towards Russia, but also noticed that the whispers of reform and revolution, already causing agitation in south China, had had little effect on the indolent peoples of the desert. He noted that there were Japanese elements in Chinese society, but that the Russians were still more highly regarded – the Chinese had not forgiven the Japanese for the war of 1894–5. Mannerheim predicted that education would soon improve when Chinese foreign students returned from abroad, but also that many of those students would have learned about the world in Japan and might impart a Japanese worldview upon their students.

Mannerheim's report is so thorough that he even outlined his predictions of how a Russian invasion of Central Asia might fare. He foresaw that a surprise Russian attack across the Tian Shan Mountains at Kashgar would easily overwhelm the poorly trained, badly managed Chinese forces in the region. In western China, Mannerheim's assessment of the potential enemy was damning – in many cases, he thought that firearms practice was merely cosmetic or entirely neglected, and that there would be little resistance. Mannerheim anticipated slightly better resistance at Urumqi, although not all that much, and suggested that an attack might establish an easily defensible stronghold as far east as Hami. Beyond Hami, he did not predict quite so easy a time.

However, Mannerheim made no attempt to talk up the importance of his findings. Western China, he wrote, was of merely tactical consequence. Any war between China and Russia would be fought in Manchuria, between the industrial cities of the Russian east and Beijing itself. Fighting in Central Asia would be a mere sideshow, but one in which swift Russian gains against poor troops would win powerful propaganda victories against the Chinese enemy, and force Beijing to draw troops away from the true front in Manchuria to fight a rearguard action over the deserts of the west. Moreover, as Mannerheim had noticed time and again during his travels, *nobody* truly ruled the Gobi and the Taklamakan. Instead, the vast, empty region passed by default into the hands of whoever held the handful of wells and oasis towns strung across its northern reaches – in a sense, thus, it was conquerable only on paper.

Such a detail would be an irritation to an administrator, but was priceless to a military tactician. Mannerheim both acknowledged and analysed the implication – that Chinese Turkestan (i.e. Xinjiang) could be swiftly 'occupied', but never truly ruled, and easily returned to China as ballast in negotiations after any future war.

For the first time in his career, Mannerheim demonstrated a truly brilliant military mind at work, outlining a strategy that turned the empty wastes of Central Asia into vital currency, not only for distracting an enemy in wartime, but for buying concessions after an armistice:[18]

> The annexation to our Asiatic possessions of this very extensive territory, with a sparse population and vast deserts, would hardly interest us … but Xinjiang province in our hands at the time when peace was declared would surely be an inestimably weighty argument, regardless of the result of operations in the main, i.e. the Manchurian, theatre of war.[19]

Mannerheim's military report is one of the most fascinating documents of his life, a speculative assessment of the progress of a war that was destined never to happen. The Chinese were lucky indeed that the Tsar's empire crumbled when it did; armed with Mannerheim's strategy, a Russian aggressor could have fatally divided Chinese defenders. It is no surprise that Mannerheim was decorated for his two-year mission; he had fought and won, at least on paper, a general's victory without firing a shot.

Mannerheim's report quelled Russian fears about the possible danger presented by China. His notes on Japan were filed away in case of trouble. And then, they were largely forgotten. With hindsight, we now know that neither China nor Japan were to present much danger for the Russians in the early 20th century, because the Russians would soon be preoccupied with troubles of their own. Including his time in Manchuria, Mannerheim had devoted over four years to military matters in the Far East, but his adversaries there were mere paper dragons. For the rest of his life, enemies closer to home would present a far greater threat.

After leave in Finland and Sweden, Mannerheim was posted to his new command in 1909, the 13th Vladimir Uhlans, in the small town of Novominsk, 25 miles outside Warsaw. Unlike their new commanding officer, the soldiers of the 13th had not fought in the Russo-Japanese War, and Mannerheim was astonished at their old-fashioned approach to warfare. He wasted no time in demanding that they incorporate the lessons that fellow soldiers had learned the hard way in Manchuria. Mannerheim thought that the 13th was living in a time-warp, pretending that a cavalryman's job still revolved around sword-waving charges. He subjected his men to a rude awakening, drilling them in the use of their rifles, and the very different role that cavalrymen might expect to fill in modern warfare. As he had discussed with his Japanese interlocutor on the Kyoto train, cavalrymen were now better regarded as infantrymen with the power to leap ahead of soldiers on the ground, using their horses to achieve forward positions, and then dismounting to fight as regular infantry.

Mannerheim made it a personal rule never to discuss politics with the Poles. As a Finn, he largely agreed with their wariness of Russia, and was troubled by what might be a view of Finland's near future, with a generation of schoolchildren growing up speaking Russian, their native language a distant, discouraged second place. His regular contact with prominent Poles in St Petersburg endeared him to his new hosts, and his proximity to the capital made his life in Novominsk much more agreeable than his previous service in the remote Kalisz barracks. He was soon admitted to Cercle de Chasse, 'the Jockey Club of Poland' as he called it, and his regular outings with locals led to several concerned reports to the Russian police. 'The Governor-General, however, consigned them to the waste-basket' as Mannerheim's achievements with his soldiers greatly outweighed any gossip over his friends. Notably, Mannerheim may have been protected by another family connection – the governor-general was George Scalon de Coligny, a relative by marriage of Mannerheim's influential godmother Alfhild.[20]

Two years after arriving in Novominsk, the change in Mannerheim's men reached the notice of the Inspector of Cavalry, who recommended him for a further promotion. Major-General Mannerheim was now stationed in Warsaw itself as the commander of the Tsar's Uhlans of the Guard, one of the best regiments in the Russian army. He repeated his successes there, and enjoyed his new command so much that he even turned down the chance to command a brigade in Russia itself. Instead, he stayed in Warsaw, where he was eventually appointed as commander of the Brigade of Cavalry – a body incorporating his former regiment, a regiment of hussars and a horse artillery unit.

Peacetime allowed Mannerheim to devote a little time to revisiting his Asian experiences. There was no opportunity for him to edit his travel diaries, although he may have been discouraged in doing so – his official inclusion within the Pelliot expedition might be a ruse that the Tsar hoped to repeat with other spies. Instead, Mannerheim tried without success to interest Finnish ethnologists in a collection of sketches of Chinese deities that he had commissioned from Léon van Dijk in Lanzhou. However, the managers of the Antell Collection in Helsinki snootily observed that they had asked for Central Asian, not Chinese materials. Mannerheim protested that '... nothing as complete as my collection exists in printed form. Academician Radloff has offered me the opportunity to have them published through the care of the St Petersburg Academy of Sciences. Personally I would prefer that this publication be produced in Finland and that this collection of drawings would not be separated from my other collections ...'[21] Despite his protests, and the veiled threat that he might give the glory to the Russians, he was unable to bring himself to pass the pictures on. His grand sinological project, a compendium of Chinese mythology, would not be published until 1993, long after his death.

The Tsar did not forget Mannerheim. They met on several later occasions, when his men were appointed as guards during the Imperial Family's trips to their hunting lodge near Warsaw. He was even invited to join in the Tsar's hunting expeditions, and gained an additional posting – and with it special insignia on his epaulettes that afforded him instant access to the imperial presence without the usual red tape. This appointment to the 'suite' of the Tsar made Mannerheim one of the highest-ranking Finns in Russian imperial service.

He was however, still plagued by the after-effects of his active life. As he neared his fifties, he experienced increasingly painful bouts of the rheumatism that had first afflicted him in Manchuria. His many youthful riding injuries exacerbated the effect, and Mannerheim faced the very real fear that he would soon become a horseman who was unable to ride a horse. In the summer of 1914 he awarded himself a sojourn in the German spa of Wiesbaden in the hope of soothing his 'witch's arrows'.

He arrived shortly after the news that Archduke Franz Ferdinand of Austria had been assassinated in Sarajevo. 'One felt war psychosis growing with every day that passed, and the public showed their hostile feelings towards Russian visitors more and more openly.'[22]

On his way back to Poland, Mannerheim decided to kill a few hours in Berlin by visiting Woltmann, a horse-dealer he had come to know well during his days in the Chevalier Guards. Woltmann was happy to see him, but worryingly commented that he had little stock for Mannerheim to see, as he had just sold 150 horses to the German army. It was not the number that troubled Mannerheim, but the quality – he knew from his own experience that the peacetime German cavalry budget could not afford horses of Woltmann's standard. He hurried back to rejoin his regiment on manoeuvres, but may have pushed himself a little too far in his efforts to prepare for war. While leading a practice charge, he was thrown from his horse and sprained his ankle.

On 29 July 1914, Mannerheim was at a dinner at a Warsaw club. One of the hosts assured his guests that a compromise was sure to be reached in the negotiations, and that the stand-off between the Great Powers would not lead to war. Even as he spoke, a messenger arrived with a note for Mannerheim, ordering him to report immediately to his brigade headquarters merely to read a telegram.

He arrived to discover a code that related to orders kept within a locked, fireproof cabinet. The sealed orders gave him and his men six hours to depart upriver to Lublin. They were on the move in four, with the hobbling Mannerheim forced to travel in a car.[23]

His regiment arrived by train in Krasnik, near the Austro-Hungarian border of Galicia, a day ahead of the German declaration of war. Mannerheim hoped against hope that the conflict would be a short one, since he was well aware that the Russian military was ill equipped to fight for long.[24]

The war in Poland was a dispiriting experience. Mannerheim's regiment achieved great things in the south against the Austrians, successfully fighting a number of actions that delayed the advancing enemy for a critical six days, allowing troops to deploy and dig in at better defensive positions elsewhere. The cavalry, as he had often predicted since Manchuria, fought in a very different style to that of previous wars, using their horses to reach areas in rapid time, and then dismounting to fight as infantry on the ground. Mannerheim himself was a notable presence in the fighting, and became a common sight among the men, smoking a cigar and offering words of encouragement.

His fearlessness was to win him several more medals, but had elements of the madcap recklessness that had led to reprimands in his youth. It was, surely, dangerous for a commander to be so close to danger, but Mannerheim expected his men to display the same cavalier disregard for their own safety as he so often did for his own. His presence at the front line spurred his men into impressive feats, but sometimes also to early deaths.

In September, Mannerheim received a rude awakening. He thought that one of his favourites, a prize-winning horseman called Bibikov, was too slow in taking an enemy position in a forest. He asked Bibikov the nature of the delay, and Bibikov neutrally supplied the information that only 14 men in his squadron of lancers were left alive.

'Are you afraid?' demanded Mannerheim.

Bibikov did not reply, but led his tattered squadron back into the dense forest, where he was almost immediately cut down by a salvo from enemy infantry. In a scene of almost Homeric anguish, Mannerheim was described by several observers as 'heartbroken' when he saw Bibikov's body, kissing the dead youth and musing that it was he, Mannerheim, who should have died.[25]

Mannerheim's bravado was not uncommon among cavalry officers, whose training was infamously geared towards fearless charges against impossible odds. But it was a mentality that sat badly with the war of 1914–18, which is remembered today not for swift-moving cavalrymen, but for the long, immobile hell of trench warfare. Even in Poland, where the war had a more old-fashioned cast to it, Mannerheim was soon protesting at the waste. The Russians were losing more officers than expected, replacements arrived barely trained, and supplies of artillery shells were often too low to provide adequate cover. Mannerheim seemed unused to, or perhaps unprepared for, the brutal effects of war on the civilian population. Russian troops pursued a scorched-earth policy in retreat, causing Mannerheim to bear witness to the wanton destruction of farms, towns and homes belonging to Polish subjects.

In October, Mannerheim deliberately disobeyed orders when he realised that a division ahead of him had unexpectedly fled before an Austrian assault. Instead of withdrawing, he ordered his men to hold their positions, thereby allowing other regiments to make their getaway. 'I succeeded in holding the enemy until the infantry brigades were safe', he wrote. 'From the very beginning of this engagement it was a severe test for my regiments to see our own troops retreating past them, and an even greater one when the sound of fighting began to be heard in their rear, but they never failed, and this was the salvation of the infantry.'[26]

Not long afterwards, an exhausted Mannerheim was woken up by one of his subordinates with the news that he had been awarded the 4th Class of the Order of St George for his quick thinking. Despite Mannerheim's successes in the south, however, a joint Austrian and German offensive in the north was swiftly gaining ground. The Russians and Poles pushed back, and the retreating Germans pursued a scorched-earth policy, destroying railways, roads and communications as they went in order to inconvenience their Russian pursuers.

November 1914 began with both sides practically restored to their pre-war lines, but with large tracts of Poland in ruins. As his regiment recaptured Polish territory, Mannerheim found himself riding through familiar forests; he was on land owned by the Marquis Wielopolski, where he had hunted in peacetime. Ahead of him, he knew, was a river, and then the picturesque town of Chroberz and Wielopolski's castle.

'I tried to be very careful with where we aimed our bombing,' he wrote, 'and did not wish to cause it damage.' With shells still falling on the town, Mannerheim and a group of his officers managed to cross the river and enter the castle, which was all but deserted. The staff welcomed Mannerheim and his cavalry as liberators and offered them a feast of Polish *bigos* stew, which Mannerheim, from past experience, knew would have taken over ten hours to cook, and hence must have been prepared for the retreating Austrian enemies. 'It was ... amusing,' he wrote, 'to note that our Austrian friends had enjoyed a cordial reception at the same castle, and even the same table just one hour before us.' [27]

Mannerheim chased his quarry to the outskirts of Krakow, drawing on his peacetime experience of the region to great effect. On one occasion, he was able to capture an entire squadron of enemy hussars through the simple expedient of allowing them to ride into a swamp. As the bedraggled Germans sloshed out of the mud, their beautiful uniforms ruined, Mannerheim's men took them prisoner.

Unknown to Mannerheim, some of his old associates from China were also doing their part for the war effort. Léon van Dijk, who had sworn never to leave China, was serving in France as a chaplain for the many hundreds of Chinese workers in the trenches. Meanwhile, the Dalai Lama, back in Tibet since 1913, had offered 1,000 Tibetans to fight alongside the British. His offer was politely declined, although he did mobilise other forces in the Himalayas, namely an army of priests, spinning prayer wheels and calling down supernatural aid against the Germans. [28]

Despite such paranormal assistance, Russian troops were

troubled by more everyday concerns. The simple necessities – food, fuel and above all ammunition for the artillery – were fast running low, prompting Mannerheim's commanding officer to observe that 'Soon we shall have to fight with sticks.' [29] Mannerheim himself began to display signs of superstition, and was once reported fretting about the presence of three candles on a dinner table – in Russia, the same number of candles that were habitually set beside a corpse awaiting burial. When one of the diners was killed the following day, Mannerheim muttered, 'See, the candles ...'

The fighting was threatening enough for Mannerheim to head back to Warsaw briefly to oversee the removal of his possessions. His apartment, where he had lived for several years surrounded by family heirlooms and the memorabilia of his Asian trip, was packed up and sent east for safekeeping.

Back on the front line, the wounding of a superior officer led to Mannerheim's appointment as acting commander of an entire cavalry division. The battlefield commission was officially confirmed in mid-1915, and Mannerheim inherited a division that he regarded as first-rate. Accordingly, he did very little to alter the organisation as it already stood – he left officers in their former posts, and did not interfere with the practices already under way. Mannerheim was now the commander of an extremely varied group of soldiers. At the pinnacle of excellence were the Ahtyrski Hussars, attired in strange brown cloaks that mimicked the monks' robes that the regiment's soldiers had once stolen from a monastery during the 1870s Turkish War. The hussars had a two-century pedigree, and were a world away from Mannerheim's Wild Division, which comprised six regiments of irregular and notoriously unreliable volunteers from the Caucasus. On paper, his command now spanned thousands of men, but some of the battalions being added to his purview were only paper dragons. Many were only at half strength after a year of fighting, and more still had been patched with under-trained new recruits.

A second wounded superior led to yet another battlefield promotion for Mannerheim, during a hot summer that saw the men under his command facing constant enemy attacks. By August, however, Mannerheim was practically crippled by his recurring rheumatism, and he spent a few weeks recuperating at a spa in Odessa. His sister Sophie joined him, but although he enjoyed the family reunion, he was greatly troubled by the news he picked up from his fellow patients.

Mannerheim discovered that the conditions in his own division were far from unique. The army's true fighting strength had been reduced by half a million men, although on paper many still showed higher staffing levels. This was because many had been assigned with new recruits, who either arrived at the front line under-trained and unsuited for action, or wallowed in garrisons waiting to be assigned. With hindsight, Mannerheim would note that these unhappy conscripts, forced to ship out to regiments that could not train, equip or use them, spent many days in idleness, 'and formed a valuable breeding-ground for revolutionary agitation.'[30]

Russian industry was not resupplying the army with anything like the necessary speed, and Mannerheim feared that the war effort would run out of men, matériel and resources within weeks. To make matters worse, someone had to take the blame, and it fell on the Grand Duke Nicholas Nikolaievich who had been leading the Russian forces. In an inadvisable move, the Tsar himself shunted the Grand Duke off to a provincial command, and assumed personal command of the Russian army.

The Tsar's decision was doomed from the start. Entirely inexperienced in military matters, the best he could hope to be was a figurehead while real soldiers fought on his behalf. But his decision to put himself visibly in charge would be a fatal blow to his standing with the people. Every mistake the army made, every retreat and delay, was now something that could be blamed on the Tsar himself, a monarch who had previously boasted that his command of the Russian Empire was a matter of God's will. The Tsar's absence at the war also contributed to whispers of revolution. The Russian parliament was suspended, leading many political decisions to be proclaimed by imperial decree. To fill in the organisational gaps in local government, many industrial concerns began appointing committees – the forerunners of the later *soviets*.

Back in the saddle after Odessa, Mannerheim was ordered south into Romania where his division scored a series of spectacular victories despite low supplies. There were, however, already intimations of some of the politicking that was soon to come. Mannerheim was aghast when a fellow Russian general simply retreated without a word, leaving Mannerheim and his Romanian allies to plug the massive gap left in the lines. The Romanians later decorated Mannerheim for his actions, although, to Mannerheim's disgust, the disappearing general evaded any punishment. The general later claimed that his actions had been a vote of no confidence in the Romanian allies, and that he had decided to find a Russian superior to whom he could report the situation. It was, noted Mannerheim sourly, 'certainly a highly original method of extricating oneself from a difficult situation!'.[31] Mannerheim was even more angered by the news, reported in the newspapers, that a group of Finnish youths had travelled to Germany and enlisted in the German army, where they were serving as the 27th Royal Prussian Jäger Battalion. Mannerheim was scandalised by the idea that inhabitants of the Grand Duchy of Finland, whose Grand Duke was the Tsar himself, could betray their ruler in so cavalier a manner.[32]

When Mannerheim's division was pulled out of the line for recuperation, he was granted leave to make a brief visit to Finland. Changing trains in St Petersburg was no simple matter; as a member of the Tsar's retinue, he was obliged to seek an audience in transit. He was admitted to the presence of Tsar Nicholas, and expected to be grilled about military events by his commander-in-chief. Instead, Mannerheim reported that the Tsar was 'noticeably absent-minded' and seemed entirely preoccupied.

Mannerheim received a better welcome from the Empress, although she, too, seemed weak and prematurely aged. In a private audience, she listened to Mannerheim's tales from the front, while the 13-year-old Tsarevitch sat beside her. At one point, Mannerheim was surprised to hear the Empress refer to a general as a deserter. It was only later that Mannerheim discovered that the man in question had indeed gone over to the enemy. He was not the only one. The disastrous progress of the war in Poland had impacted badly on the Tsar's reputation. Some of his own noblemen had urged him to consider constitutional reform, which he flatly refused, leading to the ironic position where even several members of the nobility began to speak of revolution. For the first time, the Tsar's government admitted that there were revolutionaries in Russia, provoking a series of crackdowns and arrests aimed at agitators.

The winter of 1916–17 was cold, fuel was in short supply, and hundreds of locomotive boilers had burst through mismanagement and general wear and tear. Hence, transport was inadequate, heating was threatened for the general populace, and the absence of trains was leading to food shortages in the capital. Mannerheim found things far more amenable in Finland, where many of his old comrades seemed remarkably calm. Although he did not know it at the time, this was because many of them had already realised that a revolution was inevitable.

Mannerheim dined with his friends in Helsinki in January 1917, unaware that many of them were already part of the conspiracy. Already, 2,000 Finnish volunteers had been sent abroad to train, in the full expectation that they would be required on Finnish soil to fight against a Russian counter-attack after a revolution. In a matter of months, Mannerheim's career in the Russian military would be gone forever, along with the imperial Russia that had employed him for over two decades.

7

The End of Empire

The weeks that followed were the most traumatic that Mannerheim faced in his life. Although he would go on to fight in several more wars, the collapse of the Russian Empire saw the end of an entire way of existence. Mannerheim disapproved of the moves to make Finland more Russian, but he was an inherent supporter of the status quo in which he had reached maturity. He had seen no essential problem in the Grand Duchy of Finland remaining autonomous within the Russian Empire. He had sworn loyalty to the Tsar, who was both the Emperor of Russia and the Grand Duke of Finland, and for Mannerheim the problem ended there.

Mannerheim believed in monarchy, in discipline, in authority, and in the chain of command. He had little time for democracy itself – in later life he would be a reluctant defender of the rights of the lower classes to despise privileged men such as himself. He was unlikely ever to sympathise with the complaints of the Russian proletariat. He had been horror-struck at the collapse of military discipline during the short-lived revolution of 1905, and shunned the 'Reds' who spoke of Karl Marx, the Red Flag and universal equality. Mannerheim, like many other remnants of the old aristocracy, identified himself, for want of a better term, as a 'White', in a split that would soon engulf all the Russian Empire.

Revolution was not on Mannerheim's mind when he returned to St Petersburg on 10 March 1917, by the Gregorian calendar. Under Russia's Julian calendar, it was still late February – the popular uprising now known as the February Revolution was under way.

Many industrial and commercial concerns had been suspended, and there were demonstrations in the street against 'the German woman' – the Empress, whom agitators regarded as an enemy agent in the Tsar's family. It was not the first time there had been unrest in the streets, and Mannerheim does not appear to have taken it any more seriously than any previous protest. In the Russian parliament (the Duma) there were continued demands for further political reforms, but Mannerheim was more interested in getting a ticket to the ballet. It was, he mused, an 'almost impossible feat', and yet he got a seat for a performance the following evening.[1]

It would be one of the last ballets to be performed in the realm of the Tsar. Mannerheim left the show after the curtain came down, but had trouble finding a car to take him to his hotel. In a gesture of old-time camaraderie, also soon doomed to perish, a fellow officer offered to give him a lift. Much had changed in the city since Mannerheim had first arrived – it did not even have the same name. St Petersburg was now officially Petrograd, in an attempt to make the Tsar's capital sound less German to Russian ears. Some shops were boarded up – the result of raids by starving locals, for whom food prices had soared with the shortages created by so many menfolk away fighting the Germans. When Mannerheim had been a young cadet, the streets had bustled with horse-drawn vehicles. Now, the motor car had all but taken over. Even for a Sunday night, the capital was strangely quiet. There were soldiers in the long street of Nevsky Prospect, but they were not promenading as they might have once done. Instead, they were on duty, watching the streets for signs of trouble to come – the local garrison had already been put on alert. Mannerheim dropped in at an officers' club, only to find that no other soldiers calling in that night.

He awoke on the morning of 12 March, washed and dressed, donning his general's uniform and spurs. There was a commotion outside, and when Mannerheim drew the curtains he found the street beneath his window alive with protesters wearing red armbands and waving red banners. Even as Mannerheim stared in surprise at the men in the street, he realised that some of them were staring back at him and commenting on his officer's uniform.

An agitated hotel porter banged on Mannerheim's door. He

breathlessly explained that the uprising had begun, that the soldiers had refused to fire on the revolutionaries, and that the Reds were now hunting down officers of the old order. Mannerheim had already been spotted, and the Reds had been asking the porter which room was his.

The porter's words probably saved his life. Mannerheim tore the conspicuous spurs off his riding boots, and wrapped himself in a voluminous overcoat that, fortunately, had no military insignia. He jammed a fur hat on his head and raced down the back stairs to the building's rear entrance.

There was smoke in the air on the cold spring day. The soldiers had arrested or murdered their own superior officers, and the gaols had been emptied of both political prisoners and true criminals. Police stations and government buildings had been attacked by mobs and often set on fire.

Mannerheim walked as calmly as he could to the newly opened office of a friend of his, the industrialist Emanuel Nobel, nephew of the inventor of dynamite. Mannerheim found Nobel and an unidentified Frenchman trying to plot their next move. Eventually the three agreed that the centre of town was unsafe, and that they would be better off at Nobel's home on the other side of the river Neva. They walked through the chaotic streets towards the bridge, but fatefully stopped at the smouldering ruins of a police station to read a revolutionary poster. There, they were grabbed by a gang of revolutionaries, who demanded that a passing military patrol check their papers.

The Frenchman presented his first, and tense moments passed while the self-appointed law enforcers tried to make sense of his foreign-language documents. Eventually, it was agreed that the Frenchman was probably not the sort of enemy of the state that the revolutionaries were looking for, and the gang turned to Nobel. Used to being obeyed, Nobel informed them that he was a Swede, and that they were welcome to come with him to his home to check his passport there.

The inquisitors left Mannerheim until last. He gave them an answer in the style of Nobel's, claiming that he was newly arrived from Finland, but that his passport was in his luggage at the station.

He did not have his luggage with him, he lied, because the city was in such chaos that he was unable to get a cab, but the men could come with him to the station to see for themselves. Mannerheim's answer, like Nobel's, was calculated to get them onto the opposite bank of the Neva – the 'Finland Station', from which trains departed to Helsinki, was in the same district as Nobel's house.

The bluff worked. The leader of the paramilitary patrol had better, more revolutionary things to do than pad along with three non-Russians to the other side of the river, and waved them through. Once across the river, Nobel invited Mannerheim to his home, but Mannerheim gallantly refused. Nobel was in little direct danger from the Russians for as long as he was not implicated in any counter-revolutionary activities, but if he were found harbouring a general from the Tsar's army, he might share that general's fate.

Instead, Mannerheim sneaked through the back streets to the house of a fellow Finn. The night sky was red with the flames of arson, and there was a threatening carnival atmosphere in the streets. Most houses were dark or muted, some were on fire, and small groups huddled together for warmth by bonfires in the streets. The bells of fire engines rang in the distance, although it was unclear how they would be greeted if they tried to put out burning buildings that had belonged to the old order. Meanwhile, motor cars flying red flags hurtled past in the streets, loaded with armed men, mutinous soldiers, and cackling companions that Mannerheim would only describe as 'women from brothels'.[2]

One corner of the Petrograd streets was forever Finland, as Mannerheim found himself sheltering in a Finnish officer's house, along with a retired Finnish general and Mannerheim's own brother-in-law, Mikael Gripenberg, who had unluckily arrived by train that day and was now trapped amid the unrest.

The following morning, 13 March, , there were the awful sounds of gunfire from the centre of the city, in what Mannerheim would later understand to have been the last stand of the police and soldiers who remained loyal to the Tsar. Most of them were boys and new recruits, commanded by officers who were only in town in the first place while they recuperated from wounds received in the war.

The telecommunications system, which had not been working the night before, sprang back into life, leading Mannerheim to throw on a dressing gown and sit in the draughty entrance hall trying to reach his aide-de-camp on the telephone.

Suddenly, a group of men barged into the house, demanding to know if it were true that a 'Finnish general' was in the building. Mannerheim's host told them the half-truth that a retired, elderly Finnish general was indeed staying with him as a lodger, but that he was not in at that present time. Refusing to take his word for it, the men insisted on searching the whole building, while Mannerheim lurked conspicuously in the hall, now hoping against hope that his aide-de-camp would not ring him back. Finding nothing incriminating in the house, the men came back downstairs again, and waited in the hall for the last of their number to return from the upper floors.

Embarrassed by the silence, Mannerheim asked them in Russian why they were looking for a Finnish general. Instead of answering the question, the revolutionary looked down at Mannerheim's feet, and asked him why he was wearing cavalry boots. 'These days,' replied Mannerheim, 'one was lucky to have any kinds of boots at all.'[3] Miraculously, the reply seemed to satisfy the revolutionaries, and they piled out of the house once more.

It was another day before Mannerheim re-established contact with his aide-de-camp, who sent a car for him on 14 March. Mannerheim was taken back to his hotel, now back under government control, although there was still some debate over who the 'government' was. The Tsar was still at large, somewhere out at his General Headquarters, although the Tsarina and the Tsarevitch, along with other members of the Imperial Family (many of whom had come down with measles), had been placed under arrest at Tsarskoe Selo. The first Order of the Day of the Soviets was announced, (1 March Julian/14 March Gregorian) which was that the army was now under the command of Soldiers' Councils. Committees were now in charge of all hardware and provisions, and there was no longer any need to salute superiors.

Amid such chaos, Mannerheim decided to return to the front line in Romania, which required him to take a train eastwards to the Moscow hub of the Russian networks, there to take a second train back west again towards Romania.[4] He was thus in Moscow, sitting in a sleigh outside the Brest-bound train station as a witness to the first Red demonstration in Moscow itself. It was, he observed in his *Memoirs*, a dreadful irony that he had walked in the same street just eleven years before, ahead of the newly crowned Tsar Nicholas. It was also, he recalled, the same street in which he had heard the news of the disaster at Khodynka Field, and where he had seen the gruesome carts of corpses carrying away the unfortunate victims of that day. Now, on a brisk March morning, he watched crowds of Moscow people waving red banners, calling for reform and revolution. Mannerheim, it seems, had hoped that the upheavals in Petrograd had merely been a slight shift, like the unwelcome protests that had led to earlier reforms in 1905. But in Moscow, he began to appreciate that life in Russia had changed forever.

It was in Moscow that Mannerheim heard news that shook him to the core. Tsar Nicholas II had been forced to abdicate, offering the throne instead to his brother, Grand Duke Michael. The Grand Duke, however, refused to accept the crown without the unanimous support of the people, as witnessed by the decision of the Duma as to whether Russia would go on as a monarchy, or become a republic. Mannerheim was convinced, rightly, that Russia would stumble further towards republicanism, and tried to persuade a number of fellow officers that the time was right to begin organising a counter-revolutionary movement. He found no takers, at least for the moment – his fellow officers still hoped that things would blow over, as they had in 1905.

Back among his men, Mannerheim found the Russian troops in a state of anarchy. Russian soldiers in the Romania regiments now had the right to question their orders, to go on strike, and to 'free speech'. This soon manifested itself as looting, as up to a million soldiers going absent without leave, and many desertions. In the latter case, it was thought that many of the soldiers had heard that the lands of the wealthy would be parcelled out among the deserving poor, and were determined to rush back to Petrograd or Moscow in order to be at the front of the queue.

Remarkably, discipline in Mannerheim's own command

remained relatively strong. With the nature of the Russian government still under question, Mannerheim was promoted to lieutenant-general, and told to await orders for a new offensive. In April America had entered the war, and hope remained among the Russian soldiers that they would be able to turn the tide against Germany despite their problems at home. But even if Mannerheim's own troops stayed loyal – continuing to salute him even when out of uniform – he had a presentiment of further trouble elsewhere. On one occasion, his men were due to be relieved in the trenches by another regiment, only to be told by the company commander that his men had refused to take up Mannerheim's positions. Mannerheim duly ordered his own artillery to fire a few warning shots at the positions of the reluctant Russians. It secured the handover, although it was plainly no way to run an army.[5]

News drifted back to the lines of further unrest in urban Russia. Vladimir Lenin had tried, unsuccessfully, to mount a coup in July. Then, in September, Mannerheim's old acquaintance from his China days, Lavr Kornilov, now commander-in-chief of the Russian army, mounted a disastrous coup attempt to which the beleagured government responded by arming the Red Guards of the Bolsheviks, creating a new armed group in the capital that would prove crucial when the Bolsheviks themselves made a grab for power a few weeks later.. One of Mannerheim's own men was arrested by a Soldiers' Council, after unwisely saying some words in support of the monarchy in an officers' club. Mannerheim came to his aid, and tried to have the committee members punished for attacking an officer, but found himself unable to enforce even that simple discipline. The men were arrested, but by a commanding officer who promised them that they could return to their previous posting after they had had their punishment. Mannerheim, who had wanted them thrown out of the regiment for good, was left seething at the new regime's lack of understanding of the need to keep a body of soldiers ready to die for each other, and not at each other's throats.

The event left Mannerheim unsure whether there really was any future for him in the Russian army, if indeed there would be a Russian army for much longer. He began to speculate whether it was time to take the step that he had long promised his family he would try – returning to Finland to seek a new life there.

In September, Mannerheim received notification that he had been transferred to the reserve, 'on grounds of opposition to present conditions'.[6] It was tantamount to an enforced retirement for the fifty-year-old officer, and he doubted that either he or the Russian authorities would be interested in his services while the Bolsheviks were in power. Mannerheim was also more troubled than many of his fellow officers by the arrest and abdication of the Tsar. Nicholas II had not been a distant monarch to Mannerheim, but a man he had personally guarded for many years, a companion on shooting trips and a figure of some reverence. Historical accounts record that Mannerheim realised that imperialist Russia was lost, and decided to flee for his native Finland. However, that was only his second choice. His first was to organise a counter-revolution from within Russia in 1917.

Mannerheim was still pondering these issues on a fine October day, when his horse stumbled. The creature fell, causing Mannerheim to twist his ankle badly in the stirrup – an injury that was sure to make it difficult for him to walk for the next couple of months. Without full authorisation, he took himself out of the front line to recuperate in Odessa, where he found himself in the presence of many officers who had been similarly marginalized by the change in political attitudes.

During his stay in Odessa, Mannerheim had an encounter with a fortune-teller. He had no interest in such matters, and indeed, had been intensely disapproving of Anastasie's association with spiritualists in St Petersburg after the death of their infant son. But thanks to Mannerheim's association with the Red Cross and his involvement in the expatriate social scene in Odessa, he found himself at a tea party given by the humanitarian relief worker Lady Muriel Paget, who treated her guests to a séance.

Participants were invited to submit questions about their fates, futures and families to the medium, who made a great show of going into a trance, her arms hanging limply at her sides while she barked replies in a low, unearthly voice, apparently with great effort. Mannerheim politely maintained a decorous air, as he was too much of a gentleman to scoff, although he did observe in private that the entire charade seemed to him to be 'nonsense'. 'I kept my gravity with great difficulty', confessed Mannerheim, although many years later, he was impressed enough with the woman's predictions to repeat them in his memoirs:

> I was to receive the command of an army and lead it to victory. After receiving great honours and a high position, I was to relinquish the latter of my own accord, but before long an important mission would take me to two great Western countries, where my efforts would be crowned with success. I would return to a higher position than the one I had when I departed, but again it would be of short duration. Many years later, I was again to rise to a very high position.[7]

He was still 'recuperating' in Odessa the following month when news arrived of a further revolution. The overthrowers had themselves been overthrown, the 'White' Kerensky Provisional Government falling to the 'Red' Bolsheviks – thanks to the vagaries of Julian/Gregorian dating, this November uprising is remembered as the *October* Revolution.

In military units all over the empire, committees of soldiers were embracing the revolutionary fervour, resisting their officers and, in some cases, even turning on them. With the Bolsheviks now holding Petrograd, many of Mannerheim's fellow officers were fleeing east to join the counter-revolutionary 'White' army. Mannerheim, however, decided to head north towards Finland. Fearlessly, he decided to travel in the manner to which he had become accustomed. Even though Reds all over the old empire were lynching officers, Mannerheim donned a full general's uniform, and rented himself a private carriage on the railway to the north. It was not private for long, as he was somehow soon joined by a pair of British Red Cross nurses from Paget's circle, along with a British naval officer, three Romanians on their way to Japan, and Mannerheim's aide-de-camp and batman.

It was to be a difficult journey for the unlikely group. Their carriage broke down, but the batman, as skilled in scrounging and bullying as his job required, was able to find them another one, along with provisions to last them for the six more days it would take their train to limp along at reduced speed. They arrived at Mogilev to find a fresh pool of blood on the station platform – Bolsheviks had shot the Chief of Staff moments before their arrival. Mannerheim had briefly known the unfortunate victim in Poland, and regarded the sorry affair as yet one more example of the collapse into anarchy under the Reds.

Mannerheim found Petrograd in an even worse state than when he had left it, with vagrant and insubordinate soldiers lurking around the station. He pulled out a banknote and ordered two of them to carry his luggage and find him a cab, archly observing that money still talked in the new republic.

In Petrograd, Mannerheim tried to find a member of the aristocracy who was prepared to consider leading a counter-revolution. But he found the old representatives of the imperial order docile and complacent. He dined at an officers' club with high-ranking aristocrats including two Grand Dukes, conversation at table revolving around the recent arrest of one of their fellow members, a prince in the Chevalier Guards who was a brother of the King of Serbia.

'If one of the Grand Dukes raised the standard of revolt against the Bolsheviks, enormous numbers would rally round him', suggested Mannerheim, only to meet with apathy from the other diners. 'In any case', he added, 'it is better to fall with a sword in one's hand than to be shot in the back or have one's throat cut.'[8]

On 6 December 1917, the news came that one part of the old empire had decided to make a stand. The Grand Duchy of Finland declared independence, after a reconvened Senate passed a motion in its favour by a thin margin of only twelve votes. Socialists in Finland had counselled closer ties with Russia, not because of the imperial past, but because of the Soviet future. They were, however, defeated by the small majority. Mannerheim, along with many other officials, suspected that the Reds would not go quietly, and feared that they might call on the resources that could be offered by the many hundreds of Russian soldiers still billeted on Finnish territory.

Finding no takers for his talk of counter-revolution, Mannerheim hoped to get out of Russia for good and run for Finland. However, since he had no travel documents beyond a pass ordering him to Petrograd to have his ankle examined, he would need to get a permit to leave the capital from the Supreme Council of the Bolsheviks.

Something made Mannerheim stay away from them. The Supreme Council had based itself in the Smolny Institute, a former aristocratic girls' boarding school by the river Neva. Mannerheim knew it well as it had been the place where his sister Annika had died many years before. He could not bring himself to approach it, and instead tried to get a passport from the Secretariat for Finland. The Secretariat's hands were tied, however, leading Mannerheim to try another cunning ruse – he went to see the army's General Staff, and tried to get them to *order* him to Finland.

Mannerheim found himself in the old General Staff offices, facing a group of disillusioned, frightened men who were not even wearing their uniforms. When they, too, proved unable to help him, he told them that he had heard that Finland, as per the rhetoric of the revolution, was now a free state independent of the Tsar. With that in mind, Mannerheim told them that he felt that he no longer belonged in the Russian army. He got no answer for his thirty years of service beyond an exasperated shrug.

That night, Mannerheim went to the Finland Station, and again handed over some money to loitering soldiers to act as his baggage handlers. With no papers and no permission to leave town, he marched confidently up to the table at the platform entrance, and presented the soldiers there with his military pass. The soldiers, to Mannerheim's great relief, were Ingrians – local inhabitants of the St Petersburg region, whose presence predated the coming of Tsarist Russians in search of a port. They were more Finnish than Russian and, as Mannerheim realised with mounting joy, almost entirely illiterate. The pass he had given them was written in Russian, and neither of the Ingrians had any clue what the Cyrillic letters said. This was lucky, as if they had, they would have known that it only gave Mannerheim permission to come into St Petersburg, not to leave it again. Mannerheim spoke in Finnish to the two men – his

Finnish was not fluent, but it was good enough for him to answer some basic questions. The useless pass was returned to him with a smile, and he was waved through. Mannerheim was free.

During his long journey from Romania, Mannerheim had occasionally mused that his military career was over. He was fifty years old, and Russia was dead to him – there had already been talk of some sort of civilian position for him in Finland. However, by the time his train pulled into a cold, wet Helsinki in December 1917, he had regained some of his martial bearing. Mannerheim had left Russia telling everyone, including himself, that his soldiering days were over. But when he arrived in Helsinki, he was unable to stop thinking in terms of strategies.

It was plain to Mannerheim that, rhetoric aside, the new masters of Russia would not allow Finland to remain free for long. Once he had kitted himself out in Helsinki with documents that made it plain he was a Finnish citizen, he rushed back to St Petersburg for meetings with the French military attaché, to discuss the possibility of arms shipments to an independent Finland.

'It was not a question', wrote Mannerheim, 'of whether Finland would be dragged into the revolution, but when.' [9] In Finland's own parliament, the 'Red' or Social Democrat faction had 92 seats, against just 108 among the 'White' or bourgeois/conservative parties. There were, it seemed, only 16 representatives that prevented the Finnish government from *volunteering* to rejoin the Russian sphere, and no guarantee that this would not happen after the next election, should the Reds gain ground.

Meanwhile, even though the Soviet state had supposedly recognised Finland's right to detach itself from what had been the Tsar's empire, there were still nests of Russian troops dotted all over the former Grand Duchy. There were also agitators in Finnish cities determined to turn the urban populations against Finland's rural heartland. The left-wing newspaper *Työmies* (Working Man) published dangerous allegations that Finnish farmers were restricting their own production in order to ensure that 'the workers can die of hunger next winter'. The paper itself admitted that these were unsubstantiated rumours, but it added to a climate of great tension.[10]

The Russian soldiers still in Finland were unwelcome visitors with uncertain aims and unclear authority. Some, like Mannerheim, were Finns who had joined the Russian service. However, that had been an unpopular career move since the time of the assassination of Governor-General Bobrikov, and many more of the soldiers were ethnic Russians. These latter were deeply unpopular with the Finns, and anti-Russian propaganda had reached the stage that Finnish women were advised to avoid associating with them lest the liaison produce monstrously disfigured children.

Many of the soldiers, deprived of any semblance of discipline, were now acting like drunken hooligans – on this both the left- and right-wing press agreed. There was looting in many cities, and attempts to stop this military mayhem using local volunteers soon turned into partisan recruiting exercises for what would become rival militia, the Red Guards and White Guards. Peacekeeping divided along similar partisan lines. On the day that a group of Whites in Malmi apprehended a Red looter and brought him to justice, the Reds took it as a lynching, and reciprocated by shooting a White guardsman as he was minding his own business in a different street.[11]

All over Finland, particularly in the coastal region where smuggling was easier, old weapons were broken out of storage. A number of antiquated Swiss rifles surfaced in villages on the west coast, where they had been brought a decade earlier by anti-Tsarist revolutionaries on the *John Grafton*. Some were now in the hands of the local Whites, others with local Reds – with the Tsar gone, it was not clear how he would be replaced. Bolshevik revolutionaries had proclaimed a general strike in the autumn, and sent squads of men with 5-inch nails into the streets of Jyväskylä to hammer shut the doors of any businesses that remained defiantly open.

Although both White and Red parties in Helsinki had agreed on a head of state, in the form of Pehr Svinhufvud, and indeed on a declaration of independence for Finland, the divisions between Red and White in Finland made most laws impossible to enforce. In any centre of population, both factions proclaimed themselves to be the rightful agents of the government's will, and refused to acknowledge the other. In Tampere, a Red stronghold, Red militia looted a train carrying horses for the mounted police, and sold them in order to increase their own funds. Similar requisitions were reported in Lahti and other towns. Both sides acknowledged that good folk were mixed in with hooligans and criminals, but neither was able to turn upon the bad elements in their own midst.

This was the situation into which Mannerheim was propelled as he left Russia. Although much of Mannerheim's personal possessions were in storage, and he had no Finnish residence, he was welcomed at the homes of relatives. He stayed with his sister Sophie, and then moved into an apartment that belonged to his half-sister Marguerite and her husband Mikael Gripenberg.

In Helsinki, Mannerheim was soon co-opted onto the Military Committee, a group of activists largely comprising officers from the Finnish army that had been disbanded in 1901. The Committee had grown from an illegal club, to a semi-official pressure group, to an advisory body in swift steps since the Revolution. In January, less than a month after Mannerheim's return, the Committee was officially tasked with creating a Finnish army to resist Russian aggression. Mannerheim could not have timed his arrival better – he reached Helsinki a week before Christmas; the Committee gained its new mission on 7 January 1918, the day after Epiphany.

Although Mannerheim had not known of the Committee, the Committee certainly knew of him, and had even considered him *in absentia* as a potential commander-in-chief of the Finnish forces. Were it not for Mannerheim's backdated promotion on a Manchurian battlefield, he might have been trapped a couple of ranks down the chain of command, as yet another middle-ranking officer. But Mukden had put him a critical rank ahead of his rivals, and paid off over a decade later, delivering him back to the Finns as a lieutenant-general in their time of need. Volunteering for the Russo-Japanese War thirteen years earlier bore fruit that he could not have imagined or predicted.

Some in the Committee had misgivings about Mannerheim, however, assuming that he might have gone native in his years in St Petersburg. Mannerheim soon developed similar qualms about the Committee, whose members he largely regarded as stuffed shirts. Over the course of three meetings, Mannerheim swiftly grew tired of the endless negotiations and wrangles over petty matters while, he was sure, the Bolsheviks were plotting direct and violent action.

While Mannerheim certainly respected the Committee in principle, he was disappointed in the quality of its recruits. Few of the soldiers had been on a battlefield within the last two decades. They either had no experience at all, or far too much of it in half-remembered 19th-century skirmishes using outmoded technology and tactics. Mannerheim wanted immediate action, and he needed real soldiers. He was then informed by the Committee that some were already on their way.

The Finnish independence movement was far more organised than Mannerheim had realised, and he, along with most of the rest of Europe, had been taken in by a great deception in 1916. Mannerheim himself had fulminated at the news that Finns had gone to join the German army – it had not occurred to him that the 27th Royal Prussian Jäger Battalion were patriots accepting a German offer to train for what they regarded as inevitable strife in their homeland. The 2,000 volunteers who had left to join the Germans had not done so out of hatred for the Tsar, but out of a shared loved for an independent Finland. Mannerheim immediately asked the Military Committee to order the 27th Battalion home, as the time was right for it.

However, Mannerheim was tired of the Committee's indecisiveness. The members were fully aware of the danger they were in (the three meetings they had were held in different, secret locations), but Mannerheim was convinced that the Reds were not similarly wasting time. 'Any day', he said, 'we might be surprised and arrested, and what would become of our movement if its organising centre no longer existed?'[12] Instead, Mannerheim wanted all the loyal and important Finns out of Helsinki as soon as possible. He suggested they make for the west coast, to organise a defensive position in Vaasa, at the heart of a region opposed to the Reds. Red rhetoric favoured the city worker and the disaffected urban poor, and was sure to win support among the cities of the south. Mannerheim counselled a retrenchment to an area where the Reds would never get a sympathetic hearing, among the strong-willed, testy farmers and foresters of the north.

Mannerheim was used to giving orders, and his sense of entitlement took many in the Committee by surprise. Several stammering officers suggested that he had made some good points, and that perhaps it might be a good idea to reconvene, after some written reports and perhaps a feasibility study. Mannerheim rose to his feet and lit a cigar. There would be no report from him: 'It was high time for action and not writing.' [13]

Two days later, Mannerheim got what he wanted. The Military Committee recognised that it needed someone like him who could think ahead and take the decisions that truly mattered. The chairman resigned in favour of the cigar-smoking baron, and Mannerheim called on Svinhufvud, the head of state, to tell him of the plans. In a reflection of the tense situation in Helsinki, no written record was made of the meeting – a fact which would cause strain later, when Mannerheim was accused of exceeding his brief, and Svinhufvud of going back on his word. For now, however, Svinhufvud agreed that Mannerheim should implement a plan to 'keep order' in Finland, with the understanding that the keeping of order would largely rest on somehow disarming, neutralising or removing the Russian troops already on Finnish soil, and then somehow dealing with the Reds.

8

The White Devil

The coming months would see not so much a battle for order as a battle for control of Finland itself. For Mannerheim, money was not as big a problem as it could have been. He convened a meeting of prominent bankers, and advised them that they had a choice: they could bankroll the White resistance, and see an independent Finland; or they could refuse to do so, in which case the Reds would soon be in power, and their money would be entirely worthless. The rich men at the meeting preferred to stay rich, and lined him up with enough credit for the time being.

Mannerheim boarded a train for Vaasa, using papers that gave his name as Gustaf Malmberg and stated his occupation as a businessman. There were Russian soldiers at every station on the route and Mannerheim and his fellow passengers were asked to present their papers several times. By the time the train reached Tampere, Mannerheim was asleep in his berth, and when jolted awake by the arrival of a new group of inspectors he inadvertently replied to their first question in Russian. This immediately roused their suspicions, and they insisted on questioning him further.

Thinking fast, he agreed to come with them, but claimed that he was not fully dressed, and drew the curtains so he could put on some clothes. In fact, he was frantically passing a case of incriminating documents to his aide, in the hope that they could conceal it from the inevitable search. Just when it appeared that Mannerheim could not hold off the suspicious patrol any longer, the men were confronted by an unknown Finnish railwayman, who berated them for holding up the train to look at papers that were perfectly in order, saving Mannerheim from further interrogation and probable arrest.[1]

In Vaasa, Mannerheim immediately began organising his staff, operating out of local council buildings. As with the Military Committee in Helsinki, Mannerheim was frustrated by the available manpower – old, semi-retired officers, provincial also-rans, and eager but inexperienced youngsters. He put his legendary charm to use in persuading men to take posts that were beneath their rank, and did what he could to secure arms. Some 50 of the German-trained Jägers had already arrived in Finland with 9,000 rifles and a small number of pistols and machine guns, bought in the autumn in anticipation of trouble.

Ideologically, Finland was a difficult case for the Russian revolutionaries. Part of Lenin's anti-imperialist rhetoric centred on the freedom of old Russian possessions. It was thus his public claim that Finland was not part of Russian territory, but that he hoped that it would gain a socialist government that would make it an ally and supporter of the Communists. As part of this public position, it was incumbent on Lenin to claim that Russian soldiers still in Finland were neutrals and not an invading army. Josef Stalin, however, had other ideas. Even though the Bolsheviks recognised Finland's independence on paper, Stalin, as People's Commissar for Nationalities' Affairs, sent Finnish Reds a message that strongly implied they should take armed action.

> Socialist power ... alone can sustain itself and conquer. In such an atmosphere, there can be only one kind of tactic – that of Danton: 'Audacity, audacity and again audacity'. And should you need our help we shall give it to you, extending to you a fraternal hand. Of this you may be certain.[2]

Finland was not yet at war – in fact, war was never officially declared, as neither side wished to recognise its opponent as a legitimate enemy. Instead, the various interest groups continued to eye each other suspiciously. Local militia began to coalesce into a Defence Corps: the 'White' militia in support of an independent

Finland. Similar groups formed among sympathisers with the Bolsheviks, as the 'Red Guards'. A third group comprised the Russian soldiers on Finnish soil who, while supposedly neutral, were regarded as a danger by the Whites and a potential ally by the Reds. Some Russian soldiers took Stalin's hint and voluntarily 'resigned' from the Russian army in order to lend support to the Red Guards who were already preparing to seize control of Finnish population centres. Mannerheim was already planning to order his volunteer force to disarm the Russians, but kept holding off in late January, amid vague claims from the Helsinki government that negotiations were still proceeding with the Reds and, should talks work out to everyone's satisfaction, there would be no need for more direct action.

On 27 January 1918, Mannerheim received a message from Svinhufvud, instructing him to delay action again. Mannerheim pointedly ignored the order, putting it in his pocket. He had lost patience with Svinhufvud's prevarications, and suspected that every day he waited only allowed his enemies to gain ground. Instead, he gave the order to his own men to seize and disarm the Russian garrisons in Vaasa and in the semi-circle of nearby towns linked to it by rail. It was Mannerheim's intention for the operation to be over by the next morning.

By coincidence, he was not the only person planning a swift operation. The Red Guards also struck that night, seizing control of Helsinki on a cold Sunday evening when most workers were at home. On Monday morning it was announced that parliament had been disbanded, to be replaced by a Communist commissariat. Only four politicians successfully escaped, largely through the simple chance of being out of town. Others were arrested or confined to their homes.

If there had been plans for similar actions in the Vaasa area, they never happened. By midday on 28 January, the news was out – the Reds had taken Helsinki, but the Vaasa area was in the hands of Mannerheim's Whites. Mannerheim wasted no time in sending more men along the coastal railway line, to Kokkola, Oulu and Tornio at the Swedish border. They similarly disarmed the Russian garrisons in those regions, effectively putting all of

Finland north of Tampere in Mannerheim's hands. The strategy that Mannerheim had followed was remarkably similar to the one that he had outlined for a Russian attack on Chinese Turkestan. There were thousands of square miles of forests and lakes in north Finland, but only one railway that extended all the way to the border with Sweden. Mannerheim seized the three towns that had Russian garrisons in the days that followed news of the Red coup in Helsinki. Even though he had struck at the same time, his act was largely regarded in the north as a brave defence of Finnish interests against Red aggressors.

With Svinhufvud and others still in Helsinki, it was unclear who was really in overall charge. In the early days, the disbanded politicians left Mannerheim to it, although as more elected officials made it to Mannerheim's sanctuary, they began to feel that with danger now largely past, Mannerheim was overstepping his authority. With it no longer clear if Mannerheim really had the authority to become commander-in-chief, he operated under a title that was more of a nickname than anything else – the White General.

Many of the politicians had to make a circuitous route from occupied Helsinki to what now appeared to be the new centre of government. Svinhufvud, in particular, had an adventurous sojourn in the Helsinki suburbs, squirreled away in several apartments owned by sympathetic Whites. He was, however, determined to get away to Vaasa where Mannerheim was running the defence of White Finland.

Svinhufvud's first escape attempt, on 5 February 1918, was a bizarre charade in which he and his fellow fugitive politician Jalmar Castrén posed as businessmen who fancied a joyride in an aeroplane. After suitable bribes to the Russian staff of a naval airfield, Svinhufvud and Castrén were picked up in Helsinki by a car sent by the Russians themselves, and hence not questioned at any Red checkpoints. At the airfield itself, the two surprised politicians clambered aboard a plane to make their escape. Although not necessarily White sympathisers, the Russians at the airfield cared little enough for the Bolshevik cause to take motor parts and other gifts in payment for looking the other way. The flight, however, only lasted a few seconds before the mistaken pouring of antifreeze into

the motor caused it to stall, necessitating an emergency landing. 'I shall never go up in one of those Russian machines again,' fumed Svinhufvud, as he was ferried back to his hiding place.[3]

Eventually, the capture of Reval (Tallinn) by German forces put a sympathetic harbour only a few miles away across the Gulf of Finland in Estonia. Svinhufvud and Castrén were smuggled aboard the icebreaker *Tarmo*, a vessel with an all-Finnish crew but for a Russian commander and eight Russian marines. As a further example of the lack of cooperation between Russians and Finnish Reds, when Finnish Bolsheviks discovered the plan, they were rudely refused permission to examine the ship themselves. After a false start, the *Tarmo* got underway on 2 March. Finnish Reds tried to refuse it permission to leave the harbour, but were told off by the marines for interfering in a Russian matter. Once the voyage was under way, the marines were surprised at breakfast by White Finn gunmen, and surrendered without a fight. Svinhufvud and Castrén then travelled to Vaasa via Berlin; while the Reds learned so little from the event that the Whites repeated the hijacking with a second icebreaker later in the month.

Such shenanigans belie the awful cost of the Red occupation of Helsinki, during which some 1,649 people died for their White sympathies. Historians identify two distinct waves of what became known as the Red Terror, with most deaths clustered at the beginning of the occupation in February, and another increase in April as war intensified. Some of the deaths were deserters or suspected 'defectors' to the Whites. Many of the murders in Red rural areas seem to have had less to do with politics than with long-standing grudges and the settling of scores; most killers and victims seemed to know one another. Other 'Red' deaths may have concealed a criminal element – some shopkeepers were killed in what may have been political lynchings, but could equally have been lootings wearing an idealistic cloak. Criminal elements similarly embraced the Red banner in order to hunt down policemen and judges against whom they had a grudge. Some, like one of Mannerheim's von Julin cousins found dead near Turku, seem to have been murdered simply for being aristocrats. In a brutal form of time management, many murders seem to have been committed by Red Guards who did not want to go through the paperwork of processing an arrestee – some were suspects shot while supposedly on their way to questioning.[4]

The Red Terror was sure to keep many bourgeois Finns in line in Red-occupied areas. There was plenty of the stick, but little of the carrot, although there was one bizarre promise made in February 1918. A fantastic proclamation from Lenin himself was made known, that Red Finland returning to Soviet authority would receive Eastern Karelia, a border region of ethnic Finns, as a sort of bonus. The message was clear, that joining the Soviets would see Finland's territory expand, even if the Finns would have to deal with the inconvenience of giving up their sovereignty. To those Finns, particularly among the uneducated, who had given little thought to whether a Finn, Swede or Russian was the head of state in the past, the offer must have been tempting. Mannerheim was obliged to respond with a boast of his own, that he would not sheathe his sword until Karelia was part of Finnish territory. This was all very well, but Mannerheim had not even secured control of south Finland yet, let alone planning to conquer an entire new province.[5]

Mannerheim fully intended to lead an attack to retake the south at an indeterminate future point, and was smart enough to plan far ahead. Even though to get to Helsinki he would have to take Tampere first, his thoughts were already on the nature of a potential Red Helsinki, and how it might resist his own forces. In particular, he was worried about the potential of Sveaborg, the vast island stronghold just off the city's coastline. Sveaborg had over 200 gun emplacements scattered across it, designed to protect Helsinki from a marine assault, but with potentially devastating implications if, say, they were to be turned upon the city itself in the midst of a putative White Finn assault. Consequently, Mannerheim ordered a group to infiltrate the island and neutralise its guns before the Reds in Helsinki had time to occupy Sveaborg themselves.

The operation could not have succeeded without the participation of sympathetic Russian officers – Mannerheim was not the only one by far – and a group of Polish soldiers, who were bribed to take over the island's telephone exchange. With a pass issued by a Russian colonel, in the blank space of which enterprising Finns had typed an additional order to disarm the guns, the infiltrators began passing from battery to battery. Once inside, they flashed their augmented credentials and dismounted the breech blocks from the guns, rendering them impossible to fire. At one of the first gun batteries, the artillerymen protested and insisted on calling through to headquarters for confirmation. Instead, their call was put straight through to the Polish-occupied phone exchange, and they were told not to interfere.

The disarming of the guns of Sveaborg is one of the most remarkable stories of the Finnish Civil War, not the least because it was not a single night's operation but took almost a month. Weeks later, by the time the Red Guards took control of the island, the guns were almost entirely disabled, and the 'temporary' measure had been rendered substantially more permanent by careful vandalism of the boxes in which the breech blocks had been stored.[6]

Meanwhile, back in Vaasa, the cabal of escaped politicians proclaimed themselves to be the legitimate government of Finland, and that Mannerheim was the commander-in-chief of Finland's army of liberation. Mannerheim had been behaving as the commander-in-chief since he fled Helsinki, but appreciated the expansion of his official role from the vaguer directives of Svinhufvud. Mannerheim, however, had little time for the rump government, whose members were already acting as if the trouble was all but over. Asked by the acting president to estimate how long it would take to wrest control of the south, Mannerheim estimated three and a half months. His answer, however, was not a statement of military confidence, but an admission that he had almost no resources – 16 weeks, he thought, might be enough time to recruit and train a force that could oppose the Reds in the south.

One of his most taxing organisational problems was not about food or arms, but language. The Swedish-speaking minority of Finns amounted to perhaps 11 per cent of the population in 1918, but were heavily over-represented in the officer class, particularly in the upper ranks. What few Finnish-speaking officers survived were largely relics of the Finnish army which had been disbanded by the Tsar a generation earlier – in most cases, they were unfit for command. Swedish was the *lingua franca* at Mannerheim's headquarters, and was the language in which orders were originally written. This soon caused problems with the rank and file of the White Guards, most of whom were proud Finns, and many of whom began to chafe at taking orders in Swedish from former officers of the Russian army. This was, they argued, no way for an independent country to function. Admitting that the Finnish soldiers had a point, Mannerheim ordered all military communiqués to be made in Finnish, even though this often necessitated writing them in Swedish, having them translated – Mannerheim himself did not learn passable Finnish until his fifties – and then translating any replies. Mannerheim was used to such efforts from his days commanding *Hong Huzi* in Manchuria, but others regarded it as a pointless exercise.[7]

The language issue was important, but not life threatening. Of far greater controversy and seriousness was the issue of military justice. Mannerheim faced the difficult decision of fighting two forms of war. The battle for the south of Finland was straightforward, in the sense that there was a front line, and soldiers shooting at each other across it. Any captured enemies were, it might be assumed, prisoners of war, and were often treated as such. However, since civil war had never been officially declared, and both Whites and Reds regarded themselves as the rightful government of Finland suppressing insurgents, conditions were substantially less clear behind the lines. Tensions between Whites and Reds began with reprisals and lynchings, and threatened to escalate as both sides gained better weapons for dealing death.

Mannerheim's sister Sophie remained in Helsinki where, despite her surname, she was entirely unharmed by the Reds. Instead, she was permitted to set up a hospital and work without interference. 'I hope with all my heart,' she wrote to Mannerheim, 'that there will be no kind of counter-measures instituted, when the Whites have won. Many have joined the Reds out of genuine conviction.'[8]

Mannerheim did not want reprisals either, but he had no patience for Red espionage behind White lines. His orders of February 1918 made it clear that Red sabotage or armed resistance in

White areas would be met with summary executions. But perhaps he was not quite prepared for the sheer number of executions, or the number of acts in his territory that his zealous troops would define as espionage. One author, V Kilpi, counselling calm, warned that 'the zealous justice fanatics forget that the punishment which they demand, if it is to be fundamental and impartial, will affect one half of the Finnish nation, a half without which the nation cannot function.'[9]

The Finnish religious community, which one might have expected to stand up for human rights, was also split by the conflict. Some priests preached sermons of forgiveness and caution, noting, like Kilpi, that whatever the outcome of the civil conflict, the two halves of Finland would be obliged to live together in the aftermath. Others were less inclined to turn the other cheek – a priest in Kajaani suggested that all Red leaders should be shot, regardless of whether they had shed the blood of others or not.[10]

Religious intolerance was born, at least in part, from the priests' own understanding of the Red attitude towards all religion, although the concept of 'the opium of the masses' does not seem to have been known to all Finns. In one memorable incident, the Young Women's Christian Society of the eastern city of Mikkeli sent an earnest message to Mannerheim. They understood, they wrote, that the 'betrayers of the fatherland' were likely to be shot on the spot, but asked if it were possible for traitors at least to be allowed to see a priest before their execution.[11]

Mannerheim, who had been saddled with an 'advisory council' of soldiers by the Vaasa government, put the council to work on the ethical position of recognising Reds as enemies. The issue became all the more crucial when the Whites began conscripting troops for their own war effort, and inevitably gained Red attitudes, relatives or even, as they put it, 'pinkish' sympathies among their own troops and within their own territories. Mannerheim's orders for troops on the front line eventually accorded his Red enemies a more humane status: 'It is to be strictly observed that an enemy who surrenders is to be treated as a prisoner of war and that no action shall stain the clean record of Finland's White army.'[12]

However, if Mannerheim was hoping to avoid any bad press,

he was thwarted. Red publications and propaganda already char-
acterised him as the 'White Devil' or the 'Butcher-in-Chief' – an
appellation that he would not shake off with Finland's working
class for several decades.

Mannerheim made sure that the news of his men's 'victories' in
the north made it to the outside world. It was important, he knew,
that the international community understand that Finland was
not volunteering for Communist rule, but opposing it. For as long
as the Reds in the south could be termed as rebels, Mannerheim
thought there was hope. However, this forced him to refuse help
from elsewhere. He turned down an offer from Sweden to mediate
in the conflict, as Mannerheim did not wish to offer the Reds the
concession of treating them as political equals. Furthermore, it
was the prevarication over 'negotiations' that had let the Reds take
Helsinki, and Mannerheim was not prepared to give more ground.
Mannerheim appreciated foreign help in dealing with the Reds,
but was careful to specify what was acceptable. He waited expect-
antly for the return of the main body of the 27th Royal Prussian
Jäger Battalion, but only because he counted them as Finns in exile.
He did not want Germany to send its own troops to Finland, as the
presence of German troops would drag Finland into the ongoing
First World War. He was also taken by surprise when a supposedly
neutral neighbour sent unwelcome troops onto Finnish territory.

On 10 February, a group of Mannerheim's men had reached
the strategically crucial Åland islands in the middle of the Baltic.
The islands had been part of the Grand Duchy of Finland, and the
inhabitants were Swedish-speaking Finns like Mannerheim. As
per their orders, the Whites began disarming the Russians on the
islands, only to discover that Sweden had sent a force of its own in
order to prevent the islanders from coming to harm.

When Mannerheim learned what had happened, he remonstrated with the Swedish government, arguing that they had no
right to interfere in an internal Finnish matter. He suspected that
Sweden was hoping to take advantage of the Finnish situation
to seize the islands for itself. His suspicions were hardly allayed
when his men returned to the Finnish mainland, claiming to have
done so on Mannerheim's own orders. Mannerheim's telegrams to

Åland took a circuitous route via Stockholm, and the most recent had been carefully doctored by Swedish agents to make it look as if he had ordered his men to retreat.

Finnish control of the islands was only established by the arrival of 80 of the long-awaited Jägers from Germany – a welcome restoration of Finnish sovereignty, albeit with with an unhelpful implication. The Jägers not only made it look as if Finland needed foreign assistance, but led many of those who cheered them on to expect more help from friendly Germany, and more intrigues from Sweden.

Mannerheim was, however, unable to conceal his delight when the largest group of Jägers arrived at Vaasa in February. Such highly trained, experienced soldiers were precisely what he needed to help train up the ramshackle units of volunteers and conscripts scattered throughout the Finnish countryside. He had a desperate shortage of officers, and wanted to split the Jägers up to diverse destinations immediately. The Jägers, however, had rather hoped that they would serve as a single crack unit, and had no desire to be packed off to remote fishing villages and mining towns to drill, as they saw it, yokels with pitchforks and broom handles.

Mannerheim got his own way eventually, but the Jägers were merely the first whispers of other German interference. Mannerheim had no objection to Finns with German training; what worried him was the implications if his government invited in the German army itself. Mannerheim vigorously asserted his wish for a Finns-only force before the rump parliament, arguing that it was vital for the people of Finland to fight their own battle, not least as a means of uniting the country's deep divisions, and that he was 'absolutely convinced' that the Finns could do it. He was opposed in the meeting by the Jägers' pro-German leader, Wilhelm Thesleff, with whom he was constantly at odds for the rest of the war. Mannerheim felt so strongly about the need for Finland to work through its Civil War alone that he even threatened to resign, daring the politicians to think of a man better suited to the job. In this speech, he may have over-stepped the mark, as Thesleff was all too willing to put himself forward for Mannerheim's role as commander-in-chief. Mannerheim was forced to back off, and to consent to the arrival of German troops on Finnish soil. Nevertheless, he tried to impose conditions upon them, in particular that they should be under his overall command, and that they should not be used to suppress the insurrection. That would be left to the Finns.

Of all the cities said to have fallen to the Red Finns, the industrial centre of Tampere was the furthest to the north. It also sat on a railway line that led directly to Helsinki and was therefore to be Mannerheim's main point of attack. The fighting around Tampere took place at Easter 1918, and was so fierce that Mannerheim even found himself committing some of the Jäger troops that he had been saving for later. After losing troops to Red snipers in the buildings, the Whites began a process of indiscriminate street fighting. If movement was spotted inside a building, the Whites responded with grenades. All apprehended snipers were shot. The Red Finns, to Mannerheim's irritation, put up a much better fight than he was expecting, while he was already asking the impossible of his own troops. Despite great difficulties in the chain of command and communications, and with many untried and untested soldiers, the White Finns overcame an army of some 25,000 Reds. Enemy casualties were 1,800 dead and over 11,000 captured, versus 600 deaths among the Whites.

That was, however, only the beginning. Mannerheim reiterated his order to treat captured Reds as prisoners of war. This was often disobeyed, and a massacre followed of all Russians and identifiable Red commanders.

Meanwhile, having only grudgingly accepted the offer of German aid, Mannerheim found himself unable to avoid calling on it. The battle for Tampere took longer than he had allowed for, leading him to swallow his pride and send a message to the Jäger commander Thesleff to the effect that delay was fatal.

'I got a distress call from Mannerheim today,' noted Thesleff in his diary, 'which begs me with all my strength to hurry the affair. So, my friend, what would have happened if you had had your way and we had refused the assistance?' [13]

It is likely that the Whites would have won without German assistance. They had, after all, scored victories in Tampere and in lesser battles. However, there is no telling what compromises or changes of fortune might have been forced on Mannerheim's army without the arrival of German reinforcements. Some 10,000 men left Danzig on 30 March – 368 officers, 9,077 troops, and 350 White Guards who had fled Finland and somehow made it to German territory, usually by crossing the narrow strait to German-occupied Reval. The division gained 2,500 Germans at Reval, along with a further 300 Finnish refugees. A second, smaller force came direct from the Åland islands, and both landed with little resistance at Hanko on Finland's south-west coast early on 3 April.

Many of the Red Guards fled Helsinki rather than defend it – the city's main protection was Sveaborg, designed to ward off marine assaults not land-based attacks. There was, however, still fighting, with German reports of women wielding guns alongside the men, and even Red Cross nurses joining in the shooting. There was little structural damage, and while the Germans took some 200 casualties, there were few of the post-battle reprisals that had marred the capture of Tampere. 'I am unreservedly happy that Helsinki is free,' lied Mannerheim to his sister, immediately offering a reservation, 'even though it was not my troops that liberated it ...'.[14]

Fighting continued east along the coast, where another part of the German force had crossed from Reval. The railway remained the main bone of contention, largely because by this point the Reds required it to ensure their own safe retreat to Soviet Russia. This not only involved the soldiers, but also their families – fearing reprisals, refusing to stay behind while their menfolk fled, thousands of Red Finns formed a grim convoy on the local roads, women and children on carts where possible, accompanied, in one incident, by the grotesquely inappropriate music of an enthusiastic marching band.[15]

The battleground moved onto Karelia, that region of eastern Finland whose coat of arms has always been a symbol of east-west tensions – to this day, it is a pair of contending swordsmen. On the left or western side is a knight's arm wielding a broadsword, on the right or eastern side a barbarian's arm wielding a scimitar. It was an appropriate place to see off the Soviets.

By the end of April, the south-eastern town of Viipuri had fallen to the Whites, and the last of the Red refugees were fleeing into

Russia. Mannerheim arrived to attend a mass in the city, the cathedral of which had been previously used by the Reds as a grain store.

> Now I have arrived in Viipuri, this ancient capital of Karelia ...
> which over the centuries has received the assaults of the hordes
> which came from the east ... a feeling of joy and gratitude con-
> quers my mind because the flag of Finland flies over this castle. ...
> Through your blood, brave army, Finland has now become equal
> with other European nations. Now the Finns, with their heads held
> high, step forth as masters of their own country.[16]

But who, one might ask, was the master of the Finns? On the
outskirts of Viipuri, two captured Reds began to tell their men
that help would soon be on the way from Russia. 'To preserve
discipline', they were immediately shot by the Whites. It was one
of many reprisals – the days of Red Terror were replaced by White
Terror; only the victims changed.

In the aftermath of the Civil War, the tallies of Red deaths
grew significantly higher than battlefield deaths. Over 8,000 Red
sympathisers were killed in reprisals and the settling of scores
from the coup or perhaps even before, through either summary
executions or following rulings by kangaroo courts. Some 58 of
the victims were children, another 364 were women.[17] For years
to come, Mannerheim would receive the blame for this – he was
described as the 'Hangman' or 'Butcher' of Tampere in particular,
but would also be blamed for a humanitarian disaster that followed
the end of hostilities. The Whites had taken over 80,000 prisoners,
many of them exhausted, malnourished or wounded at the time of
capture. Despite inadequate holding facilities, few of these men
were released, ironically because White agitators were insisting on
subjecting them to a fair trial. In a four-month period, over 11,000
Red prisoners died in White custody, often through neglect or the
simple lack of access to basic needs such as clean drinking water.

Mannerheim, however, marched in triumph through the streets
of Helsinki on 16 May. He was greeted by cheering crowds, and
white flowers were thrown in the path of his horse. Accompanying
him were representatives of every major unit that had fought in his

army, with the conspicuous exception of the Germans, who had not been invited. His parade was preceded by an Order of the Day in which he praised the contributions of 'the brave men of Sweden and Scandinavia' (but, once again, not the Germans) and gave a stern warning that Finland's troubles were not yet over: 'Now as before, the great questions will be decided by blood and iron ... without unity a strong army cannot be created, and only a power-ful nation can safely advance towards the future.' [18]

9

The House of the Four Winds

Mannerheim's triumph ended with an address to the Senate. Svinhufvud, the chairman of the Senate, expected him to enter the chamber alone, but he refused, and instead marched in at the head of an entourage of fellow soldiers. Already, there was talk among the politicians of removing Mannerheim from the public eye. It had been suggested that the White General might be packed off to an ambassadorial post somewhere out of the way, while the politicians got back to work. Mannerheim had little sympathy for such circumlocutions, and reminded the assembled politicians that only a few months before they had been 'powerless against robbery and plunder, and had been compelled to watch helplessly as Finnish citizens were murdered', while the politicians themselves had been 'stripped of the last shadow of power and ... forced to flee or hide away'.[1]

He saw it as his duty to address them with 'harsh words ... not watery gruel' in the name of the 'young, victorious army' which he had recently led. He spoke as the leader of the White forces that had restored order at a terrible cost:

The army holds that the only guarantee against danger is that the Finnish ship of state shall be entrusted to strong hands, beyond the reach of party wrangling, and which have no need to make compromises and bargains over the power of the government for trifles. In the ranks of the White Army stands every loyal man, in the belief that in the era which is beginning, his hopes will not be disappointed. Thousands of the white crosses in cemeteries through the distant Finnish countryside, speak their silent language. The dead demand that their sacrifice should not have been in vain.[2]

Mannerheim had already been warned that his speech went too far. He spoke to the assembly more like a Roman dictator than the servant of a democratic state, all but conferring their freedom upon them as if it was his to give. It is difficult to tell whether Mannerheim's speech was calculated career suicide, designed to impress upon the government that its problems were not over, or an arrogant riposte in the face of what he regarded as ingratitude. He and his men had accomplished an impossible task, and Finland was to remain the only 'White' state of the former Russia to maintain its independence by the mid-1920s. But Mannerheim had all but thrown down the gauntlet before the democratically elected representatives of the people – even to some Whites, his behaviour seemed dangerously aristocratic, perhaps even 'Russian'.

Svinhufvud, who was destined to become regent (i.e. interim head of state), did not take the bait. Instead he offered Mannerheim brief but curt thanks for his service. Mannerheim and the other dignitaries then left the council chamber to attend a church service. Outside in the streets, the white flowers were still falling like rain. At a later celebratory feast at the railway station, Mannerheim and Svinhufvud were seated next to each other, but did not talk.

Four days later, Mannerheim offered to step down as army commander-in-chief. It was a gentlemanly act, based on his recognition that the purpose for which he had been invested with supreme powers – the war against the Reds – was now discharged. But it was also a political act; Mannerheim was testing the new authorities. Would they accept his resignation, or would they ask him to stay, leaving the way open to negotiate terms? The politicians did not oblige him either way, and dragged him into two weeks of negotiations in which they appeared to offer him the post of commander-in-chief, but only under the acceptance of terms that he deemed insulting and counterproductive.

Mannerheim already felt outnumbered and unsupported. The enthusiasm of the soldiers for their conquering general was not repeated among the politicians. With Finland now supposedly at peace, there was no place for the special powers of the White General. Politicians paid lip-service to the idea of offering Mannerheim the role as a commander-in-chief of a reorganised Finnish army, but there were problems. Mannerheim was once more regarded as a man with unwelcome affinities. As a Swedish-speaker who had served a lifetime in the Russian army, he was a representative of both of the former authorities against which Finnish nationalism had striven. Now Finland was free of such influences, Mannerheim was less welcome.

Nor did Mannerheim think that the fighting was over. Like many on the Finnish right wing, he favoured taking the battle back to the east and reconquering eastern Karelia, which had historically been part of Finland. He had of course, already promised to do so during the Civil War, although he had not been empowered to plot foreign invasions on behalf of the Finnish government. Above all, he favoured a march on Petrograd itself, to liberate his former home from the Reds.

In this he had very little support. The Finns wished to savour their newfound independence, and did not want to invite reprisals from over the border. Meanwhile, from Russia itself, the dwindling White resistance made respectful overtures to Mannerheim, appealing on his long years of service to the Tsar, and pleading with him to bring a force of Finns charging into the east. It was, after all, such a pitifully short distance from the Finnish border to the city that had once been St Petersburg. A Finnish force, perhaps with German backing, could sweep in and snatch the old capital, giving the Whites a vital toehold in the Russian heartland. However, the White Russians refused to acknowledge the freedom of Finland itself. It was implied, and certainly not denied, that if White Russia defeated Red Russia, then Finland would be expected to return to the authority of a foreign power. The Finns had only just thrown off the Tsar and the Reds; they were not about to go to war again for the privilege of submitting to the Russians once more.

Instead, despite Mannerheim's protests, the Finnish parliament

was intent on yoking Finland closer to Germany. Only German and Finnish officers were now permitted in the army, and officers with Swedish nationality were sent home. Mannerheim was incensed that foreign men who had 'with honour carried out difficult and often thankless tasks' were now dismissed so abruptly, and rightly suspected that Swedish speakers with Finnish nationality would be next on the hit list.[3]

In a meeting that Mannerheim openly proclaimed to be a waste of his time, officials informed him that they intended to bring in German officers and support to reform the Finnish army, and that, while he was welcome to remain as commander-in-chief, he was expected to have a German Chief of the General Staff.

'Surely nobody could imagine,' wrote Mannerheim later of the affair, 'that after having created an army out of nothing and led practically untrained, badly armed, badly equipped troops to a victory gained through the fighting spirit of the Finnish soldiers … I would be a party to … orders considered necessary by a German Military Commission.'[4]

Less than two weeks after he had been received in a triumphal procession as Finland's great military hero, Mannerheim resigned, proclaiming that the Finns were creating a whole new set of problems for themselves. 'I only want to add that I am giving up my command this evening and travelling abroad tomorrow. I request the government to choose my successor at once – otherwise I shall leave the command to my nearest subordinate. Goodbye, gentlemen.'[5]

'The members of the government', he wrote, 'had not a word to say to me when I left the chamber, and no one rose to offer me his hand.'[6] However, this observation seems a little disingenuous; as his parting words makes clear, he left their presence in swift fury while the politicians looked on open-mouthed.

'Mannerheim rode ceremonially into the capital', noted his nemesis Thesleff. 'He was feted like a king and treated with respect as in a Roman Triumph, and now, after only a few days, the man is lost and has permission to give up his post.'[7]

Mannerheim was not alone, but left Helsinki in a carriage with several fellow officers who had also refused to kowtow to the new regime. He was in such a hurry that even his own supporters were surprised – a state banquet to be given in his honour was hastily called off when it was discovered he was no longer in the country.

There was little to keep Mannerheim in Finland. He had no desire to glower like Banquo's ghost at the celebrations and deliberations, and had neither property nor close family in Finland that would serve to keep him there. 'My earthly possessions', he noted, 'could easily be contained in a couple of suitcases.'[8] This hard-luck tale, while evocative and often repeated, is not strictly true – he had an entire house's-worth of possessions in storage in Poland, and would eventually retrieve them after the war.

Nor were the politicians entirely ungrateful for his services; he left Finland as the recipient of a substantial pension, equivalent to the annual salary received by the prime minister. It allowed him to live the high life abroad, and although he was no longer serving the Finnish state in any official capacity, he acted as if he did.

Mannerheim did not believe that his career was over. German defeat in the First World War was now imminent, and he foresaw with it the possible collapse of many of the politicians who had opposed him. He also worried that Finland's hard-won independence would be compromised in a post-war international community that shunned all things German. With either steadfast conviction or cunning foresight, he embarked upon a grand tour that established him in the eyes of many foreigners as a Finnish statesman and leader.

With so many Mannerheims and Nordenskiölds in Stockholm, he first went to Sweden, where King Gustav V gave him a royal audience. The King conferred Mannerheim with the Grand Cross of the Order of the Sword, presumably intending it as a great honour, although Mannerheim was uncharacteristically snide in accepting it. Smiling all the while, he mentioned to the King that he had rather hoped to receive the Order 20 years earlier, when he had been the leading officer at a Chevalier Guards banquet given in the King's honour when he was still merely the Crown Prince. King Gustav appeared, at least in public, to accept this lesson in etiquette as a joke, although Mannerheim did not give up. He noted, for example, that his decoration was supposedly for services

rendered to Sweden during the War of Liberation – Mannerheim was curious as to how the King of Sweden thought Finland's independence was to Sweden's benefit.

The King offered the diplomatic reply that Mannerheim's victory had brought peace to the Swedes and that, as the ruler of the Swedes, it was his duty to thank Mannerheim for the good treatment he had given to Swedish volunteers. That was good enough for Mannerheim, at least for the moment, but he carefully accepted the decoration in the spirit that King Gustav had claimed. He immediately cabled the new commander-in-chief of the Finnish army to inform him that the King of Sweden had bestowed the decoration on himself as the *representative* of all Finns, and not on Mannerheim the Swedish-speaking leader. Of course, accepting the decoration on behalf of his men only increased Mannerheim's standing with them.

Mannerheim met with British, American and French diplomats in Stockholm, but was careful to distance himself from the Germans. He presented himself to them as a man who had been forced to accept German assistance during the Civil War, but who could not in all conscience bear his country's continued drift into the German sphere of influence. With the First World War now turning against the Kaiser, Mannerheim was a popular figure with the Allies. A document from the British Foreign Office minister Esme Howard noted, 'It is fairly clear that he is our friend, and his influence in Finland will probably revive in time.'[9]

The only thing Mannerheim wanted from the Germans was his furniture. He would require German permission to retrieve his possessions from occupied Poland, and applied for permission to do so. The Germans, however, were all too happy to be seen to be in talks with such a prominent Finn, and invited him to visit the front line and meet the Kaiser. Keen to remain in the good books of his Allied friends, Mannerheim used his contraction of Spanish 'flu in August as a suitable excuse to call off his German visit. Instead he joined an old friend, Hjalmar Linder, on a hunting party in Norway, where Mannerheim promptly fell in love with Linder's half-sister Catharina 'Kitty' Linder.

Kitty was 20 years younger than Mannerheim but clearly

returned his affections. However, the romance of the Norwegian mountains began to dissipate when the couple returned to civilisation. Mannerheim's conspicuously public role led him to insist on a degree of secrecy, and in the eyes of the Russian Orthodox Church he was still married to Anastasie. Mannerheim promised to get a divorce, liable to be considerably easier in the newly independent state of Finland, but withdrew his application when Anastasie let him know by letter from Paris that she was going to contest it. Although honour may have been involved, money may also have been a factor – with the girls grown up and moved out, Anastasie was determined to live on in the manner to which she had become accustomed. The world was clogged with White Russians fallen on hard times. Former duchesses were working as waitresses in Istanbul and Shanghai, blue-eyed baronets were begging by the side of Chinese roads. The upheavals of the Revolution had killed millions, but also flung millions more into foreign countries. Mannerheim was fortunate in that he could run for Finland, a country which he had helped achieve its independence, and which now supported him. Anastasie wanted a piece of that money, and threatened to make Mannerheim's life difficult.

Mannerheim had by now moved out of the Grand Hotel in Stockholm, where he had been staying since his arrival, and into an apartment in the city. He wrote love letters to Kitty Linder in French, and mused hopefully that 1919 would see his divorce finalised and 'bring the fulfilment of our wishes and happiness'.[10] But even as he wrote of his plans for the future with his young paramour, the Finns courted him once more.

As he had predicted, the decision of the Helsinki politicians to hitch their infant nation close to the German empire was already looking unwise. On 9 October 1918, the Finnish Senate had officially offered the Finnish crown to the German Prince Frederick Charles of Hesse (1868–1940), brother-in-law of the Kaiser. It was hoped that Frederick Charles would help establish Finland as the world's newest monarchy, stave off any suggestion of returning to Russian rule, and keep the Swedes at bay.

Finland's government was too caught up in its internal problems and its birth pangs to enjoy adequate intelligence of someone else's war, and too politically naïve to take on the significance of the fact that Germany was already on the brink of defeat. 'It must in fairness', wrote Mannerheim, 'be admitted that Finland ... did not possess ... foreign political and military information which would have been required for an objective orientation.'[11] However, with Germany only a month away from defeat at the hands of the Allies, there were already cold feet. The day before the offer was made to Prince Frederick Charles, Mannerheim had been called to a meeting in Helsinki with his old sparring partner Svinhufvud (now head of state as regent), and the serving prime minister Juho Paasikivi. Both knew that Finland would be a laughing stock if it accepted a German-born king shortly before Germany was itself defeated. It would be a diplomatic disaster.

Consequently, the election of 'King' Frederick Charles was already doomed to failure. Although the prince accepted the offer, and even made plans to marry one of his sons to a Finnish noblewoman, he did not arrive in Helsinki to take up his new position. Svinhufvud and Paasikivi begged Mannerheim to put his international fame to use while they extricated themselves from the awful position. He should immediately go to London and Paris to assure the Allies that the whole monarchy business was an unfortunate necessity, designed to keep Finland from harm from Russian and Swedish intrigue. Mannerheim was to persuade the Americans to lift a trade embargo, and to plead with the French – who had broken off relations as soon as the German connection became apparent – not to write Finland off merely because the country had suddenly acquired a German-born head of state.

Mannerheim refused to accept an official post from the beleaguered government – this was a mess of their own creating, and his resignation had been a deliberate attempt to make sure that none of the mud stuck to him. However, he did agree to undertake the mission as a private citizen, as he had done during the summer. He sailed for England via Sweden along with his brother-in-law Mikael Gripenberg, who had been appointed as his secretary. To his great irritation, he found that his fellow passengers included a delegation from Helsinki who were rushing to Germany to urge Prince Frederick Charles to accept the offer and come with all due haste. It was, protested Mannerheim, 'hardly opportune', but one of the delegates openly confessed that their best hope was to present the world with a *fait accompli*. In other words, Prince Frederick Charles might be a German today, but if he were to become a Finn soon enough, his place of birth would be less important than his new role. The delegation hurried on its way, leaving Mannerheim to make a long, wintry crossing of the North Sea that was sure to cost him valuable time.

Delayed by storms, a seething Mannerheim arrived in Aberdeen on 10 November, from where he took a train to London. He reached the capital the following day, along with the news that, as of 11 November 1918, the war was finally over. Mannerheim was now obliged to fight the peace.

With Germany defeated and already proclaimed a republic, the issue of Finland's new 'king' disappeared. Within the month, Frederick Charles had withdrawn his acceptance, leaving Finland once more without a head of state, and tainted in the eyes of the Allies. There was already talk of a great peace conference in Paris, in which the Allies and other powers would fix the shape of the world map for the coming century. The victorious Great Powers – particularly the United States, United Kingdom and France – were determined to steer matters in such a way as to create a new world order. Their own allies took precedence, their commonwealths and sundry neighbours. As a newly created and as yet unrecognised country, Finland was not even invited to occupy a seat at the peace conference. Instead, it faced intrigues from Swedes and Russian sympathisers, and risked being counted as a German ally unless Mannerheim tried some deft manoeuvres.

Back in Helsinki, Svinhufvud gave Mannerheim the best possible support available to him. He resigned as regent on 10 December, along with Prime Minister Paasikivi's cabinet, and urged his fellow politicians to look to their constitution for a solution. Thanks to Finland's convoluted political history, its rules and regulations had been drawn up neither by Russians nor Finns. In fact, fragments of the Finnish constitution dated back to the days of the Swedish monarchy, and allowed for the election of a regent in times of need. Since Finland had just lost its only 'king', was friendless in the wake of the war, and needed a head of state who commanded respect with the many doubting foreign powers at the Peace Conference, the time was right to create a new regent to fight Finland's corner. After a lively debate, Mannerheim was elected regent of Finland by a margin of 73 votes to 27. At the time, he was already in London pleading Finland's cause.

Mannerheim's sudden, surprising appointment as head of state gave his arguments and friendships with the foreign powers a much-needed weight of authority. At meetings in London and Paris, he let both the British and French believe that negotiations with Frederick Charles had been broken off at their instigation. He pleaded for grain shipments to hold off famine in Finland and, most of all, he argued for the recognition of Finland as an independent country, regardless of the opposition of the contending powers in Russia. In meetings with Lord Robert Cecil, who had been the British Minister of Blockade, Mannerheim adroitly argued in favour of the commencement of grain shipments to Finland. Cecil complained that the Allied powers were now obliged to provide grain for all Europe, including their enemies, but that the Allies would only do so for those countries that maintained internal order – a deliberate attempt to exclude the Allies from responsibility for the situation in Russia, then still at civil war. 'To this,' wrote Mannerheim, 'I replied that the importation of grain was the first requirement for the maintenance of order. Starving masses easily fall prey to Bolshevism and anarchy.'[12]

Cecil, who would eventually become one of the lynchpins of the League of Nations, was swayed by Mannerheim's argument for the prevention of further conflict. As for the recognition of Finland as a state, Mannerheim got little out of the British beyond vague assurances, but managed to sway the French into agreeing to recognise Finnish independence, on the understanding that the country would be purged of German influences.

He returned to Finland shortly before Christmas 1918, coincidentally arriving on the same day as the first shipment of relief grain from the Allies. Once again, Mannerheim was hailed as a conquering hero, particularly among the Swedish-speaking peoples of south-western Finland. In truth, however, he had failed

to secure international recognition for Finland, and the struggle was still ahead of him.

Mindful of the need to give the appearance of an organised, broad state with traditions of its own, Mannerheim appointed the artist Akseli Gallen-Kallela as his aide-de-camp. Gallen-Kallela had volunteered to fight for the Whites in the Civil War, and gained an unexpected reward when he was asked by the new regent to provide designs for the new republic. Finland needed flags, medals, and uniforms in order to impress upon its neighbours that it was no mere flash in the pan. Consequently, the man who had once painted frescoes of newly-invented Finnish heroes in Paris, and the notorious 'stamp of mourning' would now design the medals to be worn by real heroes, and the insignia that would grace real Finnish stamps.

One of Mannerheim's first public acts as regent was to visit Sweden in February 1919. Despite undertaking an official state visit, he was obliged to slum it in the icebreaker *Tarmo*, the same vessel that had spirited Svinhufvud out of Helsinki the previous year. Like all such vessels, the *Tarmo* was a glorified battering ram, designed for smashing a path through a freezing sea by getting up a good speed and crunching down on the edge of the ice. This required a reinforced, armoured hull, stripped-down conditions inside and a flattened keel that left it distinctly unstable in rough seas. It was, Mannerheim observed sarcastically, 'hardly a pleasure yacht ... but ... if we should meet with ice obstruction on the way, we had no occasion to fear a loss of valuable time.'[13]

Conscious of the power of the printed image and of the presence of photographers at the dockside, Mannerheim determined to arrive as a uniformed officer, resplendent with his best medals – it was impossible for Mannerheim to wear all his decorations at once, there were so many of them – with the Grand Cross of the Order of the Sword most visible. The new Finnish army uniform had only just been designed by Gallen-Kallela and there was such a shortage of materials in Finland that Mannerheim's was one of only a handful in existence that was cut from the correct khaki cloth.[14]

While Mannerheim's uniformed figure, a Swedish medal prominent on his chest, may have looked impressive enough, the

Swedes were attired far more sensibly for a Stockholm winter. King Gustav V was buttoned up inside a massive greatcoat and a towering ceremonial hat, and the temperature was enough of a shock to Mannerheim's system to give him an awful cold. Nevertheless, he was intent upon winning hearts and minds in Finland. Now that he, too, was a head of state, he presented King Gustav with a medal of his own. He was particularly proud of this new honour fashioned by Akseli Gallen-Kallela, the White Rose of Finland, fastened by a chain of Finnish swastika links, originally interspersed with eight rosettes – one for each of Finland's historical districts. But in a cunning flourish, Mannerheim had decided that the chain should have *nine* rosettes; why not, he reasoned, make it clear that the Åland islands were also part of Finland, and had been widely regarded as such since the 16th century?

The islands remained a sore point between the two countries, and Mannerheim refused to give them up. The Swedes were already pushing their own cause with the powers assembling for the Paris Peace Conference, and hoped to cajole the international community into accepting that a Swedish-speaking community, off the coast of Sweden, should be regarded as a province of Sweden. In return, it was hoped that the Finns could be fobbed off with a nominal grant of territory on their eastern borders – a chunk of Finnish-speaking Karelia, perhaps, which the Russians would hardly miss.

Mannerheim countered this by accepting that the islands were of great importance to Sweden, and also that in the event of any battles with the east – Russia – he would be heavily reliant on the land route through Sweden for supplies. With an eye on keeping things friendly, he offered that they cooperate on the fortification of the islands, but King Gustav refused. Any form of military action with Finland would compromise Sweden's neutrality, and the Swedes resolved to refer the matter to the Paris Peace Conference.

By this point, Mannerheim was bedridden with the 'flu. King Gustav put the palace at his disposal, but Mannerheim hobbled back to the *Tarmo*, where he spent a miserable two days shivering with fever, swathed in blankets. His only consolation came from the Swedish newspapers, which, like King Gustav himself, were prepared to ignore the continued impasse over the Åland islands, and spoke of 'Sweden's debt of gratitude to the man who, above all others, had the honour of having stemmed the tied of barbarian aggression from the east.'[15]

Mannerheim had a less pleasant reception in Copenhagen in December, where he and King Christian X were pelted by snowballs as the royal carriage drove them from the train station to the palace. Mannerheim offered no direct suggestion of who his attackers were, but makes it clear in his memoirs that this was no act of horseplay, but a political demonstration. The hooligans with snowballs were left-wing sympathisers, keen to make it clear that radicals in other countries matched the antipathy felt for the 'White Devil' among the Finnish Reds. While Mannerheim was in Copenhagen, adding the Danish Order of the Elephant to his growing collection of medals, but also still nursing the 'flu, he received word that radicals in Norway, next on his itinerary, were planning more than mere snowballs for him. Protestors had disrupted power and water in Oslo, and advisors fretted that there would be a serious attempt on Mannerheim's life. Neither Mannerheim nor the Norwegian royals wanted to call off his planned trip, but with his illness still refusing to abate, it was decided to cut short his grand tour.

Regent Mannerheim returned to a Finland that was going to the polls for a parliamentary election on 1 March 1919. Conservative parties largely sympathetic to him still had an overall majority, but enough votes had gone to the left wing for the idea of a monarchy to be permanently shelved. Mannerheim sourly observed that he was almost as unwelcome in the parliament as in the army. The agrarian factions mistrusted him for not being a native Finnish speaker, while the Social Democrats despised him for his stance against all Reds; notoriously, Regent Mannerheim had even tried to prevent trade unions from flying red flags. Mannerheim was also feared by many factions who feared that a strong military man, a monarchist, adored by large sectors of the country's fighting men, might be viewed as the perfect figurehead for a coup, dictatorship or new tyranny.

Such suspicions were not unfounded. In June 1919, the new

government reached the final stages of negotiating Finland's new constitution. Mannerheim disapproved with many of its points, sometimes on minor points of order, but largely because of the clear indication that Finland would not be intervening in the Russian Civil War. Any hopes Mannerheim had of leading a Finnish force east, recapturing St Petersburg and delivering a death blow to the Reds, were fading. Finland was safe, but the Russia where Mannerheim had served for most of his career was gone forever. Soon, he would be called upon for his last act as regent, to approve the new constitution and stand down so that the Finns could elect their first president.

There was, inevitably, a temptation for him to play politics. If he were to refuse to approve the constitution, he could force a new election, and hope that the result left him with a parliament that was more ready to give him his way. In July, he was approached by a group of activists who had plotted an acrobatic series of loopholes in protocol. They thought that he could delay confirmation of the constitution, dissolve parliament, but then confirm the constitution with no parliament in place to argue with him one way or the other. Mannerheim would effectively be dictator, and could then single-handedly declare war on Russia. It was, presumably, expected that his many loyal soldiers from the Civil War would come out in support, and that nobody would dare oppose him.

Mannerheim had no desire to be the tyrant of Finland, although his passion to defeat the Reds was strong enough for him to consider bending the rules to such an outrageous extent. He consulted with a policy adviser, but was shown the fatal flaw in the scheme – once the constitution had been confirmed, Regent Mannerheim would lose the power to declare war, and would have to wait for a new parliament to be elected before he could do so. Nor could he expect the conservatives to support him, as the centre factions would never countenance such brinkmanship, and that would put the conservatives in the minority. Grumbling that 'a soldier cannot act in politics without the support of any political party', Mannerheim gave his seal of approval to the constitution.[16]

Mannerheim claims in his memoirs that he had every intention of retiring from active life, worn out by a career in soldiering, the deprivations of the Civil War and the ceaseless manoeuvrings of his regency and party politics. However, he was soon subjected to what he calls 'severe pressure' from friends and associates, who demanded that he stand as a candidate in the upcoming election for the new position of president. To do otherwise, he was told, would be to betray those who had placed their trust in him, leading them in a Civil War, only to abandon them to a government in which the largest single party was the Social Democrats – Red sympathisers.

'And what about the rest of us,' demanded his friend Rudolf Walden. 'Do you suppose that I am in the government for fun?'[17]

Mannerheim did what he could to improve his public image beyond his usual supporters. The existence of a Russian wife, albeit one with whom he had barely spoken for nearly 20 years, was deemed unhelpful, and he finally secured the long-requested divorce from Anastasie.[18]

The election, on 25 July 1919, however, did not go in Mannerheim's favour. He had the support of most conservatives and the Swedish-speaking factions, but was heavily outvoted in the final count. His opponent, KJ Ståhlberg, beat him by 143 votes to 50 and was sworn in as Finland's first president the following day. Accordingly, Mannerheim now stepped down as regent.

Mannerheim had had a presentiment that he would not win. On the day of the election he was far to the north in a spa near Iisalmi. The victorious Ståhlberg sent him an open letter that thanked him for freeing Finland from its enemies, for fighting its corner in foreign policy, for saving the country from famine and for laying the foundations of its independence. Sophie Mannerheim was with her brother in Iislami to witness his disappointment. Mannerheim's failure to become president lost him his last chance to drag the Finns into war in Russia, but also put paid to many social programmes he had hoped to establish. Mannerheim was still deeply suspicious of the far left, and warned that it was impossible to deal easily with adversaries who hoped to dismantle the very system that permitted them freedom.

Mannerheim still enjoyed great popular support from the Whites. When he travelled to Helsinki in August, crowds met him all along his route. The Defence Corps, civilian veterans of the Civil War, pointedly made him their honorary commander-in-chief, and welcomed him in a ceremony that ruffled feathers with the government. The White General, he was told, was 'the only one whose will could be law to them' – ominous words to hear so soon after someone else had been elected to government office.

In September 1919, Mannerheim made sure that he dropped in on prominent friends in London and Paris, at the tail end of deliberations at the Paris Peace Conference. With a president having been elected in free elections, and the regent having stood down as was his duty, Finland now enjoyed political recognition from Britain, America, France, Italy and Japan, and other nations were swiftly following suit. In a meeting with the British Minister of War, Winston Churchill, Mannerheim recounted a series of horror stories about the Russian Revolution, and nimbly continued his narrative into the Finnish Civil War. He departed confident that Churchill agreed with him about the threat presented by Communism.

Mannerheim was in Paris at precisely the right time to influence deliberations over the Åland islands. Press coverage heavily favoured Swedish demands on the islands, but Mannerheim scored a forgotten victory by paying a call on Georges Clemenceau, the French prime minister and the leading light of the Peace Conference. Clemenceau had unwisely observed to the French Chamber of Deputies that he was sure that the Peace Conference would settle the Åland question in Sweden's favour.

Mannerheim immediately requested an audience with Clemenceau, which was granted with 'flattering speed'.[19] Speaking perfect French, Mannerheim recounted the many generations in which Finland had functioned as a shield for Sweden, protecting it and Europe beyond from many menaces from the east. He noted, as he was wont to do, that the Ålands had been part of Finland for hundreds of years, and also that while Finland had been diligently fighting the tide of Bolshevism in the war, Sweden had stood idly by and remained neutral.

Of course, Finland had not been involved directly involved in the war, either, but Mannerheim's rhetoric successfully persuaded

Clemenceau that Finland was a better friend than Sweden, and that the Swedes had behaved treacherously in seeking to filch the Ålands while Finland underwent a national crisis. At least in part because of Mannerheim's stealthy arguments, the Åland islands did not form part of the deliberations of the Peace Conference. Instead, the matter was referred to the infant League of Nations, where the islands were eventually granted to Finland.[20]

Having won an entire province without having to draw his sword, on his return to Finland, Mannerheim was once again offered the post of commander-in-chief of the Finnish army, but declined on the grounds that he could not serve an administration with which he had so many disagreements. Based on his own assessment of how a future war would need to be fought, he wanted command of the army *and* militia, control over the appointments of officers and also of political surveillance. Plainly, he regarded the most important issue in Finland's defence to be the Red menace; Mannerheim wanted to lead a crusade on Petrograd (i.e. St Petersburg), and regarded it as the most important issue facing Finland's future integrity. Without a defeat of the Reds *outside* Finland, Mannerheim foresaw that Finland would be threatened again. However, Ståhlberg's government was even less willing to authorise war on Petrograd than that which Mannerheim had headed himself.

Mannerheim was now a private citizen, for the first time since he had left the cadet school in his youth. There was no love lost between him and Ståhlberg, and Mannerheim refused all invitations to attend state occasions during Ståhlberg's presidency. Mannerheim also managed to irritate Mrs Ståhlberg, who was entirely immune to his dashing officer's charm, and was convinced that Mannerheim would plot a coup if given half a chance. He had a similar lack of luck with Kitty Linder, who had moved to Munich to be with her mother and sister. Although their letters remained affectionate, the ardour had cooled in the year since their first meeting, and Miss Linder never became the next Mrs Mannerheim. In fact, some foreign dignitaries had recently mistaken Mannerheim's daughter Sophy for his wife – Sophy had helped her father entertain at some public functions during his regency, and several had misread the implications of their shared surname. In years to come, Mannerheim's sister Sophie would also be mistaken for his wife, or even the 'queen of Finland', as she undertook many foreign appearances on behalf of the Red Cross and other humanitarian organisations.

Mannerheim threw himself into charitable works, setting up the General Mannerheim League for Child Welfare with Sophie and other notables. Mannerheim initially opposed the use of his name on such an organisation, but conceded when he was told that fundraising would be all the easier. Mannerheim was deeply mindful that he had been a leader in a civil war that had created many thousands of orphans, but also of the poor physical condition of many of the Finns who fought in it. 'It seems to me,' he wrote, 'that all our sacrifices will have been in vain unless we can thoroughly rebuild this society ... that has been so sorely tried and tossed in the storms.'[21]

Mannerheim regarded child welfare as a sterling investment in Finland's future, not only in the creation of a healthy population, but in the healing of old wounds between the Reds and Whites. The only fly in the ointment was Mrs Ståhlberg, who insisted on setting up a rival child welfare organisation of her own. Mannerheim called it a 'well-aimed intrigue' that deprived him of the chance to organise a single nationally coordinated charity for orphans.[22]

He was also a staunch supporter of the Red Cross, and had never forgotten the assistance that he had received from the Red Cross doctor Richard Faltin, who had treated a much younger Mannerheim in a field hospital in Manchuria. The same Faltin was now vice-chairman of the Red Cross, and soon co-opted Mannerheim into the organisation as a prominent celebrity. In turn, Mannerheim was able to bring in other notable Finns, such as his former aide-de-camp, the artist Akseli Gallen-Kallela, and the composer Jean Sibelius, to assist with fundraising events. 'This work', he wrote, 'has given me satisfaction, and I am thankful to have been able to serve my country in this manner at a time when the authorities did not require my services.'[23]

Ståhlberg was ousted from office in 1925, but Mannerheim remained distant from the government. His feelings on the menace presented by Russia had not changed, and his unwelcome comments on it sometimes made their way into the press. The mistrust of Mannerheim even extended to his portrait in the Council of State, where some politicians objected to the sight of a uniformed general among the other images of elder statesmen in evening dress. Mannerheim first found out when someone tried to purchase a more acceptable portrait of him from Akseli Gallen-Kalela, and wryly observed that he was even a thorn in their flesh when he was made of oils.

Tiring of state dinners, and mildly disapproving of Finland's flirtation with the prohibition of alcohol (which lasted from 1919 to 1934), Mannerheim took advantage of his wealth and freedom to travel.[24] In particular, he was sure to make himself conveniently absent from Finland on important state anniversaries and elections. His other travels took him to many European countries, and further afield on hunting trips to Alaska, India and briefly Burma. He was particularly charmed by India, which reminded him unsurprisingly of Kipling's *Jungle Book*, while his love of mountain scenery was rewarded with vistas of the Himalayas. He was almost killed in an accident outside Algiers in 1923, when the car he was in crashed into a wall and flung him over a small cliff. With a broken collarbone, broken leg and several broken ribs, Mannerheim could not be moved until help arrived four hours later, and was forced to lie prone on the damp ground, while the wrecked car teetered precariously above him. He was eventually taken to a local hospital, but the accident left one leg permanently shorter than the other. Thereafter, he was obliged to correct a limp with a raised shoe, and rode a horse with one stirrup slightly higher than the other.

The trip to Africa may have not only been a simple vacation, for Mannerheim had plans to leave Finland behind him for good. In 1925, he made overtures to the French legation in Norway, in an attempt to discuss joining the French Foreign Legion. He expressed an interest in serving under Hubert Lyautey, the Marshal of France, in Africa, but was told that he was unsuitable. He would have had to be given a minimum rank of lieutenant-colonel, for which he already exceeded the retirement age; he was now 58 years old.[25]

In 1928, Mannerheim had had every intention of being out of the country on the tenth anniversary of the Civil War, to avoid the

celebrations and the likely protests that would accompany them. Instead, he was persuaded to linger, largely in order to please the many thousands of Whites who expected to see him at the parade. However, behind the scenes, there were further intrigues, as one faction of politicians argued that the White General should be presented with the honorary rank of field marshal to mark the occasion, while an equally vehement faction rejected the idea as 'too warlike'. Mannerheim remained aloof from the argument, and had the last laugh when the officers' corps unilaterally presented him with a field marshal's baton. While the politicians continued to distrust him, the soldiers remained cheekily loyal.[26]

Without an official residence in Helsinki, Mannerheim drifted back to the south-western Finland of his childhood. He spent increasing amounts of time in the Hanko region close both to the Louhisaari of his birthplace, and also to a villa that had been a summer retreat for his Uncle Albert. Eventually, Mannerheim took up more permanent residence, buying Iso Mäntysaari (Great Pine Island), renovating its two villas and paying for the building of an access road. Mannerheim loved the forest and the white sand beach beneath his airy house – sometimes a little too airy, with the strong gusts coming off the nearby Baltic Sea.

He eventually renamed the island Stormhällen, or Stormy Rock, and enjoyed it as a perfect retreat from the world – perfect but for the noise that occasionally drifted across the strait from a nearby island that was the location of an establishment called Café Afrika, named for the almost Saharan quality of the sand dunes over which the clientele had to cross in order to enter. With a somewhat bohemian reputation, Café Afrika was rumoured to be a haven for bootleggers, and served a suspiciously fortified tea that often had its customers singing boozily in the summer nights. Eventually tiring of the noise, Mannerheim bought the café and remodelled it as a classier establishment, serving coffee and cakes, and no longer a magnet for illicit drinkers. He furnished the café as if it were a French seaside bistro, and renamed it *De Fyra Vindarnas Hus*, 'The House of the Four Winds', in a moment of whimsical chinoiserie.[27]

Mannerheim spent several happy summers on his island, where he took full advantage of the nearby café. His staff even set up a bell on Stormy Rock, so that The House of the Four Winds could be notified in advance of its owner was beginning his morning walk, and could have his breakfast eggs boiled and ready as he was ferried across.

In 1931, however, he was called back to public service. Svinhufvud was elected as Finland's third president, and waited less than a day to contact Mannerheim and offer him the command of the country's armed forces. Mannerheim declined yet again, not wishing to supplant the able incumbent Hugo Österman, but the precedent had been set. Mannerheim was no longer *persona non grata* in Helsinki. He was invited to take an active part in serving his country, and left his island retreat once more for the capital.

10

The Jaws of Peril

Mannerheim remained deeply wary about the political situation in Europe, and called the 1930s his 'eight years of racing the storm.'[1] He told Svinhufvud that he had no wish to be commander-in-chief of Finnish forces in peacetime, but that he would gladly serve as chairman of the Defence Council during Svinhufvud's administration.

'We are now living in tense times,' Mannerheim wrote. 'If sensational effects do not ensue from some other country, then Hitler is sure to see to it himself. And amid all this unrest, the disarmament conference sits like Buddha, serene in its meditation, ruling on limits in the very arms and matériel for the weak that the belligerent shall use to bring them down!'[2]

Mannerheim was referring to the Geneva Disarmament Conference, convened by the League of Nations in 1932, and largely paralysed after the withdrawal of Hitler's Germany in 1933 from both the Conference and the League. The Soviet military was expanding on a rapid scale, and Nazism was on the rise in Germany. Many smaller states had invested all their hopes in the League of Nations, and some, such as Norway and Denmark, were merrily dismantling their military apparatus. Mannerheim did not share such confidence in the League, and regarded it as a toothless organisation that would be able to do little more than whine from the sidelines while belligerent nations took whatever they wanted. Ironically, the ruling on the Åland islands, ensuring they kept Finnish sovereignty, was one of the few successes of the League of Nations before the 1930s saw a series of diplomatic disasters.

As Mannerheim had predicted many years earlier, Manchuria was the flashpoint of a new conflict in the Far East. In 1936, the Japanese, who had never really left the region, blew up a section of railway near Mukden – ironically, a railway that they were supposed to be guarding. This was then used as a pretext to attack supposed 'Chinese' saboteurs in the area, and would eventually lead to the occupation of Manchuria, and its establishment as a Japanese puppet state.

That was merely the one of many intrigues in the turbulent 1930s. Italy had invaded Abyssinia; Bolivia and Paraguay went to war over the belief that there was oil in the border district of Chaco; civil war broke out in Spain. 'One sees storm signals from almost everywhere,' Mannerheim wrote, 'as well as complete inability to attain real understanding on any point.'[3] The League enjoyed no authority at all over Germany and Japan, while America and the Soviet Union did not even join. Far from steering diplomatic relations in the 1930s, the League seemed instead to be merely an observer.

Within Finland during the same period, the tensions between Reds and Whites were not over. Mannerheim found himself to be the target of a spiteful song, performed as part of a Communist meeting in Lapua. He was thus also associated with the right-wing backlash, the Lapua Movement, in which White supporters openly attacked the government for its soft stance on Communism. Finnish farmers marched in protest in Helsinki, and threatened direct action when the government dithered on an anti-Communist press law. Svinhufvud lost patience with the agitators, challenging them to take Mannerheim as their unelected leader, unsupported by parliament, to see if that would be any use to Finland's fragile democracy. Indeed, some of the supporters of the Lapua Movement were the same kingmakers who had tried to lure Mannerheim into becoming dictator in 1919.

Mannerheim was present at the farmers' Helsinki march, and lent his support to what he regarded as a dignified protest movement in favour of old-time values. 'I have difficulty,' he wrote, 'in understanding the beauty in the existence which people are preparing after they have pushed aside such values as religion,

country, history, in a word everything that civilisation and culture have given us.'[4]

But while Mannerheim broadly supported the idea of controls on Communists, the Lapua Movement was swinging significantly further to the right. After a general election that saw an increase in rightist parties in the Finnish parliament, the Finnish right wing flexed its muscles again. On 27 February 1932, uniformed members of the Defence Corps (i.e. the organisation that had once been the 'White Guards') were among a gang that broke up a lawful, peaceful meeting of Social Democrats at Mäntsälä. The fight escalated into an open revolt, with the Whites standing off against the largely sympathetic army companies sent to keep order. The Whites soon discovered that the very controls they had demanded for use against Communists could also be used against them. Svinhufvud brought the Whites to heel by invoking the self-same security law for which they had themselves agitated.

Having been considered honorary commander-in-chief of the Defence Corps ever since he had been presented with an honorary field marshal's baton in 1928, Mannerheim was sure to have an opinion about events, but he was careful to say nothing against either the rebels or Svinhufvud's law enforcers.

In 1933, in recognition of his long years of service to Finland, Mannerheim was finally given the honorary post of field marshal by the government rather than his men. The deliberations over the title had been made in secret, without Mannerheim's knowledge, so that he was both honoured and surprised when the news reached him. Any pride was short-lived, however, when Mannerheim read the small print: the title brought with it a stamp duty charge of 4,000 Finnish marks, an entire month's salary for the chairman of the Defence Council. 'It's a good job they haven't made me a more important man,' grumbled Mannerheim.[5]

Although Mannerheim now received a second, official field marshal's baton as a badge of office, in years to come he often preferred to use the one that had been given him in 1928 by his soldiers. He would claim, perhaps with a degree of dry sarcasm, that the first baton was lighter and easier to carry.

Mannerheim was surprised to see that the left-wing press did not react to his appointment with quite the antipathy that he might have expected. He responded in kind, and alluded in several speeches to the need to heal the wounds between Reds and Whites that had endured since the Civil War. It was, he argued, futile to cling to bad memories about where a man had stood in 1918. Red or White, Mannerheim wanted all his countrymen to stand as Finns, ready to resist any dangers that might come from abroad. He summed up this conciliatory position in a stirring speech:

> Where war is waged, life is trodden down and property devastated. The all-destroying strength of modern weapons confers on modern war its ghastly grandeur ... Where chivalry and magnanimity are lacking and hatred commands the sword, there is no room for a lasting peace. But we live at a troubled and threatening time ... So let us extend an open hand to everyone who wants to work and do his duty in this country. A patriotic spirit, expressed in the will to defend the country and to stand in the ranks like a man if some day it has to be defended, is all we ask. We do not need to ask any longer what position a man took fifteen years ago.[6]

It was blatantly obvious which danger Mannerheim had in mind. He spent much of the early 1930s arguing with politicians that they were wrong to cut military spending in the misplaced belief that Finland was safe from further conflict. Mannerheim was adamant that when a new threat came, it would come from Russia and that it would do so overland, across the 45-mile-wide land bridge that led from the Finnish border to the city once known as St Petersburg or Petrograd – now Leningrad.

'The Karelian Isthmus was Finland's lock – our Thermopylae,' wrote Mannerheim. The area lacked any rocky foundation, making it unfeasible to build a line of permanent fortifications like France's Maginot Line. It was, however, ideal for temporary barriers and strongpoints. The entire isthmus was riddled with lakes and marshes, choking all roads into still narrower points.

Mannerheim thought that it would be possible for Finnish forces to hold the isthmus, as long as there were enough of them, and they had enough time and resources to dig in. He fretted that a strong enough force of enemy tanks could all too easily rush across the gently undulating ground, or even across icy lakes in winter.

Increases, rather than reductions, in budgets would have been preferable, but Mannerheim had to work with what he had. Returning from a study tour of the Karelian Isthmus, he urged the government to think of the defence of Finland in territorial terms. The Finnish army was concentrated in a few large pockets, which might easily be bombed, captured or even bypassed by hostile forces. Instead, Mannerheim recommended spreading the Finnish army out so thinly that no observer could identify where it was. He counselled for an increased reliance on the Defence Corps, noting that an aggressor (Soviet Russia being the only real candidate) would find the going immensely slow if every hamlet and every village was a strongpoint defended by armed, trained locals with intimate knowledge of the local terrain. While some in the government regarded the Defence Corps as a worryingly vociferous militia, Mannerheim saw them as the core of any defence of Finland, an unstoppable force that would rise from the land like the vipers contending with Ilmarinen in Akseli Gallen-Kallela's famous picture.

With the end of Svinhufvud's term as president, Mannerheim thought that it might be time for him to retire himself. He was now 69 years old, although he looked remarkably spry. Mannerheim had the outward appearance of a much younger man, which he took great pains to maintain. It was even suggested, by an English lady who saw him up close, that he dyed his hair and applied a little rouge to his lips to keep them bright and youthful for the cameras of the press.[7] He slept on a humble camp bed, in an attempt to keep hard support for his back. He rode every day unless prevented from doing so by other duties, and took care to conceal his many aches, pains and injuries from the public gaze. He was looking forward, in his old age, to finally compiling and editing the many books of observations and diaries from his half-forgotten ride across Central Asia and China some thirty years before, and was thus mildly disappointed, but also touched, when the new president begged him to stay in his post.

Mannerheim tried his luck, asking for a series of reforms to his position as chairman of the Defence Council that would transform it from an advisory post to one with actual executive authority. This was denied, but he was persuaded to stay on anyway.

Mannerheim's 70th birthday, 4 June 1937, was an expensive occasion for him, costing him over two months' salary for the hiring of four assistants, as well as postage and telegraph fees, to answer letters from his many well-wishers. He would have much preferred to be conveniently abroad, but reluctantly agreed to some public celebrations with accompanying pomp and ceremony for its public relations value in uniting the country. A mildly embarrassed Mannerheim left his Helsinki residence in the morning to find two pretty young girls in white dresses earnestly strewing flowers in his path. He marched in the centre of Helsinki (the rain clouds obligingly clearing in time for the big parade), and later attended a celebration in his honour at Helsinki's Exhibition Hall. The day ended with a party at Mannerheim's Helsinki residence, with the last straggler not departing until past three the following morning.

With such a crushing social whirl, not to mention his ongoing duties on the Defence Council, Mannerheim gave up all hope of work on his Asian papers. In 1937 he donated them all to the Finno-Ugrian Society, leaving them to others to deal with. Admirers soon began to plan something suitably impressive for Mannerheim's 75th birthday, for which the Finno-Ugrian Society hoped to publish a bound edition of his Asian diary, with a companion volume of reports and papers of some of his ethnographic acquisitions. Mannerheim's involvement in the publication of the papers, however, would be minimal, limited to the dashing off of a hasty foreword in 1940, by which time he was otherwise occupied.

Mannerheim, meanwhile, felt that he was achieving nothing with the Defence Council. Arms and equipment budgets had continued to be cut, and he noted with some alarm that the Finnish army did not have a single anti-tank gun. The Finns only had a handful of tanks, and those were veritable antiques, and while there had been moves to get an aircraft factory up and running in Jyväskylä, this itself was a cost-cutting measure that only served to delay the actual arrival of any planes. By June 1939, Mannerheim felt he had achieved all that he could and in a letter to the president, he noted that his very prominent public role risked becoming counterproductive, in that it might 'lull many into an unjustified sense of security'. He agreed to stay on in his post, but, he repeated his concerns whenever possible. At a dinner in Viipuri, he spoke as if war had already been declared:

> Even the dreamer who has lived in the belief of eternal peace is beginning to wake up and realise the brutal realism of the twentieth century. The rights of nations are not defended by means of declarations and phrases. There must be the desire to defend one's country by deeds and sacrifices.[8]

The Soviet Union, and in particular its new foreign minister Vyacheslav Molotov, began to make outrageous demands on Finland, purportedly in the interests of balancing the growing power of Nazi Germany. The Soviet Union in the Baltic was haunted by the ghosts of the Tsar's old empire; the borders were weak and vulnerable without Finland to shield them. Leningrad sat at the far end of the long Gulf of Finland, leading the Soviets to 'request' that Finland hand over the strategic Hanko Peninsula to keep watch over the narrow straits. While the Finns prevaricated, on 17 September 1939 the Soviet Union attacked Poland, and, when Estonia was found to be sheltering an escaped Polish submarine, Estonia soon followed. Reval (now Tallinn), only 18 miles from Helsinki across the Gulf of Finland, fell under Soviet rule, in a 'treaty of mutual assistance' that effectively ended Estonian independence for the next six decades. Other Baltic States soon collapsed, in a repetitive cycle of bluster, feigned outrage, concessions gained and then boundaries over-stepped. When Latvia, too, fell to the Soviets, a Finnish representative was summoned to Moscow to discuss 'strategic questions'. These amounted to demands for Finnish territory of benefit to the Soviet navy – specifically the south-western Hanko Peninsula, the nearby port at Lappvik, several islands in the Gulf of Finland, and the agreement of a treaty of non-aggression.

Similar treaties had been of little use in protecting the Baltic States from Soviet bullying. Nor were the Finns pleased to hear that the Soviets no longer accepted the countries' shared border on the Karelian Isthmus. Instead, the Soviets wanted the Finns to pull back their border significantly inland, demolishing the obstructive fortifications on the way. It was tantamount to asking the Finns to pave a road for Russian tanks into Viipuri and south Finland.

Mannerheim was appalled, but not surprised at the level of Soviet arrogance. When told that the redrawing of territorial boundaries would require parliamentary assent, Soviet negotiators simply told Finnish diplomats to make sure they achieved it. When the Finns expressed their doubts that parliament would agree to the handing over of mainland territory like Hanko to a foreign power, the Soviets offered to slice a canal through one end of the peninsula, thereby making it an island and hence easier to hand over![9]

Mannerheim's role as chairman of the Defence Council was becoming untenable, but, once again, he was persuaded to stay on as negotiations with the Soviets took on aspects of a farce. By November the deadlock was complete. 'We civilians don't seem to be making progress,' said Molotov ominously. 'Now it is time for the soldiers to negotiate.' A few days later, he waved off the Finns with a merry 'Cheerio.'

Mannerheim could not take it any more. 'While everything has pointed to a giant conflict approaching,' he wrote, 'the indispensable demands of our defence have been treated with little understanding, and with a parsimony which left a great deal neglected. Even now, questions regarding the most urgent necessities of the armed forces are treated in as leisurely a manner as if we lived in normal times.'[10]

Now aged 72, Mannerheim stood down at last as chairman of the Defence Council, and re-entered private life. He would remain there for all of two days.

Even as Mannerheim had been drafting his letter of resignation, Soviet artillerymen in the Karelian Isthmus had been executing the next move. They opened fire on their own soldiers, killing four men and wounding nine others in an impressive display of self-inflicted gunnery, blowing some impressive craters in the ground near the small village of Mainila.

Immediately, the Soviets protested that it was an act of Finnish aggression. This was news to the Finns, who did not have any artillery of their own in range of Mainila. Indeed, when Finnish observers examined the craters, they discovered that the shells had clearly been fired from the south-east, in other words from far behind Russian lines.

Molotov announced that the Russians could not stand back and endure such an act of naked aggression, and broke off diplomatic ties with Finland. Even as Finnish diplomats attempted to smooth over the crisis and offered new concessions, Soviet troops were already on the move. Amassed for some time all along the shared Finnish-Russian border, the Soviets advanced at the close of November. Russia and Finland were at war. 'We are so few, and they are so many,' said one Finn. 'Where will we find the room to bury them all?' [11]

Mannerheim did not need to receive an official report to learn of the outbreak of war. He heard it himself on 30 November 1939, as a Soviet air squadron hurtled out of the sea from a base in Estonia and dropped bombs on an unsuspecting Helsinki. News of artillery barrages and massive troop movements swiftly followed. The Red Army was advancing on several points, both in the Karelian Isthmus and north in the long reaches of the forests. It was the defence of the Karelian Isthmus that would attract the attention of the world's press, as the Finns staunchly held what was soon known around the world as the Mannerheim Line.

Mannerheim went to the Presidential Palace to get his job back. In a grave meeting with President Kyösti Kallio, 'I told him that in the face of the enemy attack, I naturally withdrew my request to be relieved of my post if the President and the government felt they needed my services.' The president took him on the spot, and parliament swiftly gave its assent later that morning – Mannerheim was now, once again, commander-in-chief of the Finnish forces.

Nothing united Finland like the Soviet attack on Helsinki. There were many women and children counted among the 65 deaths of that first air raid, which was followed by a rain of leaflets calling Finland to rise up against the 'White Guard' clique of Mannerheim and his associates. Soviet propagandists do not seem to have done their homework – later leaflets promised the workers of Finland an eight-hour working day under Communism, something they had been enjoying for the past twenty years.

Meanwhile, the Finns were told that a new Finnish government had been set up in the 'city of Terijoki', actually a tiny hamlet so close to the Karelian border that it was practically on the outskirts of Leningrad, and one which Mannerheim distinctly recalled evacuating during preparations for defence. Terijoki, it seemed, had been suddenly and miraculously repopulated with Soviet sympathisers, including Otto Kuusinen, a Finnish Communist and Stalin's former ghostwriter. The Terijoki Finns were ready to proclaim themselves as the Finnish Democratic Republic, in a move that also spectacularly backfired. If the Soviets recognised Terijoki, then they would effectively cancel their recognition of the legitimate government of Finland, leaving Mannerheim's government with no choice but to fight – it being impossible to negotiate with a government one does not recognise. More crucially, the sleight of hand over Terijoki even served to alienate Finnish Communists. Arvo Tuominen, a prominent Red and the leader of the illegal Finnish Communist Party, could not bring himself to support a power-grab that was so plainly arranged by the authorities rather than being the legitimate will of the people. Instead, he cabled other Finnish Communists with an order to resist the Soviet Union. Mannerheim now enjoyed the support even of his staunchest former enemies.

Mannerheim initially set up his headquarters in the eastern Finnish town of Mikkeli. Although that is now where the modern Headquarters Museum is, in the Winter War Mannerheim's staff were spread out across several city blocks, all the better to thwart bombers. The communications centre, codenamed *Lokki* ('Seagull'), was buried within a hollowed-out hill a hundred paces from the school where Mannerheim had his own base. In later months, Mannerheim's headquarters would become more mobile, and he would make greater use of his personalised train carriage, which came with office space and sleeping quarters. When visiting the front line, he dressed like his men in snow camouflage and a white cape, and was often forced to hunch low in the midst of air raids.

Mannerheim had always enjoyed the respect and adulation of

the officer class and the former Whites. But the Winter War found him a new set of admirers from an unlikely quarter. Working-class Finns, many of whom might have suffered during the Civil War at the hands of the Whites, were heard to express their relief that it was Mannerheim who was in charge of removing the Russians from Finnish soil. 'I hate to admit it,' said one to historian Wolf Halsti, 'but it's a damned good thing the old butcher-in-chief is still around for this show.' [12]

Even if Mannerheim could expect unified command, his resources suffered greatly from a decade of cutbacks. At the outbreak of the war, he estimated that the Finnish army did not have enough artillery shells to last a month, and had similarly low quantities of aircraft oil. Fuel and rifle rounds amounted to no more than two months' worth. [13]

Soviet propaganda made light of Finland's limited resources. Molotov, the Soviet foreign minister, continued to spin Soviet aggression against Finland. In one radio broadcast he made the outrageous claim that Russian aircraft were not 'bombing' Helsinki at all, but merely dropping food parcels to help the poor starving Finns. In sarcastic response, the Finns began to refer to the Soviet RRAB-3 incendiary cluster bomb as the 'Molotov bread-basket'. Out on the front line, Finnish soldiers came up with something in return. In imitation of Republicans in the Spanish Civil War, they fashioned a crude explosive device using a bottle of flammable liquid with an ignition fuse, designed to smash on impact. The most effective, knocked up with a little help from the Finnish drinks industry, was a volatile blend of petrol, kerosene, tar for extra staying power, and chloride of potassium. An additional vial of sulphuric acid was taped to the bottle, designed to ignite the entire concoction when the bottle smashed. They called these bottle-bombs 'Molotov cocktails' in honour of the man for whom they would most like to mix one. [14]

The Russians, who heavily outnumbered the Finns, were initially overconfident. In the first encounters, artillery bombardment began towards the end of the day, with Russian soldiers rushing in during the fading light of the afternoon. The Finns, however, countered with searchlights in the darkness, and lured the Russians into the 'open terrain' of frozen lakes. The Russian tanks presented the greatest danger, but after their initial surprise, the Finns discovered that the tanks, too, had their weak points. They could be disabled by logs jammed into their bogie wheels, or by satchel charges left on the treads. In one infamous incident, a lone Finn was seen calmly standing in the path of a lumbering tank, carefully sighting a pistol in between the viewing-slits on the front of the tank.[15]

The Soviets might have had larger amounts of equipment, but that did not make them better soldiers. With the exception of a few units brought in from Siberia, many of the Russian soldiers were unused to skis, and some met a macabre end as a result of the basic physics of throwing a grenade while sliding forward. Their equipment was not always state of the art. Some of the ammunition captured from the Russians was labelled in Japanese, and appeared to have made a long journey from Manchuria, where it had presumably been purloined some thirty years earlier.

The Soviets also lacked more crucial supplies, including food. Some divisions had little to survive on except biscuits and the meat of their own horses. In one notorious incident near Tolvajärvi in Karelia, a battalion of Russians surprised and overran a Finnish field kitchen. The staff fled, but the Russians did not pursue them, instead falling ravenously on the steaming cauldrons of sausage soup that the cooks had left behind. Unfortunately for the Russians, they had chosen to steal sausages close to the location of Colonel Aaro Pajari, a veteran of the Civil War who could make a soldier out of anyone. While the starving Russians ate, Pajari rounded up a motley crew of artillery officers, store clerks, supply sergeants and even medics, and led them in a vicious midnight counter-attack, largely at knifepoint, with a few soldiers picking off stragglers with small-arms fire.[16]

The Finns soon exploited the Russian habit of concentrating their infantry behind the tanks, by sighting their guns on areas of ground to the rear of their armour and waiting for it to be full of soft human targets. The Russian columns, with their reliance on armour, were also forced to stick to the forest roads, while the Finns skied through the forests in search of weak points. Nor were the Finns averse to laying false roads across what the Russians

would inevitably discover to be a frozen lake, mere moments before Finnish explosives blew up the 'road' and sank the tanks.

As the weeks wore on, it became apparent that the Finns were not going to give up easily. Despite overwhelming odds, outnumbered at least five to one, the Finns fought the Russians to a standstill on the Mannerheim Line. There were similar victories elsewhere. In the skies, the Finns adopted an almost foolhardy policy of sending at least one of their antiquated fighters up against any Russian sortie. Sometimes, the Finns were shot down, but on enough occasions a lucky shot brought down an overconfident bomber. On 6 January 1940, the lone Finnish ace Jorma Sarvanto shot down six Soviet bombers in four minutes. By the end of the Winter War in March, the sight of a single Finnish plane was often enough to persuade an entire Soviet squadron to drop its load and run. Confirmed kills in the Winter War totalled 240 Soviet planes to Finnish losses of 26.[17]

The Arctic front in the very far north saw the Soviets make swift initial advances. They were, however, doomed to face Kurt Wallenius, a prominent right-winger who had been one of the ringleaders of the Mäntsälä uprising, for which he had served two years in prison. Although he was no friend of Mannerheim, Wallenius fought a continuous rearguard action, delaying the Soviets for as long as he could, before a vicious ski-borne counterattack. His Finns had managed to get within a hundred yards of the Soviet forces without being noticed, and fell upon them with such speed that they captured vast quantities of Russian arms and armour. Among the Russian dead, his men found soldiers wearing felt buskins that would have been next to useless in the bitter Lapland cold.

South of the Arctic, where the Russians had hoped to cut Finland in half and sprint for Oulu on the coast of the Baltic Sea, they had instead been massacred at Suomussalmi on the Raate Road, laid low by Finns in the trees and frostbite in the air. Finns on the Raate Road erupted from the trees mere yards from the Russian line, ghostly in their all-white snow camouflage. Demolition teams hurled packs of explosives into the nearest vehicles, and fled back into the trees on the other side. It was only as the smoke cleared and the casualties were counted, that the Russians realised that their own wrecked vehicles now blocked the narrow forest road. As the Russians frantically tried to get the road clear and the column moving, more white figures charged out of the forest.

The Finns called such encirclement tactics *motti* – from the name for a bundle of firewood. In repeated ambushes and assaults on the Soviets, the tactic bunched troops up in vulnerable positions, and stalled the armoured vehicles in place for days. There was no super-fast *blitzkrieg* in Finland. Instead, the Soviet armour often proved to be a liability, jammed or broken down on desolate, snowbound roads, in one of the coldest winters Europe had seen for a century.

Initially Mannerheim did not believe the figures. It was, he thought, most unlikely that the Finns could only suffer minor casualties while the Russians perished in their thousands. In one case, he directly queried a front-line commander's claim to have killed a thousand Russians on one night in Taipale. Shortly afterwards, he received a sarcastic communiqué informing him that the Finns had collected a thousand Russian rifles from the bodies, some of them a little battered, and that whenever Mannerheim was ready, he was welcome to come down and count them. 'I did not think,' observed Mannerheim with a sad smile, 'that my men were so good, or that the Russians could be so bad.' [18]

If Mannerheim was swollen with pride for his troops he was sure to show it, although he could also be abrasive in private. He had begun his command with a screaming row with his subordinate and predecessor as commander-in-chief, Hugo Österman, which ended with both men threatening to resign, only to back down and get on with the job at hand.

The Finns like to remember Mannerheim as a man who was keen to give credit where it was due, not just to the soldiers in the line, but to those in the rear, the nurses and auxiliaries. After the war, Mannerheim even awarded a collective medal to the mothers of Finland; a copy of the signed citation still hangs in all Finnish churches. At headquarters, he was quick to reward achievement and equally quick to remove those who could not take the pace. He was, in most cases, at least twenty years older than the men he was commanding, and was as tough on them as he often was on himself.

One officer famously worked all night preparing a detailed report that Mannerheim had ordered as fast as possible. When the exhausted officer presented it to him, Mannerheim took it without a word and continued working at his desk. Somewhat taken aback, the officer asked if the report was what the field marshal had in mind. 'Yes,' said Mannerheim bluntly. 'Do you expect me to kiss you?' [19]

The conflict in Finland had attracted the notice of the world's press, which was largely in favour of the Finns. Just as the international community had supported the plucky Japanese underdog in the Russo-Japanese War, there was no love lost over Soviet bullying. Journalists were largely concentrated in a Helsinki hotel, far from the Mannerheim Line and, to their annoyance, from Mannerheim himself. Instead, they were left to graze on dispassionate and dull press releases from the Finns themselves.

One journalist received an irate order from his editor to get out of the hotel bar and find the real story, which was sure to be with Finland's venerable, heroic field marshal. He sent a cable back in which he gave his frank appraisal of Mannerheim's availability: 'Mannerheim impossible. Shall I try Jesus Christ?' [20]

Some reporters, however, had managed to get through, particularly in the Arctic north, where temperatures sank as low as minus 42°C, but there were better lines of communication to neutral Norway and Sweden. *Life* magazine ran an article on the defenders of the north, and helped introduce a new word into general use – *sisu*, that Finnish word best translated as 'guts' – the kind of bloody-minded, terrifying guts that will allow a man to stand calmly in the snow and take careful aim with a handgun at the armoured slits of an oncoming tank. Although Finland was fighting alone, there were increasing calls in the international community for someone, anyone to come to its aid.

On 20 January 1940, Winston Churchill noted that the Finnish successes in the Winter War had provided the rest of the world with a valuable lesson in the weaknesses of the Soviet army. 'Everyone can see how Communism rots the soul of a nation,' he said, 'how it makes it abject and hungry in peace, and proves it base and abominable in war. We cannot tell what the fate of Finland may be, but no more mournful spectacle could be presented than ... this splendid northern race ... worn down ...by the dull brutish force of overwhelming numbers.'

There was now, it seemed, a very real possibility that Finland would receive aid from other powers. Already some limited supplies had arrived from France and Britain, and a volunteer corps was being set up in London.

'Only Finland,' thundered Churchill, 'superb, nay, sublime in the jaws of peril – Finland shows what free men can do.'[21]

11

The Eye of the Storm

B ehind the scenes, Mannerheim was still holding out for more than words from the Allies. When a French military attaché arrived with a consignment of supplies, Mannerheim's first remark as he shook his hand was a dour, 'Are you here to prolong our agony?'

Mannerheim had no illusions about the Finns' prospects. He sagely observed that nobody needed to tell him about the Russian army, as he had served in it himself for thirty years.[1] The Soviet plans for Finland were a mirror image of those that Mannerheim himself had written for the war that never took place between the Tsar's Russia and the Chinese Empire. The Russian strategy in Finland, not unlike the young Mannerheim's own outline of a Russian attack on Central Asia, seemed to be planned as a massive, desperate grab for territory, which could then be used as a bargaining chip when hostilities ceased. If the battle did not now draw to a close, then the melting of the snows would give the Soviets many more avenues into Finland, which the Finns would be unlikely to be able to stop. When the Winter War ground to a halt in March 1940, the Soviets had made a daring, suicidal stab towards the important south-eastern city of Viipuri, advancing both on the land of the Isthmus and on the sea ice. Tired and feverish, Mannerheim surprised his generals and the Helsinki ministers by suggesting that now was the time to seek peace terms from Moscow.

His reasoning was sound. Finnish strength was already on the wane, but the Soviets did not know how much longer the Finns would last. There were already whispers that the international community might send more aid to the Finns, and it was in the Russians' interests to conclude a peace as swiftly as possible. At this juncture, the Finns had not actually 'lost', and hence they could afford to be a lot more demanding than they might be if, say, they waited until the Red Army was a stone's throw from Helsinki.

The bitter, bloody four months of the Winter War had demonstrated very clearly that Finland would not surrender without a fight. The Soviets were already making overtures, through discrete diplomatic channels, that would amount to a reversal of the diplomatic status of the Terijoki puppet government. Throughout the war, Moscow had refused to entertain any diplomatic entreaties from Finland that did not come through Terijoki. Now, Moscow abandoned Terijoki and began negotiations with Helsinki. The lie that had been the Finnish Democratic Republic, at least, was now over.

On 12 March 1940, the belligerents signed the Peace of Moscow, and the Winter War was over. The terms were greeted with shock and surprise in Finland, where the population had been buoyed up for months with positive, censored headlines that only played up Finnish successes. It was thus something of a surprise when the news came that the Karelian Isthmus was to be ceded to Russia, along with Viipuri, Finland's second city, and territory on the northern shores of Lake Ladoga. To many, it felt like a defeat, and a betrayal.

The capitulation was particularly galling to Finnish politicians who had been far away from the front lines, and who had assumed that Finnish soldiers could continue to hold off indefinitely millions of Russians with little more than Molotov cocktails and *sisu*. In fact, the Finnish forces were on the brink of collapse, and Mannerheim was right to call it a day when he did. In an inclusive, non-partisan speech read out on the radio, copied out and pinned to the walls of churches all over the country, he told Finns everywhere what he thought of his fellow countrymen:

> I have fought on many battlefields but I have not seen your equals as warriors. I am proud of you as if you were my own children, as proud of the man from the northern tundras as of the sons of the

broad plains of Ostrobothnia, the forests of Karelia, the smiling tracts of Savo, the rich farms of Häme and Satakunta, the lands of Uusimaa and South-West Finland with their whispering birches. I am as proud of the factory worker and the son of the poor cottage as I am of the rich man's contribution of life and limb.[2]

Mannerheim did not shrink from laying the blame for the current conditions where he thought it belonged, at the feet of the men who had opposed his warnings for the preceding decade. Even while praising the superhuman efforts of the Finnish population, he noted that they had been forced to 'produce what was wanting, to conduct lines of defence that did not exist, to seek help which did not come'.

The storm, said Mannerheim, that was 'now sweeping over the world', had been approaching for many years, and he had been racing against its tide. Mannerheim was not making such claims in order to score cheap points against political opponents. Instead, he was warning, as subtly as he could, that the war was not over: 'We must be ready as before to defend our diminished fatherland with the same determination and strength ...'[3]

With the end of the war, Mannerheim should in theory have given up his post of commander-in-chief. Despite this constitutional requirement, he did not do so, nor did the government ask him to resign. Instead, he continued to function in a heightened executive role, despite Finland's supposed reversion to peacetime status. Part of this role included plans for Finland's future defence. After the death of many thousands of Finns in the Winter War, Mannerheim finally got his way, with defence procurement taken out of the hands of the minister of defence and placed directly in Mannerheim's hands. Nor were the politicians liable to ask too many questions – to do so, they were warned, might irritate the field marshal and lead to his resignation before Finland's safety was assured.

The Finnish army remained mobilised, its strength in the field dropping from 195,000 to 109,000, but its forces still largely concentrated on the Russian border. Some equipment ordered from abroad during the Winter War arrived late, but was incorporated

into the regrouped brigades, with significantly more anti-tank guns, mortars and aircraft.

Meanwhile, the Second World War continued to redraw the map elsewhere. Norway and Denmark, despite their neutrality, fell to Nazi occupation in April, cutting Finland off from any supply route from the Scandinavian coast or through the Baltic. Any hope that Finland may once have had of receiving British aid through Norway was now gone. Henceforth, anything arriving from the west in Finland needed to come through German lines. Having only barely repulsed the Soviets, Finland now had to rely solely on German supply routes for both fuel and grain. France fell in June 1940. Across the Gulf of Finland, the Baltic States – Latvia, Lithuania and Estonia – were officially incorporated into the Soviet Union.

Mannerheim was unsurprised to see that 'peace' with the Soviets was far from easy. In June, the Soviets began making new demands about the Hanko Peninsula, and also for nickel mining rights in the northern district of Petsamo. The Finnish government fearfully begged the press not to report such activities, although there was little they could do to cover up the case of the *Kaleva*, a Finnish passenger plane shot down by Russian fighters in the Gulf of Finland. At the time, the plane's loss was reported as an accident, although the involvement of the Russians was soon known. The full story did not come out for several years; the Russians had deliberately shot the plane down in order to retrieve documents carried by a French diplomat on board.

In August, Mannerheim was plunged into a bizarre charade in which he was told to expect important information. A telegram gave him the name of an individual at Malm airfield who would have a letter for him. This in turn told him he would be meeting a German lieutenant-colonel, who presented him that night with a letter from *Reichsmarschall* Hermann Goering.

Goering's letter requested that Mannerheim assent to the transit through Finland of Nazi 'items' – men, for example, on vacation or perhaps recuperating from an illness or wounds. The Swedes had already agreed something similar, and it would be a kind gesture. In return, the Nazis might be able to arrange some reciprocal deals – other 'items', for example, like tanks.[4] Mannerheim saw the letter's implications for what they were – more far-reaching than mere business deals and train journeys. Nor was he authorised to make decisions on Finnish foreign policy. The government in Helsinki, however, was eager to accept the German offer, and was soon signing deals with Berlin. Materiels intended for Finnish use in the Winter War but seized by the Germans in Norway were now freed up for Finland.

As the months passed, it became apparent that Germany and the Soviet Union were drifting further apart. In their own mutual interest, Helsinki and Berlin began to discuss the possibilities of a combined action in the event of a new attack from Moscow. Purely hypothetically, it was suggested that in the event of a new Soviet attack on Finland, the Finns could hold the line, as they had done before, until German aid arrived. A combined Finnish-German force could then press a dual attack on Leningrad. No stranger to hypothetical conflicts, Mannerheim could also see how this would look in Moscow. If Germany were to attack Russia, then one of Moscow's first acts would be to secure its north-west flank, by attacking Finland. Whatever happened, Finland would be in the eye of the storm. Whichever way the wind blew, the storm was going to start up again.

'I remembered Stalin's words to our delegation in the autumn of 1939,' wrote Mannerheim. '"I well understand that you wish to remain neutral, but I can assure you that it is not at all possible. The Great Powers will simply not allow it." ... Finland was no longer free to decide about her own fate.'[5]

Finland, as one of its own idioms would have it, was caught between 'the ditch and the duck pond' – the two options were equally unattractive. Although Mannerheim appreciated that the Nazis were currently all that were keeping the Soviets out of Europe, he had made no secret of his distaste for them. He had already sent two cases of his papers to Stockholm for safekeeping – seemingly out of fear that they might not go down well with his new German 'friends'. In an echo of the formation of the 27th Royal Prussian Jäger Battalion a generation earlier, a group of Finnish soldiers left to study in Germany, forming a Finnish battalion of the

Waffen-SS. As in the days of the Jägers, Mannerheim disapproved – not least because he wanted the men for the defence of his own country, not training to support the Nazi war effort elsewhere – but he was overruled.[6]

With no help forthcoming from the Allies, and Soviet forces massing on the Finnish frontier, Mannerheim was prepared to consider agreeing with the Germans that Helsinki and Berlin shared a common enemy. However, he was careful to stress that this did not make Finland and Nazi Germany allies. He refused the position of supreme commander of the Finnish forces, since that would have placed him in the Nazi chain of command. He permitted a German liaison officer at his own headquarters, and permitted German battalions transit through Finland to attack the Soviet Union, but shied away from any formal, written accord. It was stressed, on several occasions, that Finland and Germany happened to be fighting different wars on the same front. Finland reserved the right to conclude its own peace with the Soviet Union, independent of what the Germans might wish – this clause, in the agreement that the two powers signed in September 1940, was to cause great discord in the later days of the war.

There was a hiatus until 22 June 1941, when the Germans launched a massive attack upon the Soviet Union from bases in Romania, Poland and Finland. The fact that German forces were using Finnish bases was enough of an excuse for the Soviets to commence air raids against Finland. Similarly, the fact that the Soviets had 'initiated' an attack on Finland was enough of an excuse for Mannerheim to order his own men back into battle. In European history books the conflict is usually remembered simply as Operation *Barbarossa,* part of the German campaign against Russia in the Second World War. However, to the Finns it was *Jatkosota*, the Continuation War, a new phase in the conflict with the Soviet Union that was now seen to have been only temporarily halted by the Peace of Moscow.

German troops in the north of Finland were soon forced on to the defensive after running into greater Soviet opposition than expected. The Finns in the south fared considerably better. With immensely better equipment, and anti-tank squads and vital air and artillery support, Finnish forces poured into the Karelian Isthmus and almost encircled Lake Ladoga. Within weeks, the Finnish forces had not only recaptured the territory that had been lost, but advanced significantly further into parts of Russia that had not previously been under Finnish rule. The Continuation War now saw the Soviets on the defensive, with the Finns taking up position within a few miles of Leningrad itself. The rationale for the continued advance was to seize airbases within range of Finland and thus reduce bombing raids, although a more believable and simpler motive is blunt revenge.

Mannerheim remained a reluctant 'co-belligerent' of the Nazis. He refused to cooperate in attempts to persecute Jews under his jurisdiction, but was forced to bite his tongue on many minor occasions in the face of Nazi bluster. Mannerheim had always had a reputation for gentlemanly reserve – when faced with an opinion with which he disagreed, he was known to glance briefly away and change the subject. He found himself adopting this conversational tactic on many occasions with his new associates.

Naturally, the decision of the Finns to fight alongside the Nazis was not well received by Allied governments. Winston Churchill, who had been prevented from sending aid to the Finns through Norway and Sweden, and who had every respect for Mannerheim, pleaded with the field marshal not to associate himself with the Axis powers. With the Soviet Union now fighting the Nazis, too, Churchill was obliged to consider that the enemy of his enemy was his friend. This, of course, was precisely the same reasoning that had led Mannerheim to conclude the 'co-belligerency' pact with the Nazis, but that truth was of little help. Churchill was under pressure to declare war on Finland, and would have to do so unless Mannerheim could find some way to disassociate himself from war against Russia. The merest gesture, Churchill suggested, indicating the Finns were no longer combatants, would be repaid a thousandfold:

> Surely, your troops have advanced far enough for security during the war and could now halt and give leave … It is not necessary to make any public declaration, but simply leave off fighting … and

make a *de facto* exit from the war. I wish I could convince Your Excellency that we are going to beat the Nazis ... It would be most painful to the many friends of your country in England if Finland found herself in the dock with the guilty and defeated Nazis.[7]

Mannerheim's response was equally cordial and respectful. 'I would regret', he wrote, 'if these operations, carried out to safeguard Finland, would bring my country into conflict with England, and I would be deeply grieved if you will consider yourself forced to declare war on Finland. It was kind of you to send me a personal message in these trying days, and I have fully appreciated it.'[8]

Britain's war against Finland, declared on 5 December 1941, was largely for appearance's sake – a few bombs were dropped in the sea near Turku to save face. Although now officially in a state of war, Mannerheim still had a group of British servicemen under his jurisdiction. The men had joined up as volunteers during the Winter War, although they had not seen any action, and were now interned as 'enemies'. Mannerheim saw to it that the British volunteers were returned home via Sweden, even though this theoretically returned them to the war effort against the Nazis.

Behind the scenes, however, Mannerheim appears to have entirely agreed with Churchill. Some of his speeches to his men conjured up images of conquest and revenge, including one particularly controversial one in which he revisited his promise of 1918 not to sheathe his sword until East Karelia was free. But in private, he had his doubts about the need to push beyond Finland's previous boundaries, as he wrote to his sister Eva:

We have occupied a great part of the territory taken from us when peace was last concluded, and also added a fair piece of East Karelia. However, the fighting is incredibly hard ... perhaps because this time we do not have the cold and snow as allies. The Bolsheviks are fighting with an unbelievable tenacity and bitterness on every front ... joy for our victories is overshadowed by daily reports of killed and wounded. They show how many brave Finnish boys will never again see the homes that they went to war to defend.[9]

Although Leningrad lay tantalising close, an assault against it would tie the Finns inextricably to the Nazis. In 1918 Mannerheim would have given anything for the chance to advance on the city. But East Karelia was enough – it had been considered so 'Finnish' in the past that Stalin had once even toyed with the idea of giving it to the Finns anyway. The Soviet rhetoric against an independent Finland had focused on the danger that an independent Finland would present to Leningrad. Mannerheim refused to prove them right.

His decision angered the Germans, who had not enjoyed the success on their own fronts for which they had been hoping. The Finns stopped at the outskirts of Leningrad, as did the Nazis from the west, initiating a prolonged 900-day siege. Regarding his main objective, the reconquest of the previously lost territory, as now being achieved, Mannerheim remained unwilling to pursue further objectives on behalf of the Nazis. His words of regret to his sister over the loss of 'Finnish boys' masked another admission – that many of the Finnish boys themselves were questioning if they were still fighting a war of national defence, or one of foreign conquest.[10]

Churchill was not the only foreign leader putting pressure on Mannerheim. Franklin D Roosevelt had threatened that a Finland that did not halt its advance would be 'deprived of the amicable support of the United States' in future. Among the Germans, the ramifications of Mannerheim's careful choice of words in describing their 'co-belligerency' began to become clearer. Mannerheim had gone into the Continuation War acknowledging that the Finns and the Germans shared certain aims. Now he seemed ready to announce that the Finns' aims were achieved and that, consequently, the time was approaching when the pact should be dissolved.

The Nazis responded with, for want of a better a term, a charm offensive. Mannerheim was offered Third Reich medals, and badgered with calls or cables from prominent Germans hoping to lure him into further advances. On the occasion of Mannerheim's 75th birthday, 4 June 1942, he deliberately removed himself to the front to avoid unwelcome 'personal presentations'. As he had explained to his sister Eva in a letter the previous month, he also found the idea of celebrating anything during such bitter conflict to be rather

vulgar. 'Holding any sort of party at the headquarters now would simply be in bad taste,' he wrote, 'as all the men and officers are in such a tight spot, and often have to see one of their comrades being carried off.'[11] But despite his intentions, he was practically ordered by the serving Finnish president, Risto Ryti, to make sure that his train headquarters was in the vicinity of the railway sidings and airfield at Immola.

A high-ranking delegation, including Ryti himself, was on hand to confer upon Mannerheim a new title, Marshal of Finland. Mannerheim was honoured by the unique appellation – he remains the only man to have been awarded the title – and was particularly touched by the delegation that brought it. Standing before him near the carriage were not just the president, the Speaker of the Finnish parliament and many politicians, but also a deputation of Finnish trade unionists. Unlike his 'honorary' field marshal's baton, this was not solely an offering from what were once known as the Whites, but also from what might be reasonably termed Finland's Reds. 'For me,' wrote Mannerheim, 'this was a deeply valued recognition of my long labour for confidence and co-operation between opposing social groups.'[12]

Then came the bad news. An aeroplane was shortly due to land at Immola bearing the big surprise guest for the birthday celebrations that Mannerheim had tried to avoid – Adolf Hitler.

A feast was laid on in the nearby railway carriages, with special provisions for the vegetarian guest. Sipping on a mineral water while the other diners downed wine, Hitler made excuses for the lack of German assistance offered during the Winter War, pleading that the Nazis would have been split on two fronts. German forces, he explained, only really performed well in good weather, and he had not known at the time that the European front would have been shut down by bad weather. The implication, evident for all to see, was that Hitler was hoping that the siege of Leningrad might be ended by a 'Big Push' while it was still summer, before the weather turned cold again.

Hitler went on to complain about the Italians, whom he regarded as poor allies who had been more of a hindrance than a help, and whose misadventures had only served to drag men and *matériel* away from what otherwise might have been earlier German assistance for the Finns. Mannerheim, for his part, told Hitler what he was sure he already knew, that Finland had every reason to wish to stay out of any further provocation of the Soviet Union. As dinner ended, the waiters passed around cigars, refused by all the German officers, who knew that Hitler despised smoking. All eyes fell on Mannerheim, who gamely lit up in the Führer's face, and soon all the Finns followed suit.[13]

After Hitler left, Mannerheim came down with a fever for several days. He was already suffering from gout and bouts of eczema on his hands, and his teeth were troubling him in old age. As Mannerheim feared, Hitler's brief visit had been designed as a propaganda coup, and it was soon being discussed around the world. 'Nazi Germany, hard pressed by Russia,' observed the *Washington Post*, 'tried to persuade the Finns to cut the northern supply line which is feeding the Russian machine.'[14] Mannerheim was obliged to pay a return visit to Berlin, where he further irritated Hitler by paying a courtesy call on a Nazi officer who had fallen out of favour with the Führer. A second unwanted guest arrived in July, when Heinrich Himmler paid a call on the Germans still in Lapland, and insisted on offering his belated birthday greetings to Mannerheim. 'As he had arranged for a considerable number of Finnish invalids to receive special treatment in German War Hospitals,' admitted Mannerheim, 'we felt we owed him thanks.'[15] Himmler turned up accompanied by exceedingly youthful SS officers, singing the praises of new anti-tank weapons that were, one might assume, ideal for a new assault on the Soviet Union.

This, too, failed to impress the Finns. In 1943, Mannerheim announced that he forbade the formation of a new Finnish SS battalion, and that he required the presence of any German-trained Finns in his own army, not that of the Nazis. As most of the Finnish SS were home on leave at the time, this was relatively easily accomplished, but was understandably seen as a further example of cooling relations with Berlin. In secret, a Finnish diplomat in Lisbon got a message to an American diplomat that Finland would not oppose American troops if they were to land in Norway and cross over onto Finnish soil. It was tantamount to an invitation to America to take on the Nazis still in Lapland, but nothing came of it.

The Soviets, too, were aware that the Finns were drifting away from the Nazis. In June 1944, they exploited these cooling relations with a sudden lightning assault on the Karelian Isthmus, pushing back Finnish gains in the hope of giving them less territory to hold at the beginning of any negotiations. Already the suggestion was in the air that the Soviets might be prepared to agree peace if Finland retreated to the 1940 borders, both giving up on gains made in the Continuation War and ratifying the losses made in the Winter War.

With the tide of war turning against the Nazis after the disaster of Stalingrad and the summer assault of Operation *Overlord*, Finland entered into a messy set of political ruses to extricate itself from the war. President Ryti had given the Germans his word that he would not seek a separate peace with the Soviets without gaining German consent. He kept his promise, after a fashion, by resigning as president so that it was no longer his decision to make. In his place, the Finnish parliament unanimously appointed Mannerheim. Initial deliberations had focused on reinstating the regency, or even making him president for life, but Mannerheim had refused. He agreed, but even then against his will, only to lead the country out of war, before taking a long-deserved, long-postponed retirement: 'Ill as I was, and worn out by the burden of heavy responsibility I had carried for so many years, it was with great reluctance that I accepted a new responsible task, and I only did so after members of the government and other prominent politicians had repeatedly appealed to me.'[16]

The war years had taken their toll, and Mannerheim was not sure he would live to see any armistice, whether in Finland's favour or not. A stomach and lung infection back in April 1943 had led to double pneumonia and the conviction that he was going to die. He began plans to change his will, but bounced back after three weeks recuperating in Switzerland. Mannerheim now looked frail and ill; the stress-related eczema had spread from his hands to his arms and face, and the combination of winter, age and smoking created lung infections that were increasingly difficult to shift. Only a few months into his presidency, Mannerheim remained in

his post against the orders of his own doctor. He was also troubled by severe stomach pains, initially feared to be cancer, but later determined to be a particularly bad ulcer.

As commander-in-chief and head of state, Mannerheim laid down the situation for the politicians. Finland could not endure a renewed Soviet assault. The pact with Germany was no longer realistically worth anything to the Finns. The time had come to stop fighting, the better to ensure that when the Second World War came to an end Finland was not fighting on the wrong side.

With the assent of the Finnish parliament, in September 1944 Mannerheim concluded an agreement on preliminary peace terms with the Soviets. He also now refused to believe German boasts that they could continue the war against the Soviets for another decade. 'Whereas this may be possible for a population of ninety million,' he wrote to Hitler, '... we Finns are already physically unable to continue the war. The large-scale offensive launched by the Russians in June has exhausted all of our reserves. We can no longer permit such bloodshed, which imperils the continued existence of small Finland.' [17]

Germany, wrote Mannerheim, would live on, even if it were defeated. Finland's fight was a fight for its very existence, and he did not expect his country to survive if it were swallowed back into the Russian world. For this reason, even though he knew Hitler would be angry to read such words, 'our roads will probably soon part ... I regard it as my duty to lead my people out of the war ... I cherish the hope that, even though you may take exception to my letter, you will share my wish and the wish of all Finns, that the change in our relations may not give rise to animosity.' [18]

It was not to be. The Germans in Lapland had already been digging in with the full expectation that the attitude of the Finns might change. The population of Lapland fled south into central Finland or west to Sweden, ahead of the inevitable outbreak of hostilities. Even as the guns fell silent on the Karelian Isthmus, as the Soviets and Finns warily acknowledged that they were no longer fighting each other, a new war broke out between the Germans and the Finns.

The Lapland War of 1944–5 had effects far beyond Finland.

Finnish sailors in German ports abroad were arrested, and their ships impounded. Although much of the population was successfully evacuated, few buildings were left standing in Lapland, as the fleeing Germans pursued a severe scorched-earth policy. Bridges were destroyed, towns, including the district capital of Rovaniemi, were razed to the ground, and all communication lines were cut. The Germans in the north, who had fought alongside the Finns for years, and in some cases even married them, were bitterly angry about their betrayal. One German language graffito in Lapland sums up the depth of their anger: 'Thanks for nothing, Comrade!'

Some 774 Finns died in this last skirmish of Finland's prolonged conflict, while the Germans lost 1,200 men. On 31 December 1944, Mannerheim formerly gave up command of the Finnish armed forces, leaving the last days of the war to others while he dealt with an altogether thornier problem – the Soviets.

12

Marski

The Second World War ended with Finnish soldiers chasing German soldiers out of Finland, and with Finnish borders broadly returned to the boundaries decided in 1940. Finland lost the Petsamo district in the far north, a strip of territory in the east, and the Karelian Isthmus in the south, including Viipuri. Tens of thousands of Finns from the lost regions needed to be rehoused, and there were legions of wounded, maimed and orphaned citizens to accommodate. A resettlement scheme began by appropriating state land for veterans and refugees, but also threatened to impinge on the territory of Finnish farmers, who were not expecting to fight to save their homesteads from the Soviets, only to lose it to other Finns.

Meanwhile, Soviet Russia continued to badger Finland for damages and concessions. Unrealistic demands were made for the payment of war reparations in equipment and raw materials, and the Soviets insisted on the banning of several 'right-wing' organisations, including the Veterans' Association. Mannerheim was also forced to watch as two loyal Finnish officers were arrested for conspiring to stockpile arms for an armed resistance against an occupation that had not yet come – a scheme of which Mannerheim probably had foreknowledge.

Soviet diplomats presented Mannerheim with lists of Finnish 'war criminals', which he vigorously, and successfully, protested. When sent draft treaties based on Russia's deals with other countries, Mannerheim instead wrote his own deal with the Russians,

273

in Russian, in order to be sure that there were no disagreements over points of translation.

When he returned to Helsinki in 1945, Mannerheim barely recognised the city; he had spent no more than a couple of days there in nearly six years. Most of his friends were gone, and he had little time for anything except his presidential responsibilities. Nor was he free to leave on personal business. 'My wings are clipped,' he noted to his sister Eva when he was unable to attend her 75th birthday in Stockholm, urging her stiffly in English to 'make the best of it'.[1]

Much of President Mannerheim's work was conducted behind closed doors. He regarded it as unconstitutional for him to express his feelings about the upcoming elections, and limited himself to a handful of public engagements. He was spotted at the Helsinki synagogue, attending a service for fallen Jewish soldiers, and made a presidentially correct appearance at the celebrations for Ståhlberg's 80th birthday – paying his respects to the former office, not the man.

The election in March 1945 showed that Finland was still on a knife-edge – 99 socialist members were returned to parliament, against 101 non-socialists. The majority of two was not enough on most issues, and Finland soon favoured a left-wing agenda. To Mannerheim's great annoyance, the new government appointed a civilian as minister of defence, which he feared was likely to see Finnish military preparedness sink back down to dangerous levels. Many wartime representatives had refused to stand again, causing Mannerheim to gaze upon a sea of relatively new faces as he delivered his opening address to parliament. Some, to his further irritation, wore flowers with red ribbons in their buttonholes.

'Your task will be to create the conditions for the continuation of life in freedom under the law in which all citizens have equal rights and equal security,' he said. He warned them of an era ahead that would be coloured by the difficult duty to maintain friendly relations with 'our eastern neighbour'. He entreated that 'we must be able to look with confidence towards a brightening future'.[2]

With the surrender of Japan on 2 September and the end of the Second World War, Mannerheim was still unsure whether he would, as Churchill had threatened, be forced to stand in the dock alongside the Nazis. In accordance with international agreements, the Finnish parliament passed a law to punish 'the war guilty', although it was still unclear who precisely was guilty of what. The stance of the Soviet Union was that virtually everyone in Finland was guilty of waging war against Russia; among the Finns, that only Russia was guilty, and that no justice was expected.

Eventually, several Finnish politicians were prosecuted for war crimes, including a wartime president, two wartime prime ministers and a smattering of other officials. Mannerheim, despite being the commander-in-chief of the Finnish forces that fought alongside the Nazis against the Soviets, was only asked to testify and answer questions, but was not put in the dock to answer charges of his own.

It remains a mystery why Mannerheim was not put on trial at Soviet insistence. Some have made the unlikely suggestion that it was out of a sense of gratitude for stopping when he did, instead of wiping Leningrad off the map. Another possibility is that he was simply too deeply loved by the Finns, and that putting him on trial might have caused such internal unrest that, as with Emperor Hirohito in far-away Japan, he was best retained as a symbol of national continuity. Perhaps, too, there was no case to answer, or that by his actions in 1944, and the reversals of the Lapland War, he began 1945 as a *de facto* ally of the Allies, and hence saved himself from blame.

In the midst of such deliberations, Mannerheim, now 78, took a difficult journey across Europe to Portugal, where he spent six weeks recuperating at his doctor's orders. His lungs and stomach both cleared up noticeably, although during his return journey he was hospitalised in Paris en route, and arrived in Finland only to check straight into a ward in Helsinki. In a strange, and once again inexplicable, move, Mannerheim received a message in his hospital bed that the Soviet Union would not be prosecuting him for any alleged war crimes, whether he remained in office or resigned. The reason, at least officially, was that he was the one who had 'concluded the peace between Finland and the Soviet Union'.[3]

In January 1946, Mannerheim's doctor pronounced him no longer fit to serve as president. The sole hope for his failing health, it transpired, was the absence of stress, of which a presidential position delivered great doses from morning until night. The continued leftward drift of the Finnish parliament also damaged his ability to steer Finland in his own desired direction – as a right-wing president with a left-wing parliament, he was reduced to little more than a figurehead.

He presented his resignation to Prime Minister Paasikivi on 4 March 1946, citing his continued poor health, and the arguable point that he had accomplished those tasks for which he had been appointed to the presidency by parliament. Paasikivi went on the radio that night to read out Mannerheim's letter and offer his own thoughts:

> The name of President Mannerheim is deeply engraved in the history of our country ... Under his leadership and under the protection of his authority our country disengaged herself from the war. Nobody else could have carried out this task, because nobody else enjoyed as he did the confidence of the great majority of the people ... Mannerheim can retire to a well-earned rest in the consciousness that the people of Finland will not forget the exceptional services he has rendered the Fatherland.[4]

Mannerheim began his eighties still talking of responsibility and struggle. As he saw it, Finland still ran the risk of drifting irrevocably too far to the left, and he was determined to hold this off by the last means available to him – writing his memoirs.

'Was it not my duty,' he wrote, 'now that the West seemed to have forgotten the gallant Finnish people, to communicate to all our friends near and far what I knew about its indomitable battle for all that a nation holds sacred, and had not my countrymen a right to hear my interpretation of the causes that had led to the position where Finland now stood?'[5]

His decision was unsurprising, but also unwelcome to some of his successors. Mannerheim's avowed intent was to educate the Cold War world about recent Finnish history, but his memoirs were sure to attract the attention of readers back home. President Paasikivi, in particular, fretted that his illustrious predecessor would write a tell-all book that was sure to land Finland in hot water with the Soviet Union, with which relations were still strained. Mannerheim did exactly as Paasikivi had feared but was steered into being less forceful in his published comments on Bolshevism and 'Reds', and also in his attitude towards the Swedes. In private, Paasikivi grumbled that if he paid heed to every one of the field marshal's grim warnings then everyone in Finland might as well walk into the forest with a pistol and shoot themselves in the forehead.[6]

Despite the politicians' concerns, Mannerheim was left to write his memoirs in peace with the help of a small staff of assistants. He seems to have originally planned on doing so in Kirkniemi, a manor house he had bought in what is now the Helsinki suburbs, but continued ill health lured him out of Finland to Switzerland in the late 1940s. 'If on this earth there is a place to be found which is dedicated to forgetting,' he wrote to a friend, 'it is Switzerland, with all the convenience which makes life easy, hotels, communications, order, food and the beauty of the landscape, but above all, the mountains, the Alps which give the impression of being somewhere in the atmosphere, above the clouds, between earth and sky.'[7] Mannerheim also observed that Switzerland, unlike so many other parts of Europe, had been spared the damage and destruction of the war – it was, in many ways for him, a reminder of the lost Europe of his younger days.

Mannerheim's finances, however, were not as healthy as they had been. His pensions and endowments were worth barely 15 per cent of their pre-war value, and the Finnish mark continued to lose its value on the international market. The post-war years ate away at his other possessions, too. Kirkniemi's estates were reduced in size by mandatory government reforms aimed at finding land for the settlement of the many thousands of Karelian refugees. Mannerheim only clung to his residence in Helsinki (now the Mannerheim Museum) by renting out the ground floor to the staff of the War Casualty Archives.

His circle of true friends, always small, dwindled predictably in old age. 'I begin to see only graves around me,' he commented,

although his dry melancholy was economical with the truth. In fact, he spent much time in the company of a new lady companion, the elegant Countess Gertrud Arco-Valley. Some thirty years his junior, the divorcee countess was a friend of Mannerheim's younger daughter and was often seen accompanying him on his travels.

Mannerheim spent increasing amounts of time in hospital, troubled in particular by stomach and intestine problems. A perforated ulcer nearly killed him in 1946, and kidney stones and haemorrhages laid him low in 1948. He began to lose weight drastically, and is noticeably thin and frail in the photographs of him at the clinic in Val-Mont, Switzerland, where he both took spa treatments and continued to work on his memoirs.

In early 1951, Mannerheim was hospitalised again in Lausanne with a distended abdomen, and had emergency surgery for a blocked intestine. It was, he joked with his surgeon, his last battle, and one that he was likely to lose. He said his goodbyes to those around him on 27 January, and fell into a sleep from which he never awoke. His heart stopped half an hour before midnight, although in Finland's time zone it was already the following morning – the anniversary of his decisive strike against the Reds in the Finnish Civil War of 1918.

Mannerheim had left no instructions for his memorial service. Paasikivi took the initiative, and ordered a state funeral, and that Mannerheim's body should be interned in the military section of Helsinki's Hietaniemi Cemetary. It was, noted Paasikivi, only natural that the resting place of the Marshal of Finland would become a place of national pilgrimage, and entirely proper that those approaching his grave would do so through acres of Finland's heroic dead.

His coffin was brought with full military honours to the Lutheran cathedral in the centre of Helsinki, clad in the uniform of a field marshal. He went to his grave as *Suomen Marsalkka*, the Marshal of Finland. Already, the mourners were contracting the unwieldy Finnish term to the affectionate diminutive *Marski*.

Tens of thousands of mourners queued in the snow for up to six hours, waiting to pay their respects. For the funeral itself, over 100,000 Finns lined the streets, including some 6,000 reserve

officers, who all turned up in uniform, their medals polished on their chests. Mannerheim's own decorations were borne before his coffin; it took six men to carry them.

For fear of angering the Soviet Union, all but two government ministers stayed away. Mannerheim would have been more pleased by the gallant decision to include his horse in the proceedings. Talisman, Philip, Neptune and many others were long gone, and Kate, his last charger, was pregnant. Despite this, Kate was led into the procession for a brief walk in her rightful place; it was a moment of equestrian protocol that Mannerheim would have loved.

The Speaker of the Finnish parliament at the time was Karl-August Fagerholm, a Social Democrat leader and a former union leader. He was, perhaps, a curious choice to give Mannerheim's elegy – presumably also selected in order to avoid any inflammatory statements that might annoy the Soviets. Instead, Fagerholm faced down an audience of Whites and called Mannerheim a great warrior, statesman and citizen who had left his native land with a precious heritage in the form of 'the country's freedom and independence, the lodestones of his life'.[8]

With that, Mannerheim made his last journey, down the steep steps of the cathedral and to the waiting gun carriage. The procession filed on in silence, broken only by the hooves of horses and the turning of the carriage wheels on Helsinki cobblestones. His coffin was born the short distance to the cemetery at Hietaniemi, where it was laid to rest. As Mannerheim finally found peace in the cold earth of his native Finland, twin 19-gun salutes rumbled out across the bay like the peals of distant thunder.

Mannerheim in the 21st Century

Had Mannerheim's career ended in 1919 with his retirement, it would have already contained enough incident for any biographer. He had seen the birth of a new nation, and yet a decade later he returned to defend Finland in her time of need, acquiring a legendary allure thereafter. Indeed, in 2004 he was voted as the 'Greatest Finn of All Time' in a national television survey, occupying an equal position in Finland to that of Winston Churchill, Charles de Gaulle and Ronald Reagan in similar programmes in the UK, France and the United States.

Mannerheim remains a powerful presence in the centre of Helsinki. A statue of him on horseback sits on a massive granite slab outside the Finnish parliament building, positioned as if he is marching past, neither towards or away from the politicians within, but on a path of his own. In a country where other presidents are doomed to be represented by modernist abstractions, misshapen lumps and baffling metal tubes, Mannerheim's image remains resolutely old-fashioned, well proportioned and in realistic pose, his horse conspicuously and calmly walking, not charging or rearing. He is in uniform, martial but not belligerent.

Parliament and the statue both stand on what is now the Mannerheim Road (Mannerheimintie), along with the Marski hotel. There are other memorials of him scattered in unlikely places. Montreux, where he spent his final years at the private Val-Mont hospital, has gained a Parc Mannerheim dominated by an obelisk that bears a bas relief of the Lion of Finland. The cocktail of vodka, aquavit, gin and vermouth he habitually drank in Mikkeli is sold in Finland as Marski's Schnapps. His favourite salted-meat appetiser, supposedly a relic of his time in Poland, is sold in supermarkets as Marski's Vorschmak.

Not every appearance was welcomed. In the 1950s, the members of a newly elected left-wing city council in Tampere, site of his 1918 victory over the Reds, were horrified to discover that they had inherited a project to put a statue of Mannerheim in the city centre. To add White insult to Red injury, the statue was conceived in imitation of a famous painting of Mannerheim, his hands in his pockets, gazing down thoughtfully upon Tampere as the Whites retook it. Refusing to place it where their predecessors had planned, and politically unable to throw it away, the councillors placed the statue far out of town, in the middle of a remote forest, where it remains to this day.

Mannerheim is a constant source of interest to older Finns. Pensioners taking the Finnish-language tour of St Petersburg are shown the houses where he lived, and told tall tales of ballroom romances and trysts at Tsarskoe Selo's 'Chinese village'. Such stories do not form part of the fabric of other-language tours because few speakers of other languages know who Mannerheim was, or care that he was once a resident.

Even among the Finns, Mannerheim has become part of the furniture, a statue in town squares (or far, far away from them, in the case of Tampere), a portrait on grandparents' walls, or a classic book on dusty library shelves, often seen but seldom read. For irreverent young Finns, Mannerheim is the moustached old man their parents make them look at in provincial museums, when they would much rather be on a rollercoaster in a theme park.

Finland is a young country. The centenary of her independence will be marked in 2017. History before that date often has a Russian or Swedish taint, leading many Finns to lean heavily on heroes and villains of the Second World War era. Mannerheim dominates Finnish history, and is still a national icon. The Mannerheim Foundation, which oversees much of his legacy, continues to funnel his estate into charitable works, and piously guards his image. But national heroes are nationally owned, and while Mannerheim still has his admirers, he also has his detractors, and as in any country, the ever-growing legions of the indifferent.

For a population jaded by worthy accounts, modern coverage of Mannerheim veers towards the scandalous or provocative. The strangest addition of all, at least to date, is *Uralin Perhonen* (*Butterfly of the Urals*, 2008), a short, beautifully made puppet animation by Katariina Lillqvist which casually suggests that Mannerheim returned from Asia with a Kirghiz catamite, whom he hid from the jealous Anastasie and later abandoned during the Civil War. Reviews of this work in newspapers centred largely on the unfounded allegation that Mannerheim was bisexual, and ignored the far more contentious scenes in the film of him partying with the Grim Reaper in Tampere, while taking turns to shoot at Red prisoners. Critical reaction among older Finns was largely one of head-shaking despair; among the young, a greater interest in reality television shows on the other channel, although the damage was still done. Mention one is writing a book on Mannerheim to a young 21st-century Finn, and the first question one invariably hears is, 'Was he gay?'

Nevertheless, Mannerheim remains a war hero to many Finns, a nation whose wariness of Russia continues to support national conscription for adult males. Mannerheim would surely crack a smile if he were to tour the Finnish officers' school in modern-day Hamina – the institution that once expelled him now has his portrait in every one of its classrooms.

In the 21st century, Finns are no longer afraid of speaking out against what was the Soviet Union, a threat that has long passed. Nor are some afraid of speaking out against Mannerheim himself. Like all public icons, his fortune waxes and wanes, but his adventurous life is sure to make him an enduring icon of Finland as the nation enters her second century.

Pieces of the Mannerheim story remain all over Finland. The House of the Four Winds still stands on its island. His Helsinki residence is now a museum (Mannerheim Museum), as is the Mikkeli school from which he ran the Winter War. Even the *Tarmo*, that battered old hulk that took him to Stockholm, can still be found at the docks in Kotka.

Remarkably, one can even trace his steps in China and Japan. It is still possible to visit the arrayed idols of Sanjūsangendō, although government agents will no longer chase you from the dockside at Shimonoseki. I have stood, like Mannerheim, before the tower of the Famen temple, and outside the cracked façade of the Cave of the Sun and Moon on Mount Hua. I travelled to the Forest of Steles in Xi'an, and the mosque where Mannerheim once photographed the lead imam. My Chinese driver, curious about this strange itinerary, had never heard the word 'Finland', but soon brightened up when I explained: 'The Land of Nokia'.

There is still time, still stories to be told, that it might be known as the 'The Land of Mannerheim', and not merely in China. This book is my small contribution.

Note on Names

Carl Gustaf Emil Mannerheim rarely used his full name. As a younger son of a count, he was technically a baron. He was never Carl; that was reserved for his elder brother, although among family members, Carl was usually called Calle. Nor did Mannerheim habitually use the Emil, which he disliked. Instead, he signed his letters simply Gustaf or G. In the presence of Finns, particularly during his attempt to ingratiate himself with the new regime in 1918, he would sometimes use the Finnish form of the name, Kustaa. To his subordinates, particularly in later life where there could be no mistake, he signed his letters simply Mannerheim.

His name is rarely pronounced the way it looks to English speakers. Up until the end of the First World War, the accent of his Russian colleagues-in-arms transformed his name to *Kustas Mannergeim*. Among the Finns, where vowels are always assumed to adhere to strict and unbending rules, his name is properly pronounced in a way that sounds like *Munner-hame* to English ears.

In China, he was *Ma Da-Han* (馬達漢), the 'Horse Reaching China', although many older sources, including Mannerheim's own *Memoirs*, repeat the erroneous claim that the name meant 'Horse Leaping through the Clouds' or 'Horse that Jumps Over the Stars'. There was additional confusion among the Chinese from one of Mannerheim's travel documents, which transcribed his name phonetically as something like *Ma-nu-er-hai-mu*. There is a chance that some of Mannerheim's hosts in Chinese Turkestan did not find the *Han* of his name quite so endearing (it is the name of China's dominant ethnic group, unpopular in the western provinces), and that they may therefore have substituted a character of their own. In Aqsu on 21 March 1907, the local prefect called him 'Ma Tajen', which might *possibly* have been Mannerheim's mishearing of 'Ma Dayun' – 'Horse Leaping through the Clouds' (馬達雲). There is, however, no way to be sure a century later, either of what the prefect said, what he meant or what Mannerheim actually heard.[1] Meanwhile, Mannerheim commented that another phonetic rendering of his name, conferred by an official in Suzhou in December 1907, mischievously used an inappropriately rude character for the first syllable. He does not say what this was, but it could have easily been 'Drunken' (醉), 'Revolting' (罵), or even 'Reckless' (漫). The insult was noticed within days by Zeng Guangjun, and by 12 December Mannerheim had acquired still another name by way of replacement.[2] Mannerheim sent his father the table plan for his banquet with Viceroy Shen on 10 March 1908, which clearly gives his Chinese surname as a different Ma (瑪), literally meaning 'agate' or 'carnelian'.[3]

Modern Chinese writers, for whom Mannerheim is just another Second World War general, tend to use *Man-na-hai-mu* (曼納海姆), a purely phonetic cluster of characters that is not supposed to mean anything, although the separate elements spell 'Prolonged Restraint Sea Governess'. However, since the publication of Wang Jiaji's Chinese translation of excerpts from *Across Asia* in 2000, the name *Ma Da-Han* has come back into use, both in Chinese books and in articles about him – such as, for example, a commemorative piece that appeared in the *Gansu Daily* in 2007, shortly before the centenary of his arrival in Lanzhou.

I have undertaken some simplifications with other members of Mannerheim's family, who invariably had several names. Mannerheim's mother, for example, was baptised as Hedwig Charlotta Helena, but preferred to be known as Hélène, French accents and all. Mannerheim's sister Annika, who died in childhood at the Smolny Institute, was properly known as Nanny Albertina Anna Helena. The accommodating Uncle Albert was, strictly speaking, Johan Albert Edward von Julin. Like most previous Mannerheim biographers, I have taken my cue from Stig Jägerskiöld, and used the names that family members preferred to employ in private correspondence.

Other issues trouble the researcher trying to make sense of

sources in multiple languages. Place names in Finland usually have three spellings: a modern Finnish one, an older Swedish one, and a largely forgotten Russian one. Helsinki, Helsingfors and Khel'sinky are one and the same place. In most cases, I use the modern Finnish variant – Mannerheim's Swedish-language letters to his family referred to his military academy as Fredrikshamn, although this book uses its modern name of Hamina.

Many Swedish names were Fennicised to make a nationalist point, some before the 1917 revolution and others increasingly in its aftermath. Hence, the famous artist Akseli Gallen-Kallela was plain Axel Gallén until 1907; I have anachronistically used the name by which he is known to posterity. Conversely, the Chinese bandits called *Khunkhuzy* by the Russians were actually *Hong Huzi* ('Red Beards') in Mandarin. St Petersburg was renamed Petrograd in 1914, in an attempt to make it sound less German to Russian ears; it was subsequently renamed Leningrad, and is now St Petersburg again.

An entire world of pain awaits the researcher trying to make sense of Finnish, Swedish and Russian variants on Turkic, Chinese and Japanese place names, many of which already exist in English in several romanisations. There is, in fact, enough argument to fill an entire book. Luckily, that book has already been written: I have made extensive use of Harry Halén's *Analytical Index to C.G. Mannerheim's Across Asia From West to East.*

There are additional difficulties in the Russo-Japanese War, when Mannerheim and his fellow Europeans were often oblivious of the meanings of the place names around them. He crossed a river that he called the Daliaohe, omitting to mention that 'Da' simply means 'big', and 'he' simply means 'river'. Where possible, I have stripped both Finnish and Chinese prefixes and suffixes from recognisable Chinese place names. Furthermore, Russian maps were so unreliable that Mannerheim believed, and many Finnish sources continue to repeat, that he went on a mission to 'Mongolia' in 1905, even though he merely crossed to the western side of the Liao River into Jehol. Hence, I have relied where I can on contemporary Japanese maps, and used those to gauge the most accurate rendering in anachronistic Pinyin romanisation. Thus, we have the harbour town of Ying Kou, as the Chinese knew it, and not Inkon as it appears in some sources – the initial 'Y' incorrectly assumed to be a Russian accent, and the final 'n' a vestige of the Finnish genitive case. The suffix *–bu (or –bao)* simply means a walled village. Where I have been able to identify actual Chinese place names, I have used the correct spelling in the translation of Mannerheim's diaries and letters.

Notes

Introduction

1. In 1903, British agents had become convinced that the Tsar
   was moving in on Tibet, largely because a Russian subject,
   Agvan Dorzhiev, had become one of the Dalai Lama's
   closest advisers. Unbeknown to the British, Dorzhiev was
   actually playing both sides – he was, it was true, possessed
   of a Russian surname, but he was an ethnic Buryat, whose
   ancestors were from Mongolia or Siberia, and personally
   committed to the idea of a Mongol-Tibetan superstate to
   rival both China and Russia. It was he who had planted
   the idea with the Dalai Lama that Tsar Nicholas II was the
   incarnation of a Buddhist deity. A Norman, *Holder of the
   White Lotus: The Lives of the Dalai Lama* (Little, Brown:
   London: 2008) pp 337–8.
2. Mannerheim, *Across Asia from West to East in 1906–1908*,
   revised edition edited by Harry Halén (Otava, Helsinki:
   2008) p 765. All page references to *Across Asia* are to this
   English-language edition, which is the most comprehensive
   of the many versions available and considerably more
   complete than its Finnish counterpart – see my notes on
   Sources and Further Reading for details.
3. Ibid. The English translation here calls the gun a 'Browning
   revolver', although Browning did not make revolvers,
   and Mannerheim specifically mentions demonstrating
   to His Holiness how to reload a seven-round magazine.
   Mannerheim was no fool, and was genuinely giving the Dalai
   Lama one of his most valuable possessions.

4. Mannerheim, *The Memoirs of Marshal Mannerheim* (Cassell: London: 1953) p 69.

1. Mannerheim's World

1. R Brantberg, *Mannerheim: Tsaarin upseeri [In the Service of the Tsar*, literally *Officer of the Tsar]* (Kustannusosakeyhtiö Revontuli, Tampere: 2003) p 97.
2. Letter to his family, 14 September 1887, quoted in R Lehmusoksa and Ritva Lehmusoksa, *Dining With Marshal Mannerheim* (Ajatus, Helsinki: 2005) p 49, and Brantberg, *Mannerheim: Tsaarin upseeri*, p 97, although Brantberg omits the detail about Carl's coat. J Screen, *Mannerheim: The Years of Preparation* (C Hurst & Co, London: 1970) p 29, *pace* the unabridged S Jägerskiöld, *Nuori Mannerheim [Young Mannerheim]* (Otava, Helsinki: 1964) p 122, prefers the term 'apostate' to 'traitor', repeating the Finnish text which favours *luopio* – apostate, defector or renegade.
3. Mannerheim, *Päiväkirja Japanin Sodasta 1904–1905 sekä Rintamakirjeitä Omaisille [Diary from the Japanese War 1904–1905 with Letters to his Family]* (Otava, Helsinki: 1982) p 178.
4. P Aalto, *Oriental Studies in Finland 1828–1918* (Societas Scientiarum Fennica, Helsinki: 1971) pp 144–5.
5. G Kish, *North-east Passage: Adolf Erik Nordenskiöld, his life and times* (Nico Israel, Amsterdam: 1973) p 63. Louhisaari is mentioned several times in Kish's account, but under its Swedish name of Villnäs. See also Jägerskiöld, *Nuori Mannerheim*, pp 29–30.
6. Kish, *North-east Passage*, p 192.
7. Kish, *North-east Passage*, p 201.
8. Screen, *Mannerheim: The Years of Preparation*, p 24; Lehmusoksa, *Dining With Marshal Mannerheim*, p 35.
9. Mannerheim, *Memoirs*, p 4.
10. L Vlasov, *Mannerheim Pietarissa, 1887–1904 [Mannerheim in St Petersburg]* (Gummerus, Jyväskylä: 1994) p 41.

11. V Meri, *Suomen Marsalkka, C.G. Mannerheim* (Werner Söderstöm OY, Porvoo: 1988) p 142. He still required private lessons in mechanics, at which he fell behind.

12. Lehmusoksa, *Dining With Marshal Mannerheim*, p 56.

13. Meri, *Suomen Marsalkka*, p 144. It was this high score in map drawing that was to influence the selection of Mannerheim for his Asian mission of 1906–8. However, Aalto, *Oriental Studies in Finland*, p 92, notes that the Hamina cadet school generally had a reputation for turning out fine draughtsmen. Possibly early Hamina experiences helped increase Mannerheim's grades at St Petersburg.

14. Meri, *Suomen Marsalkka*, p 146.

15. Mannerheim, quoted in Brantberg, *Mannerheim: Tsaarin upseeri*, p 106.

16. L Vlasov, *Mannerheimin Elämän Naiset [The Women in Mannerheim's Life]* (Schildts, Keuruu: 2002) p 53, has the date of the drunken incident as Wednesday 19 June, Brantberg as a week earlier. Bizarrely, according to Screen, *Mannerheim: The Years of Preparation*, p 33, the School's own records continued to show Mannerheim as second in his class. S Jägerskiöld, *Mannerheim: Marshal of Finland* (University of Minnesota Press, Minneapolis: 1986) p 7, also claims that he finished second, and that he would have finished top of his class were it not for favouritism towards a Russian aristocrat. In which case, one is tempted to ask, why was no place in the Guards immediately offered to him on graduation? Mannerheim himself, in *Memoirs*, p 6, claims 'I left the School as one of the first half-dozen' – a strangely vague statement that seems almost comically designed to strike a balance between the conflicting statements of others.

17. Meri, *Suomen Marsalkka*, p 147.

18. Letter to Albert von Julin, 25 September/7 October 1889, quoted in Lehmusoksa, *Dining With Marshal Mannerheim*, p 63.

19. Letter to Albert von Julin, 7 October 1889, quoted in S Jägerskiöld, *Nuori Mannerheim [Young Mannerheim]* (Otava, Helsinki: 1964) p 158. 'All the stores are Jewish, so

it's impossible to buy anything during these holidays. If you need an apartment, furniture, clothes, guns – anything at all, you have to rely on some affable, long-robed Jew with long curls falling around his ears. Simply nothing can be achieved without Jewish fixers.'

20. Mannerheim, *Memoirs*, p 7.

21. Ibid.

22. He left for St Petersburg within weeks, although his official transfer did not arrive for several months. Consequently, Mannerheim's service in Poland shows up as two years (from August 1889, when he was assigned to his regiment, to August 1891, when he was officially reassigned), although he was actually in Kalisz for a much briefer period (October 1889 to January 1891).

23. Kish, *North-east Passage*, p 257.

24. D Keene, *Emperor of Japan: Meiji and His World 1852–1912* (Columbia University Press, New York: 2002) p 449.

25. Keene, *Emperor of Japan*, p 450.

26. Mannerheim, *Memoirs*, p 10. The translator inadvertently gives Anastasie's surname in the masculine form. Strictly speaking, she was Anastasie Arapova.

27. Vlasov, *Mannerheimin Elämän Naiset*, pp 65–6; S Jägerskiöld, *Nuori Mannerheim [Young Mannerheim]* (Otava, Helsinki: 1964) p 234; Lehmusoksa, *Dining With Marshal Mannerheim*, p 87.

28. Brantberg, *Mannerheim: Tsaarin upseeri*, p 124.

29. Letter of Hanna Lovén to Hedvig Santesson, 11 August 1892, quoted in Jägerskiöld, *Nuori Mannerheim*, p 229.

30. Kish, *North-east passage*, p 269; Letter of Eva Mannerheim to Adolf Nordenskiöld, summer 1892, quoted in Jägerskiöld, *Nuori Mannerheim*, p 230. Nordic insults can be difficult to comprehend at the best of times, but I believe this to be a reference that capitalises to some extent on 'gilding the lily'.

31. Letter of Sophie Mannerheim to Hanna Lovén, 2 January 1893, quoted in Jägerskiöld, *Nuori Mannerheim*, p 231.

32. Vlasov, *Mannerheimin Elämän Naiset*, pp 69 and 71. Vlasov favours Tasia as the diminutive of Anastasie's name, but

some other authors use Stasie – perhaps she was Tasia in Russian but Stasie in Swedish. Her mother's nickname was Nata.

33. Letter of Carl Robert Mannerheim to Johan Mannerheim, 27 March 1896, quoted in Jägerskiöld, *Nuori Mannerheim*, p 234. Vlasov, *Mannerheimin Elämän Naiset*, p 74. Jägerskiöld, *Mannerheim: Marshal of Finland*, p 11, admits that Mannerheim's association with Shuvalova 'gave rise to talk', but only mentions this *after* Anastasie had fled for France. The occasion was in March 1897, but the tension appears to have been mounting for some time.

34. Brantberg, *Mannerheim: Tsaarin upseeri*, p 133. The couple stayed at the beachfront Hôtel du Palais, looking out over the Bay of Biscay. Built originally for the wife of Napoleon III, the hotel was a favourite spot for European royalty, many of whom were enthusiastic followers of an old tradition that the salt waters of Biarritz would cure any number of unspecified ills. Baroness Mannerheim enthusiastically took to the waters. Mannerheim, meanwhile, stole away to watch something else that Biarritz was famous for – horse racing.

2. The Field of Vipers

1. O Warner, *Marshal Mannerheim & the Finns* (Weidenfeld and Nicolson, London: 1967) p 31.
2. Mannerheim, *Memoirs*, p 11.
3. Mannerheim, *Memoirs*, p 11.
4. Mannerheim, *Memoirs*, p 12.
5. Grand Duchess Olga Alexandrovna, quoted in G King, *The Court of the Last Tsar: Pomp, Power and Pageantry in the Reign of Nicholas II* (John Wiley & Sons, Hoboken: 2006) p 386.
6. King, *The Court of the Last Tsar*, p 268.
7. Mannerheim, *Memoirs*, pp 12–13. In his *Memoirs*, p 13, Mannerheim notes that he broke bones on 13 occasions in his life, but that the Berlin incident was the worst. Considering that his life was in substantially greater danger in the Algiers car accident of 1923, it was a strange claim to

make, but Mannerheim was presumably far more devastated by the suggestion that his military career was over than by the mere possibility that he would die.

8. Letter of Kaiser Wilhelm II to Tsar Nicholas II, April 1895, quoted in I Levine, *Letters from the Kaiser to the Czar* (Stokes, New York: 1920) p 10.

9. Anastasie appears to have kept much of this quiet on her return, and the alleged details of her misadventures only came out later, quite possibly when she had ample opportunity to embellish them. Letter of Eva Mannerheim Sparre to Hannah Lovén, 16 January 1902, quoted in Jägerskiöld, *Nuori Mannerheim*, pp 235–6.

10. Letter to Albert von Julin, 2 January 1902, quoted in Jägerskiöld, *Nuori Mannerheim*, p 235.

11. Letter to Eva Mannerheim Sparre, 22 December 1901, quoted in Jägerskiöld, *Nuori Mannerheim*, p 235.

12. Letter to Eva Mannerheim Sparre, 1 April 1904, quoted in Jägerskiöld, *Nuori Mannerheim*, p 236.

13. Vlasov, *Mannerheimin Elämän Naiset*, pp 244–5. According to Vlasov, Geltser gave birth to the son of an unknown father in Moscow on 7 December 1902. Supposedly the son was called Emil, although Mannerheim notoriously hated the name and rarely used it himself. Emil subsequently moved to Switzerland and then Germany. Emil's own son, Karl Gustav Emil Kramer, born in 1927, was rumoured to have been a surprise guest in the entourage of Adolf Hitler on the occasion of Mannerheim's 75th birthday in 1942. I relegate this claim to a footnote because nobody seems to take it very seriously, and it seems typical of the desperate attempts in modern times to put new and controversial spins on Mannerheim's well-documented life. Vlasov does not so much discuss the allegations as print a full-page 'picture' of a Finnish tabloid article, so it is not all that clear if he believes it, either.

14. T Polvinen, *Imperial Borderland: Bobrikov and the Attempted Russification of Finland 1898–1904* (C Hurst & Co, London: 1995) pp 186–7.

15. E Parmanen, *Taistelujen Kirja [Book of the Struggles]* (Werner Söderström OY, Porvoo: 1936) Vol 1, pp 591–4.
16. Letter to Carl Mannerheim, 27 April 1903, in Mannerheim, *Kirjeitä Seitsemän Vuosikymmenen Ajalta* [Letters from Seven Decades] (Otava, Helsinki: 1983), pp 64–5, hereafter *Kirjeitä*.
17. Letter to Carl Mannerheim, 28 June 1904, in Mannerheim, *Kirjeitä*, pp 64–5.
18. Letter of Kaiser Wilhelm II to Tsar Nicholas II, 3 January 1904, in Levine, *Letters from the Kaiser to the Czar*, pp 96, 100; see also Keene, *Emperor of Japan*, p 593.
19. Keene, *Emperor of Japan*, p 596. Supposedly, Viceroy Alexeiev had only advanced through the ranks out of the gratitude of a Romanov Grand Duke who had been arrested in a Marseilles brothel. Alexeiev nobly took the fall for behaviour that was entirely the Grand Duke's, and received in payment a fast-track through the Russian ranks. This, of course, left him entirely unsuitable to perform his duties, as the Russians would discover to their cost in the war of 1904–5.
20. Mannerheim, *Memoirs*, p 16.
21. H Aittokoski, 'Finland shaken 100 years ago by murder of Governor-General Bobrikov' in *Helsingin Sanomat*, 15 June 2004. News of the event reached Dublin on 16 June 1904, and hence was mentioned in James Joyce's *Ulysses*, which is devoted to that day in history.
22. Polvinen, *Imperial Borderland*, pp 182–3.
23. Letter to Carl Mannerheim, 28 June 1904, in Mannerheim, *Kirjeitä*, pp 72–3.

3. The Baptism of Fire

1. Unidentified letters of Gustaf Mannerheim, October 1904, in L Vlasov, *Mannerheim: upseeri ja tutkimusmatkailija, 1904–1909 [Mannerheim – Officer and Explorer]* (Gummerus, Jyväskylä: 1997) pp 7–8.
2. Letter to Carl Robert Mannerheim, 2 April 1905, quoted in Jägerskiöld, *Nuori Mannerheim*, p 340.

3. Mannerheim, *Päiväkirja Japanin sodasta*, p 21.
4. Letter to Sophie Mannerheim, 7/20 November 1904, quoted in Jägerskiöld, *Nuori Mannerheim*, p 317. The absent pages are noted in Mannerheim, *Päiväkirja Japanin Sodasta*, pp 36–7. Vlasov, *Mannerheimin Elämän Naiset*, pp 139–44, gossips luridly about several women who made Mannerheim's acquaintance in Manchuria, but is unable to identify them.
5. Mannerheim, *Päiväkirja Japanin sodasta*, pp 38–9.
6. Vlasov, *Mannerheimin Elämän Naiset*, p 139.
7. Letters to Johan Mannerheim, 13/26 November 1904, and to Carl Robert the same day, quoted in Jägerskiöld, *Nuori Mannerheim*, p 323. Mannerheim actually writes the term 'fanzaa' for his quarters, likely to have been his attempt to transliterate the Chinese *fangzi*, a room or small dwelling. Mannerheim calls the sorghum straw 'kaoliang' (i.e. *gaoliang*) as he does not know its Swedish name.
8. Letter to Johan Mannerheim, 13/27 November 1904, quoted in Jägerskiöld, *Nuori Mannerheim*, p 323.
9. Letter to Carl Robert Mannerheim, 3/16 December 1904, quoted in Jägerskiöld, *Nuori Mannerheim*, p 324.
10. Letter to Carl Robert Mannerheim, 13/26 November 1904, quoted in Jägerskiöld, *Nuori Mannerheim*, p 325.
11. Letter to Carl Robert Mannerheim, 1 December 1904, quoted in Jägerskiöld, *Nuori Mannerheim*, p 325.
12. Y Matsusaka, *The Making of Japanese Manchuria 1904–1932* (Harvard University Asia Center, Cambridge, MA: 2001) p 75.
13. Letter to Johan Mannerheim, 20 November/3 December 1904, quoted in Jägerskiöld, *Nuori Mannerheim*, p 327. At least, that is what Mannerheim claims. His Swedish original reads *schangou*, which could be 'very good' or 'very high' in Chinese, but might equally be an attempt to say *shan gou*, 'mountain dogs'. Since the Manchus have long held horsemen in respect, however, we might give him the benefit of the doubt on this occasion.

14. However, long-range reconnaissance by cavalry scouts, often ranging up to 30 miles behind enemy lines, was later cited as a major contribution to what few Russian successes there were in Manchuria. Mannerheim's superiors, Paul von Rennenkampf and Pavel Mishchenko, took the credit. See S Nidvine, 'The Russian Cavalry During the Russo-Japanese War' on the website of the Russo-Japanese War Research Society, www.russojapanesewar.com, 2002.

15. Ullrich, quoted in Jägerskiöld, *Nuori Mannerheim*, p 322.

16. Mannerheim, *Memoirs*, p 18.

17. Letter of Carl Robert Mannerheim to Johan Mannerheim, 21 January 1905, in Jägerskiöld, *Nuori Mannerheim*, p 329.

18. M Akashi, *Rakka Ryūsui: Colonel Akashi's Report on his Secret Cooperation with the Russian Revolutionary Parties during the Russo-Japanese War* (Studia Historica 31, Helsinki: 1988) p 34. Mannerheim was not officially promoted to full colonel until 1906, but we might permit some latitude for Carl's family pride, or perhaps Akashi's understanding of Russian ranks.

19. See, for example, F Singleton, *A Short History of Finland* (Cambridge University Press, Cambridge: 1998) pp 101–2; S Kurobane, *Nichi-Ro Sensō to Akashi Kosaku [The Russo-Japanese War and the Deeds of Akashi]* (Nanso-sha, Tokyo: 1976) p 193; R Deacon, *A History of the Japanese Secret Service* (Frederick Muller Limited, London: 1982) p 55. Konni Zilliacus is not to be confused with his son, who was born in exile in Japan, and would eventually become the British MP for Gateshead. Lenin's press activities were the first stirrings of the revolutionary agitation that would eventually bring him to power.

20. Letter to Johan Mannerheim, 28 December 1904, in Jägerskiöld, *Nuori Mannerheim*, p 330.

21. Or so he thought. He found the name rather poetic and even suggested to Johan that he give it to one of his horses. However, *Eldhaisen* is not a Chinese word (although it may be Manchu), and I have not found anything similar on Chinese maps. I am tempted to speculate that the Chinese

'place-name' he had heard was *Er-dai-xian*, or 'forward of the second unit'.

22. Mannerheim, *Memoirs*, p 19.

23. Mannerheim, *Memoirs*, p 19.

24. Jägerskiöld, *Nuori Mannerheim*, p 335.

25. Chinese and Japanese sources refer to the villages nearby as Heikoutai and Zhendanbao – it is the latter that appears to have been corrupted in European sources to Sandepu.

26. For the full text, see http://artsci.shu.edu/reesp/documents/ bloodysunday.htm. Suspiciously, the priest who instigated the peaceful protest was somehow smuggled out of Finland and later turned up in London at the Charing Cross Hotel. It is not impossible that the protest was yet another of Colonel Akashi's espionage projects; Singleton, *A Short History of Finland*, p 102.

27. R Connaughton, *The War of the Rising Sun and Tumbling Bear: A Military History of the Russo-Japanese War 1904–5* (Routledge, London: 1988) pp 223–4.

28. A Ignatyev, *A Subaltern in Old Russia* (Hutchinson & Co, London: 1944) p 239.

29. Letter to Sophie Mannerheim, 22 January 1905, in Jägerskiöld, *Nuori Mannerheim*, p 335.

30. Hugo Backmansson, quoted in Screen, *Mannerheim: The Years of Preparation*, p 45.

31. Letter to Carl Robert Mannerheim, 2 April 1905, quoted in Jägerskiöld, *Nuori Mannerheim*, pp 340–1.

32. Letter to Sophie Mannerheim, 20 March 1905, quoted in Jägerskiöld, *Nuori Mannerheim*, p 339.

33. Letter to Sophie Mannerheim, 19 April 1905, quoted in Jägerskiöld, *Nuori Mannerheim*, p 341.

34. Vlasov, *Mannerheim: upseeri ja tutkimusmatkailija*, p 57.

35. Mannerheim, *Päiväkirja Japanin Sodasta*, pp 134–5; letter to Carl Robert Mannerheim, 20 March/2 April 1905, in ibid, pp 161–2.

36. E Selle, *Donald of China* (Harper and Brothers, New York: 1948) pp 27–8. The journalist was William Donald, who one

day would become the chief adviser to Zhang Zuolin, the Marshal of Manchuria.

37. Letter to Eva Mannerheim Sparre, 28 April 1905, in Jägerskiöld, *Nuori Mannerheim*, pp 347–8.

4. The Tournament of Shadows

1. L Seaman, *From Tokio through Manchuria with the Japanese* (D Appleton and Company, New York: 1905) pp 69–70. Notably, in *Across Asia*, 26 June 1908, p 763, Mannerheim mentions three years later in a Chinese monastery that he is a man from Finland, only for a nearby Buddhist to exclaim, 'Aha, the government that refused to send soldiers to the Russo-Japanese war.' Considering Mannerheim's role in the war: it must have been tempting indeed for him to break cover and argue the point, but he seems to have controlled his feelings.

2. Letter to Sophie Mannerheim, 8/21 June 1905, quoted in Mannerheim, *Päiväkirja Japanin Sodasta*, pp 177–8.

3. Letter to Sophie Mannerheim, 8/21 June 1905, in Mannerheim, *Päiväkirja Japanin Sodasta*, p 179.

4. Jägerskiöld, *Nuori Mannerheim*, p 358.

5. Balmont, 'Nash Tsar'. The poem is prominent enough in Balmont's work to be reprinted in its entirety on his page in the Russian Wikipedia.

6. J Forsyth, *A History of the Peoples of Siberia: Russia's North Asian Colony 1581–1990* (Cambridge University Press, Cambridge: 1992) p 187. Clearly, the direct translation of *Japanese Emperor* had somehow transformed to *Japan Khan* in Central Asia, and hence to *Yapon-kan*.

7. Screen, *Mannerheim: The Early Years*, p 52.

8. T Bergroth, 'A Life in Uniform', in M Norrback (ed), *A Gentleman's Home: The Museum of Gustaf Mannerheim, Marshal of Finland* (Otava, Helsinki: 2001) p 62.

9. Mannerheim, *Memoirs*, p 27.

10. S Hedin, *My Life as an Explorer* (National Geographic Adventure Classics, Washington: 2003) p 1.

11. Hedin, *My Life as an Explorer*, p 2.

12. Hedin, *My Life as an Explorer*, p 32.
13. Mannerheim, *Across Asia*, 20 July 1906, p 18. Possibly to shield the still living Pelliot from Mannerheim's excoriating complaints, perhaps even out of sheer spite, Pelliot was not mentioned in editions of the book printed before 2007.
14. Being called 'a voyager with American airs', would have sent Mannerheim into conniptions if he were ever unfortunate enough to hear it – fortunately, it appears that he did not. P Pelliot, *Carnets de Route, 1906–1908* (Les Indes Savantes, Paris: 2008) pp 17, 349. There are 35 references to Mannerheim in Pelliot's travel diary, which make for a fascinating comparison with the Pelliot material restored to the revised edition of *Across Asia*. Mannerheim in *Across Asia*, 18 July 1906, p 15, does not seem to have registered that he had ruined Pelliot's attempts to ingratiate himself with the emir's son Mahmoud. Curiously, Mannerheim does not seem to have registered that Mahmoud was dressed incongruously in the uniform of a Russian military officer. Or, if he did, he does not mention it in his diary, perhaps for fear that he might draw attention to his own knowledge by noticing. Mannerheim makes a brief cameo in P Flandrin's *Les Sept Vies du mandarin français: Paul Pelliot ou la passion de l'Orient* (Éditions du Rocher, Monaco: 2008) pp 127–9, a gripping biography of Pelliot that pushes the bold, but not entirely unjustifiable thesis that, in the words of Charles Nouette, 'It was without doubt the first time that [the local Chinese] have met a European with an erudition and knowledge of their classics comparable to the most qualified men of letters among them.' The Chinese saw things differently, and eventually erected a placard in Dunhuang denouncing Pelliot as a thief. Flandrin contextualises Pelliot's growing belief during his travels that he was the best qualified man to examine the antiquities of Central Asia, but that he had arrived too late, to find the region already 'defiled' by 'visitors, spies, explorers, adventurers' and other philistines, among whose number he most certainly had begun to count Mannerheim.

15. Mannerheim, *Across Asia*, 29 July 1906, pp 24–5; Pelliot, *Carnets de Route*, p 19.

16. Pelliot, *Carnets de Route*, 10 August 1906, pp 22–4.

17. Mannerheim, *Across Asia*, 11 August 1906, p 30.

18. Mannerheim, *Across Asia*, 12 and 14 August 1906, pp 31, 36. Pelliot thought the reverse, that two of the Cossacks were Mannerheim's and that the other three were his. Pelliot, *Carnets de Route*, p 29.

19. Mannerheim, *Across Asia*, 15 August 1906, p 37. Pelliot, *Carnets de Route*, p 29. Pelliot does not mention Nouette's presence in the hunting party, nor does he give any indication that the trip was unsuccessful.

20. Pelliot, *Carnets de Route*, 21 August 1906, p 36.

21. Pelliot, *Carnets de Route*, 21 August 1906, p 36. For Mannerheim's version of events, see the entry for the preceding day in *Across Asia*, p 47.

22. Mannerheim, *Across Asia*, 19 August 1906, pp 45–6. Also Mannerheim, *Memoirs*, p 31, in which he erroneously refers to the *tomocha* game as a *baiga* (i.e. horse race). Needless to say, Pelliot saw things very differently, admitting that the locals suffered him to have the goatskin, but claiming that a rouble was actually a gesture of honour, since most other players only received 10 kopecks (a tenth of the value). Nor does he make any claim of personal prowess, regarding his horseback victory as a charade *'par politesse'*, allowed by indulgent hosts. He makes no mention of Mannerheim's greater success at the game. Pelliot, *Carnets de Route*, p 34.

23. Pelliot, *Carnets de Route*, 22 August 1906, p 38; Mannerheim, *Across Asia*, p 49.

24. Pelliot, *Carnets de Route*, 21 August 1906, p 36. Naturally, Mannerheim saw things differently, and thought that the Frenchmen had already been adding unreasonable charges to his board.

25. Pelliot, *Carnets de Route*, 26 August 1906, pp 44, 46; Mannerheim waits until 28 August before giving his own account of their dispute, which matches Pelliot's almost word-for-word: *Across Asia*, pp 55–6.

26. Mannerheim, *Across Asia*, 31 August 1906, pp 60–1. Pelliot had been behaving like this, perhaps initially without realising, for several weeks. As early as 15 August 1906, he records himself discussing the origins of mankind with a local dignitary in the languages of 'Kirghiz mixed with a bit of Russian' while 'Mannerheim retired to his tent'. However, Pelliot does not openly reveal his own feelings until 21 August, when he vents in his diary about Mannerheim's standoffish behaviour. Pelliot, *Carnets de Route*, pp 28, 36.

27. Mannerheim, *Across Asia*, 28 September 1906, p 66.

28. Mannerheim, *Across Asia*, 9 October 1906, p 71. References to Mannerheim in Pelliot's *Carnets de Route* hereafter are limited to occasional notes on his location on the Silk Road. In August 1907 (p 156), etiquette obliged Pelliot to accept a gift on Mannerheim's behalf, which he did grudgingly. Pelliot notes the receipt of letters from Mannerheim, on pp 102, 169 and 332, the second of which was apparently *'fort amiable'*. He also archly refers to 'an enigmatic dispatch asking for our news', sent to him from Mannerheim in Lanzhou (p 311 and in a letter, p 385). A letter from Nouette to Vaillant on 27 September 1907 (also included in the *Carnets de Route* on p 434) has Pelliot commandeering some 23 taels of Chinese money that Mannerheim has left in Urumqi. This may have been the closest that Pelliot came to receiving his 'subvention'.

29. Letter to Carl Robert Mannerheim, 14 June 1908, quoted in S Jägerskiöld, *Gustaf Mannerheim 1906–1917* (Otava, Helsinki: 1965) p 89. The odd juxtaposition of the 'Bible' (i.e. Old Testament) and 'New Testament' is present in Mannerheim's original text.

30. Mannerheim, *Memoirs*, p 33.

31. Mannerheim, *Across Asia*, 29 October 1906, p 83. A month later, in Pelliot's *Carnets de Route* for 5 December 1906, (p 91 and in a letter, p 365), Pelliot takes evident pleasure in meeting a local man who had been hired by Mannerheim, but released from duty after only eight hours when it became clear that Mannerheim was ill. He refers to him as Monsieur

Kouo (Guo?) – this seems to tally with the account from *Across Asia*.

32. Mannerheim, *Across Asia*, 25 January 1907, p 129 notes the end of Liu's complaints, which seem to have begun on 6 October 1906, *Across Asia*, p 69.

33. Mannerheim, *Across Asia*, 19 November 1906, p 91. The presumed quote from Confucius is from *Analects*, Book VII, verse 8: 'There is no point in teaching those who do not wish to learn nor in helping those who do not ask for it. If I present one corner of a subject, and my students cannot deduce the other three, I do not repeat my lesson.' Mannerheim returned to Yarkand and spent Christmas with Raquette, during which time he found out that one of his Chinese servants had absconded with most of his supplies, stolen from the other servants and sold off what he could. However, he only discovered this when Liu the interpreter was late for a rendezvous. On questioning Liu, Mannerheim discovered that the mandarin whose troops he had previously ridiculed had pursued the robber, arrested him and used his own money to buy back most of the stolen goods. Furthermore, the mandarin had ordered Liu not to tell Mannerheim of the incident, preferring to spend his own money in order to preserve the harmony of Mannerheim's trip, and the appearance of Khotan as a law-abiding society. Mannerheim, *Across Asia*, 19 December 1906, p 124.

34. Mannerheim, *Across Asia*, 21 November 1906, p .93.

35. Mannerheim, *Across Asia*, 10 December 1906, p 114.

5. A Horse Reaches China

1. Pelliot, letter of 8 February 1908, *Carnets de Route*, p 253.

2. Mannerheim, *Across Asia*, 27 January 1907, p 134; Mannerheim, *Memoirs*, p 33. At the time, Mannerheim believed it meant 'Horse Leaping Through Clouds', which it did not. The saga of Mannerheim's Chinese name, which is rivalled in complexity only by its futility, is dealt with in painstaking detail in my Note on Names.

3. Letter to Carl Robert Mannerheim, 14 January 1907, quoted in Jägerskiöld, *Gustaf Mannerheim 1906–1917*, p 61; also Lehmusoksa, *Dining with Marshal Mannerheim*, p 100.

4. Mannerheim, *Across Asia*, 4 February 1907, p 143.

5. Mannerheim, *Across Asia*, 8 February 1907, p 151.

6. Mannerheim, *Across Asia*, 13 February 1907, p 159.

7. See, for example, the arguments of Di Renjie in the Tang dynasty, in J Clements, *Wu: The Chinese Empress who Schemed, Seduced and Murdered her Way to Become a Living God* (Sutton Publishing, Stroud: 2007) pp 168–9.

8. Mannerheim, *Across Asia*, 4 March 1907, p 189.

9. Mannerheim, *Across Asia*, 30 Marcy 1907, p 212.

10. Mannerheim, *Across Asia*, 3 May 1907, p 253. H Halén's *An Analytical Index to C.G. Mannerheim's Across Asia from West to East in 1906–1908* (Finno-Ugrian Society, Helsinki: 2004) p 127, offers Zhao as the Pinyin romanisation of the Swedish *Tchao* from Mannerheim's original text. It is romanised as *Chao* in Halén, since he is using the Wade-Giles system there, and not the Pinyin system I have employed in this book.

11. P Hopkirk, *Foreign Devils on the Silk Road: The Search for the Lost Treasures of Central Asia* (John Murray, London: 1980) p 181, places Pelliot at Kucha for 'eight months' in 1907. Mannerheim knew exactly where Pelliot was, and plainly could not be bothered to stop by. Mannerheim and Pelliot remained in touch by letter, and fragments of their correspondence are preserved in Jägerskiöld, *Gustaf Mannerheim 1906–1917*, pp 74–7.

12. Mannerheim, *Across Asia*, 26 May 1907, p 280.

13. Mannerheim, *Across Asia*, 28 July 1907, p 348. Mannerheim seems to have been told about the prescribed mourning period, which is usually given as '25 months' in order to meet the notion of spanning three calendar years. However, courtesy of the usual confused interpreting, Mannerheim misunderstood and assumed that the dignitary would be retiring *in* 25 months, as if the mother's death was already scheduled!

14. Mannerheim, *Across Asia*, 30 July 1907, p 352. For the matter of the Oulu-Tornio railway line, see Polvinen, *Imperial Borderland*, pp 179–80.
15. Mannerheim, *Across Asia*, 9 August 1907, pp 357–8.
16. Mannerheim, *Across Asia*, 28 October 1907, p 438. The cook is not named, but since he is the 'new cook', it was presumably Chang, first mentioned at Santai on 1 September.
17. Mannerheim, *Across Asia*, 9 December 1907, p.488. Mannerheim successfully bought the man's forgiveness with a bribe, but was rightly embarrassed at his mistake.
18. Mannerheim, *Across Asia*, 20 November 1907, pp 463–4.
19. Hopkirk, *Foreign Devils on the Silk Road*, p 184.
20. H Halén, 'Baron Mannerheim's hunt for ancient Central Asian manuscripts', in P Koskikallio, and Aslo Lehmuskallio (eds), *C.G. Mannerheim in Central Asia 1906–1908* (National Board of Antiquities, Helsinki: 1999) p 50. Compare to the slightly different reading of the passage in Mannerheim, *Memoirs*, p 55 – Halén argues this is a mistranslation from the original Swedish. Dunhuang certainly receives only cursory treatment in Mannerheim's letter of 17 February 1908 to Otto Donner of the Finno-Ugrian Society, in which he dismisses its ruins in a single sentence. See Halén, 'C.G. Mannerheims brev til senator Otto Donner från Kina', in Koskikallio and Lehmuskallio (eds) *C.G. Mannerheim in Central Asia 1906–1908*, p 60.
21. Mannerheim, *Across Asia*, 20 November 1907, p 464.
22. Mannerheim, *Across Asia*, 22 November 1907, p 466.
23. Mannerheim, *Across Asia*, 29 November 1907, p 474. From this point, Mannerheim begins injecting a lot of basic Chinese into his diary. The vocabulary implies that he is learning enough to pre-empt his interpreter on many occasions. He seems proud that he is able to translate for himself the Suzhou brigadier's *bu hao* ('Not good') appraisal of Russian troops, and insists on calling a cart a *xiao che* (literally, 'little chariot'). Such fragments of vocabulary recur with increasing fluency, so that by Xi'an his notes are often all but impenetrable to a reader who does not also speak

Chinese. Early errors are also preserved in *Across Asia*.
At the Jiayuguan road marker, for example, Mannerheim
mistranslated *xiong*, 'strongest/greatest', as its homonym
'strict'. He also claimed Jiayuguan was built in the reign of
the 'Emperor Ming', rather than in the reign of the 'Ming
Emperors' – i.e. during the Ming dynasty, *c* 1372. He similarly
confuses dynasties with Emperors' names on several later
occasions in China. However, by the time he is in Luoyang
on 26 May 1908, he clearly understands appreciably more
of what his guides are telling him. He even recounts a basic
version of the city's brief period as a capital for Empress Wu
during her short-lived Zhou dynasty in the late 8th century,
although since Luoyang was also a capital in the *original*
Zhou dynasty some 2,000 years earlier, there is still some
confusion – *Across Asia*, p 722.

24. Mannerheim, *Across Asia*, 6 December 1907, p 479.
25. 'Chinese New Year's Day was celebrated a day or two after
our arrival.' Mannerheim arrived on 29 January. Chinese
New Year in 1908 fell on 2 February. Mannerheim, *Across
Asia*, 28 February 1908, p 566.
26. Mannerheim, *Across Asia*, 28 February 1908, p 571.
27. Mannerheim, *Across Asia*, 28 February 1908, p 578.
28. Mannerheim, *Across Asia*, 3 March 1908, p 585.
29. Mannerheim, *Across Asia*, 17 March 1908, p 597.
30. Mannerheim, *Memoirs*, p 61.
31. Mannerheim, *Memoirs*, p 63.
32. Mannerheim, *Across Asia*, 27 March 1908, p 625
33. Mannerheim, *Across Asia*, 28 April 1908, p 669. For the end
of mapping, see Halén, *Analytical Index*, p 153.
34. Mannerheim, *Across Asia*, 10 May 1908, p 687. Reading
Mannerheim's 'Pa-san-kung' (p 691), as *Ba xian gong* –
Temple of the Eight Immortals. The other locations are listed
in Halén's *Analytical Index*.
35. He was at the Famen temple on 24 April 1908. On 15 May,
after a night in Lintong, he rode past the burial mound of the
First Emperor, within half a mile of the site of the Terracotta
Army.

6. The Paper Dragons

1. Mannerheim, *Across Asia*, p 806.
2. Norman, *Holder of the White Lotus*, p 343.
3. Vlasov, *Mannerheim: upseeri ja tutkimusmatkailija*, p 89.
4. Mannerheim, *Memoirs*, p 71.
5. Vlasov, *Mannerheim: upseeri ja tutkimusmatkailija*, p 91,
   implies that Mannerheim and Arseniev journeyed by land
   down the Shandong peninsula. Although this is possible,
   it seems more likely that they took a ship from Tianjin to
   Zhifu. Curiously, although Arseniev, Kyoto and Shimonoseki
   are all mentioned in Mannerheim's *Memoirs* in English, p 71,
   they are dropped from the mass-market Finnish account,
   *Suomen Marsalkan Muistelmat [Memoirs of Finland's
   Marshal]* (Otava, Helsinki: 1954; reprint 2004) p 32, even
   though there is no indication in the latter that it is abridged.
6. Letter to Carl Robert Mannerheim, 13 September 1908,
   quoted in Jägerskiöld, *Gustaf Mannerheim*, pp 96–7. A
   very similar comment is recorded in Brantberg, *Tsaarin
   upseeri*, p 271, except Mannerheim supposedly says it
   directly to Arseniev. Vlasov, *Mannerheim: upseeri ja
   tutkimusmatkailija*, p 91, has the same letter, but oddly
   replaces 'bandy-legged' with 'slant-eyed' in his translation.
   Brantberg has a different itinerary for Mannerheim's Japan
   trip, suggesting that he travelled *together* with Arseniev, and
   that while in Kyoto the two men visited the Phoenix Hall
   (presumably the Byōdō-in) and the Nijō palace/castle. I have
   corrected the spelling of 'Yeiko Maru', a meaningless term
   that quaintly preserves Arseniev's Russian accent, to *Eikō
   Maru*, a Japanese ship's name: *Glorious Radiance*.
7. See, for example, J Clements, *Marco Polo* (Haus Publishing,
   London: 2006) pp 91–7.
8. Vlasov, *Mannerheim: upseeri ja tutkimusmatkailija*, p 92.
9. D Wells (ed), *Russian Views of Japan 1792–1913: An
   Anthology of Travel Writing* (Routledge/Curzon, London:
   2004) p 206.
10. Vlasov, *Mannerheim: upseeri ja tutkimusmatkailija*, p 93.
11. Vlasov, *Mannerheim: upseeri ja tutkimusmatkailija*, p 93.

12. Vlasov, *Mannerheim: upseeri ja tutkimusmatkailija*, p 94. In fact, we now know that the closest the the Japanese would come to a rematch with Russia was the Siberian Expedition of 1918–22 when the Japanese formed a large part of a multinational force sent into the Russian East, supposedly to support the last of the Tsarist forces against the Bolsheviks.

13. Vlasov calls it 'koori', seemingly unaware that *kōri* is simply Japanese for ice. Mannerheim presumably bought a snow cone, or *kakekōri* from a vendor, and got a direct and slightly misleading answer when he asked what it was. Similarly Mannerheim dined that day on a fish which he knew only by its Japanese name *tai* (red sea bream), as well as Chinese pork and peaches.

14. Vlasov, *Mannerheim: upseeri ja tutkimusmatkailija*, p 93, makes the unlikely claim that the men met at the Sannoin, which is in a relatively remote spot on Mount Kōya. But he adds that the location was also known as the Temple of the Thousand-armed Buddha, which is an alternate title for the Rengeō-in, also known as the Hall of the Lotus King, and as Sanjūsangendō. It is surely more likely that the men met at Sanjūsangendō, which is within walking distance of both Kyoto station and a temple called the Chion-in, to which Mannerheim strolled after their parting.

15. Mannerheim, *Kirjeitä*, p 78.

16. Letter to Sophie Mannerheim, October 1908, in Mannerheim, *Kirjeitä*, p 78.

17. Mannerheim, *Memoirs*, p 72. Strangely, Vlasov, *Mannerheim: upseeri ja tutkimusmatkailija*, p 97, recounts the same meeting, with a number of chatty, incidental details, including the claim that the Tsar spent the entire meeting seated, which is in direct contradiction of Mannerheim's version of events.

18. Screen, *Mannerheim: The Years of Preparation*, p 79.

19. Mannerheim, *Predvaritel'nyy otchet*, quoted in Screen, *Mannerheim: The Years of Preparation*, p 79.

20. Mannerheim, *Memoirs*, p 77.

21. Letter to Frederik Lindström, 3 March 1909, in H Halén and Bent Lerbæk Pederson, *C.G. Mannerheim's Chinese Pantheon: Materials for an Iconography of Chinese Folk Religion* (Finno-Ugrian Society, Helsinki: 1993). As a result of the Finnish committee's lack of interest and Mannerheim's refusal to allow the drawings to become a 'Russian' academic publication, they remained in his possession and were eventually donated to the Finno-Ugrian Society with his other Asian papers in 1937.
22. Mannerheim, *Memoirs*, p 78.
23. Lehmusoksa, *Dining with Marshal Mannerheim*, p 108.
24. Mannerheim, *Memoirs*, p 80.
25. Screen, *Mannerheim: The Years of Preparation*, p 102.
26. Mannerheim, *Memoirs*, p 87.
27. Letter to Marie Lubomirska, 4 December 1914, in Mannerheim, *Kirjeitä*, p 109. The same events are recounted in Mannerheim, *Memoirs*, p 88.
28. Halén and Pedersen, *C.G. Mannerheim's Chinese Pantheon*, p 6; Norman, *Holder of the White Lotus*, p 348.
29. Mannerheim, *Memoirs*, p 88.
30. Mannerheim, *Memoirs*, p 97.
31. Mannerheim, *Memoirs*, p 107.
32. Screen, *Mannerheim: The Finnish Years* (C. Hurst & Co, London: 2000) p 9.

7. The End of Empire

1. Mannerheim, *Memoirs*, p 110.
2. Mannerheim, *Memoirs*, p 112.
3. Mannerheim, *Memoirs*, p 113.
4. Mannerheim regarded the route Petrograd-Moscow-Brest as so self-evident that he does not bother to explain it in his *Memoirs*; many abridged versions of his account also drop the fact that he went to Moscow *on his way back to the Romanian front*. Hence, readers of some sources may be confused by his sudden decision to run for Moscow in the midst of the Revolution, when in fact, as noted in

Jägerskiöld, *Gustaf Mannerheim 1906–1917*, p 373, he was simply returning to work by the most convenient route.

5. Mannerheim, *Memoirs*, p 116.
6. Jägerskiöld, *Gustaf Mannerheim 1906–1917*, p 329.
7. Mannerheim, *Memoirs*, p 120.
8. Mannerheim, *Memoirs*, p 122.
9. Mannerheim, *Memoirs*, p 130.
10. A Upton, *The Finnish Revolution 1917–1918* (University of Minnesota Press, Minneapolis: 1980) p 49.
11. Upton, *The Finnish Revolution*, p 125.
12. Mannerheim, *Memoirs*, p 133.
13. Mannerheim, *Memoirs*, p 133.

8. The White Devil

1. R Luckett, *The White Generals: The White Movement and the Russian Civil War* (Longman, London: 1971) p 136.
2. Luckett, *The White Generals*, p 133.
3. Upton, *The Finnish Revolution*, p 386.
4. Upton, *The Finnish Revolution*, p 378.
5. Jägerskiöld, *Mannerheim: Marshal of Finland*, p 58. This controversial boast, made without government authorisation, would return to haunt Mannerheim during the Continuation War, when Finnish troops conquered East Karelia. See M Baryshnikov, *Mannerheim Without the Mask 1940–1944* (Johan Beckman Institute, Helsinki: 2005) pp 206–7.
6. Upton, *The Finnish Revolution*, p 388. Sveaborg is now better known by the name it was given in 1918, *Suomenlinna* (Fortress of Finland).
7. Screen, *Mannerheim: The Finnish Years*, p 25.
8. Letter from Sophie Mannerheim, 25 February 1918, quoted in Upton, *The Finnish Revolution*, p 316.
9. V Kilpi, quoted in Upton, *The Finnish Revolution*, p 317.
10. Upton, *The Finnish Revolution*, p 317.
11. Upton, *The Finnish Revolution*, p 314.
12. Upton, *The Finnish Revolution*, p 316.
13. Thesleff, quoted in Upton, *The Finnish Revolution*, p 473.

14. Letter to Sophie Mannerheim, 19 April 1918, in Mannerheim, *Kirjeitä*, p 176.
15. Upton, *The Finnish Revolution*, p 492.
16. Upton, *The Finnish Revolution*, p 511.
17. Upton, *The Finnish Revolution*, p 519.
18. Upton, *The Finnish Revolution*, p 527.

9. The House of the Four Winds

1. Upton, *The Finnish Revolution*, p 528.
2. Ibid.
3. Mannerheim, *Memoirs*, p 181.
4. Mannerheim, *Memoirs*, p 182.
5. Upton, *The Finnish Revolution*, p 534.
6. Mannerheim, *Memoirs*, pp 182–3. Mannerheim (or rather his amanuensis using official documents) 'remembers' the incident as occurring on 30 May 1918, although that was the date that his resignation was made public. If he did leave a council chamber while the politicians remained disrespectfully seated and silent, he did so on 29 May. See Screen, *Mannerheim: The Finnish Years*, p 41.
7. Upton, *The Finnish Revolution*, p 534.
8. Mannerheim, *Memoirs*, p 184.
9. Esme Howard, British minister in Stockholm, to the Foreign Office, 13 July 1918. FO 371/3206, 123376/144/56.
10. Letter to Kitty Linder, 30 December 1918, quoted in Screen, *Mannerheim: The Finnish Years*, p 87.
11. Mannerheim, *Memoirs*, pp 186–7.
12. Mannerheim, *Memoirs*, p 192.
13. Mannerheim, *Memoirs*, p 210.
14. Bergroth, 'A Life in Uniform', p 67.
15. Mannerheim, *Memoirs*, p 212.
16. Screen, *Mannerheim: The Finnish Years*, p 64.
17. Mannerheim, *Memoirs*, p 225.
18. Meri, *Suomen Marsalkka*, p 172.
19. Warner, *Marshal Mannerheim and the Finns*, p 100; R Brantberg, *Mannerheim: Sotamarsalkka 1918–1940 [The Field*

Marshal] (Kustannusosakeyhtiö Revontuli, Tampere: 2005) p 75.

20. Mannerheim, *Memoirs*, p 232.
21. V von Fersen, 'The Humanitarian Work of Baron Gustaf Mannerheim', in Norrback, *A Gentleman's Home*, p 117.
22. Letter to Johan Mannerheim, 18 February 1925, in *Kirjeitä*, p 218. Long afterwards in 1936, the contending child welfare organisations were obliged to form a loose union; see Screen, *Mannerheim: The Finnish Years*, p 96.
23. Mannerheim, *Memoirs*, p 251.
24. According to a French observer, Mannerheim was somehow exempt from the Finnish national prohibition on alcohol. See Lehmusoksa, *Dining With Marshal Mannerheim*, p 165.
25. Screen, *Mannerheim: The Finnish Years*, p 102.
26. Screen, *Mannerheim: The Finnish Years*, p 100. The protestation that the post sounded 'too warlike' is not as daft as it might appear. A Field Marshal in Finnish is a *Sotamarsalkka*, literally a 'War Marshal'.
27. Lehmusoksa, *Dining With Marshal Mannerheim*, pp 164–5. The name makes no reference to the John Buchan novel *House of the Four Winds*, which was not published until 1935, two years after Mannerheim had sold the café.

10. The Jaws of Peril

1. Mannerheim, *Memoirs*, p 265.
2. Letter to Georg Gripenberg, 21 March 1933, in *Kirjeitä*, p 237.
3. Letter to Hannes Ignatius, 1932, quoted in Jägerskiöld, *Mannerheim: Marshal of Finland*, p 87.
4. Letter to Marie Lubomirska, 9 November 1921, in Screen, *Mannerheim: The Finnish Years*, p 70.
5. Screen, *Mannerheim: The Finnish Years*, p 111.
6. Mannerheim, quoted in Jägerskiöld, *Mannerheim: Marshal of Finland*, p 101.
7. Screen, *Mannerheim: The Finnish Years*, p 89. Such cosmetic allegations do not appear to have made their way into Finnish accounts, but were a matter of some discussion between the British diplomat Duff Cooper's wife, Diana, and

her friend Brendan Bracken. Far from being a sign of vanity in Mannerheim, the story surely demonstrates how eager he was to maintain at all times an impeccable, spry public image, even when tortured by a lifetime of injuries.

8. Mannerheim, *Memoirs*, p 305.
9. Mannerheim, *Memoirs*, p 312.
10. Letter to Kyösti Kallio, 27 November 1939, in Mannerheim, *Memoirs*, p 319.
11. Warner, *Marshal Mannerheim and the Finns*, p 146.
12. W Trotter, *The Winter War: The Russo-Finnish War of 1939–40* (Aurum, London: 2003) pp 201–2.
13. Mannerheim, *Memoirs*, p 324.
14. Trotter, *The Winter War*, pp 72–3.
15. Trotter, *The Winter War*, p 157. Lieutenant Virkki is the only man in history known to have defeated a tank with a pistol, as the Soviet driver, rightly suspecting that another Finn might be sneaking up on him with a satchel charge, eventually turned and ran.
16. Trotter, *The Winter War*, p 109.
17. Trotter, *The Winter War*, p 191.
18. W Citrine, *My Finnish Diary* (Penguin Books, Harmondsworth: 1940) p 105.
19. Warner, *Marshal Mannerheim and the Finns*, p 150.
20. Trotter, *The Winter War*, p 201.
21. W Churchill, 'House of Many Mansions', speech broadcast on 20 January 1940.

11. The Eye of the Storm

1. H Denham, *Inside the Nazi Ring: A Naval Attaché in Sweden 1940–1945* (John Murray, London: 1984) p 77.
2. Mannerheim, Order of the Day No. 34, 14 March 1940, quoted in Jägerskiöld, *Mannerheim: Marshal of Finland*, p 127.
3. Mannerheim, Order of the Day No. 34, 14 March 1940, quoted in Screen, *Mannerheim: The Finnish Years*, p 159.
4. Mannerheim, *Memoirs*, p 399.
5. Mannerheim, *Memoirs*, p 409.

6. Jägerskiöld, *Mannerheim: Marshal of Finland*, p 139. However, Screen, *Mannerheim: The Finnish Years*, p 173, says quite the opposite, and that Mannerheim *encouraged* the formation of the battalion in order to promote Finnish interests in Germany. He did, however, immediately ask to have the Finns back at the beginning of the Continuation War, and refused to authorise the creation of another Nazi battalion in 1943 at the end of their enlistment. The Finnish battalion received high praise from Heinrich Himmler, who commented in his Order of the Day, 11 July 1943, 'Where a Finnish SS man stood, the enemy was always defeated.'

7. Letter from Winston Churchill, 29 November 1941, quoted in Mannerheim, *Memoirs*, p 435.

8. Letter to Winston Churchill, 2 December 1941, quoted in Mannerheim, *Memoirs*, p 436.

9. Letter to Eva Mannerheim Sparre, 7 August 1941, in *Kirjeitä*, p 320.

10. Baryshnikov, *Mannerheim Without the Mask*, p 63.

11. Letter to Eva Mannerheim Sparre, 13 May 1942, in *Kirjeitä*, pp 324–5.

12. Mannerheim, *Memoirs*, p 450.

13. Mannerheim, *Memoirs*, pp 451–3; Lehmusoksa, *Dining with Marshal Mannerheim*, p 260. Hitler's visit cannot have been that much of a 'surprise', as his vegetarian menu had been prepared by Mannerheim's staff. He was certainly, however, the last person Mannerheim would have wanted to see. For the medical after-effects, see Screen, *Mannerheim: The Finnish Years*, p 191. In a letter to Eva Mannerheim Sparre, *Kirjeitä*, p 336, Mannerheim confesses that the skin on his hands had troubled him in cold weather since his time in Manchuria.

14. Mannerheim, *Memoirs*, p 453.

15. Mannerheim, *Memoirs*, p 456.

16. Mannerheim, *Memoirs*, p 491.

17. Letter to Adolf Hitler, 2 September 1944, in Baryshnikov, *Mannerheim Without the Mask*, p 221.

18. Letter to Adolf Hitler, 2 September 1944, in Mannerheim, *Memoirs*, p 495. This is the same letter as that in Baryshnikov, Note 17 above, but a different translation.

12. Marski

1. Letter to Eva Mannerheim Sparre, June 1945, quoted in *Kirjeitä*, p 340.
2. Mannerheim, speech of 7 April 1945, quoted in Screen, *Mannerheim: The Finnish Years*, pp 220–1.
3. Screen, *Mannerheim: The Finnish Years*, p 236.
4. Mannerheim, *Memoirs*, p 512–13.
5. Mannerheim, *Memoirs*, p 240.
6. Screen, *Mannerheim: The Finnish Years*, p 247.
7. Letter to Andrée von Nottbeck, 19 May 1947, quoted in Screen, *Mannerheim: The Finnish Years*, p 245.
8. Fagerholm, speech of 4 February 1951, quoted in Screen, *Mannerheim: The Finnish Years*, p 254.

Note on Names

1. Mannerheim, 21 March 1907, *Across Asia*, p 203.
2. Mannerheim, 12 December 1907, *Across Asia*, p 495.
3. Lehmusoksa, *Dining with Marshal Mannerheim*, p 103.

Sources and Further Reading

Although Mannerheim's name is on the cover of his *Memoirs*, the ailing ex-President left much of the first draft to his assistants and only then made amendments to their text. Consequently, the book offers blunt, dispassionate recitations of facts and summaries of official reports, and lacks much of Mannerheim's personal charm. Mannerheim's *Memoirs* blandly record that he ran wartime operations out of his headquarters in Mikkeli, but one has to go there in person to spot the copy of Homer's *Odyssey* on his bookshelves, crammed in among the maps and troop manifests. There is little indication in the *Memoirs* of the prankster who once impersonated a Chinese mandarin to entertain nurses in Manchuria, or of the homesick youth who travelled for two days in order to surprise his family on Christmas Eve disguised as Santa Claus.

His *Memoirs*, then, could be considered as merely approved by, rather than 'written' by its putative author, and also contains errors – the aged Mannerheim's memories of his military service have him promoted to captain two years early, for example, and mis-date his arrival in Manchuria by a whole month, despite extant documentation to the contrary. Some incidents, such as the departure of his cook Ismail in Urumqi, are faithfully copied from his diaries; others, such as the re-hiring of Ismail only a couple of days later, are ignored. There are other slips in later life. Mannerheim made the baffling claim to Walter Citrine that he had 'missed the Boxer Rebellion' only because he was coming back home for his wedding – a strange comment to be made by a man who was not only already married at the time, but quartered in St Petersburg as an equestrian specialist. The *Memoirs* also appear to exist in slightly different forms; Finns could be forgiven for assuming that a version in their mother tongue is the most complete, but the Finnish mass-market edition of the *Memoirs* (itself a translation from Mannerheim's original Swedish) drops many incidental details that are to be found in the English version.

Mannerheim destroyed some of his correspondence in 1944 (a controversial decision that has led to much conjecture about his dealings with the Germans), and more still in 1948, when he feared that Helsinki would be next after the Communist coup in Prague. Luckily, his relatives among the Jägerskiölds, von Julins, Mannerheims and Lovéns treasured and preserved the letters they had received from him, allowing us a rich vein of primary source material. The mother lode for many Mannerheim studies, sometimes at one or two places removed, is the massive eight-volume biography by the late Stig Jägerskiöld. The work of a relative with direct access to these family archives, it is available in both Finnish and Swedish and tells Mannerheim's story in a chiefly epistolary format.

Even when researchers do not lean on Jägerskiöld, they are often steered by his decisions. Jägerskiöld was the editor of Mannerheim's published correspondence, and hence is often responsible not only for what is repeated by most other authors, but also for what is not. Jägerskiöld is so central to Mannerheim studies that readers of many books often assume that any unidentified pieces of data comes from his works, which are oft quoted but, sadly, seldom cited. Such a lack of adequate referencing has, I believe, allowed some writers to sneak supposition and speculation into their own works in the assumption that readers will believe it has *probably* come from Jägerskiöld. In this book, I have deliberately traced as many quotes as possible back to him, even though I often first encountered them without provenance in the works of others.

Older Finnish and Swedish accounts of Mannerheim are insistently respectful and deferential, and concentrate largely on his military exploits. He is a figure of such massive national importance, that many Finnish authors feel obliged to portray him as entirely free of flaws, mistakes or complaints. This has, in my opinion, backfired, and made many older accounts of this great man seem overly pious and humourless. They can also be too defensive. Much ink has been spilled, in particular, over who did what, why and when in the 1940s, a period when the Germans, Finns and Soviets were all carefully lying to one another, for which extant documents often reflect only partial truths, and where much other evidence has been carefully torched. Mannerheim's testimony at post-war trials, for example, does not entirely match that of his *Memoirs* a few years later, nor the evidence assembled even by a sympathetic biographer like Screen, and certainly not by adversaries.

Modern writing veers more towards the sensational, both in a reflection of the caprices of contemporary readers, and in attempts to humanise a figure held in godlike awe by the older generation. The collapse of the Soviet Union has led to a renewed interest in Mannerheim from Russian authors, particularly Leonid Vlasov, who has thoroughly documented Mannerheim's Russian decades in several books, often using archives and material unavailable before the 1990s. The period also introduced a number of sources that were far less admiring of Mannerheim. Hence, Russian interest has led not only to an exhibition that celebrates his St Petersburg youth, but also to Baryshnikov's persuasive polemic *Mannerheim Without the Mask*, which is heavily critical of many Finnish sources on the Continuation War.

Periods of Mannerheim's life remain unclear. The young Mannerheim was, in modern parlance, the child of a broken home, and seems to have been adept at playing his guardians against each other, judiciously selecting differing facets of the truth in order to placate his long-suffering relatives. There appear, for example, to be several versions of the shenanigans surrounding his graduation from the Nikolayevskoye Cavalry School and subsequent failure to secure an immediate place in the Chevalier Guards. For the prudent Uncle Albert in Helsinki, there was a sob story of Russian prejudice and exclusion. For the more informed godmother Alfhild Cedercreutz Scalon de Coligny, there was a messier and probably truthful tale of drunken excess and plummeting grades, which appears to have been quietly swept under the carpet by his St Petersburg relatives. The School's own records, however, show him graduating second in his class, and popular belief in modern

Finland is that he was simply a poor little Finnish boy who couldn't afford to join the Chevalier Guards straight from college. As for Mannerheim's own memoirs, written six decades after the incident, they disagree with all of the above!

Mannerheim's service in Poland, from late 1889 to early 1891, is largely a blank in his record, supposedly because there was precious little to do in Kalisz, and little worth saying about it. The published correspondence, *Kirjeitä*, by chance or design, omits almost every letter Mannerheim wrote in the 1890s; for Mannerheim's wedding, the birth of his children and his estrangement from Anastasie, one must look to quotes included in biographies, not in the published correspondence itself. Similarly, Mannerheim's fortnight in Japan in 1908 is an intriguing void between Zhifu and St Petersburg in his correspondence, although Vlasov has turned up enough information *somewhere* to account for at least a week of it.

Modern publishing has cast around for new approaches on well-worn territory, so that we can now buy an entire book devoted to Mannerheim the big game hunter, a comic about key moments in his life, including his sojourn in India and his ride across Asia, a treatise about his favourite journeys, and even a remarkably informative Mannerheim cookbook. While I was writing this book, the tabloid *Ilta Sanomat* uncovered new photographs of Hitler's 1942 visit from a family photo album, and two separate teams of enthusiastic Finns retraced Mannerheim's ride across Asia for a book, a blog and a special supplement for the broadsheet *Aamulehti*.

Mannerheim's love life is a tangled mess of contradictory information and insinuation. Although separated from Anastasie for 20 years, he remained married in the eyes of the Russian Orthodox Church, and hence discreet in the tradition of the time. By the time he secured a divorce, he was running for political office and fearful of press intrusion, so remained equally secretive thereafter. Vlasov's *Mannerheimin Elämän Naiset* rakes over dozens of possible relationships, but is strangely silent on those that Mannerheim's own archives support. His love letters to Kitty Linder, for example, are a matter of public record, but she is barely mentioned in Vlasov.

This embarrassment of riches is not repeated outside the Nordic languages. Jägerskiold's superb, exhaustive history (which devotes, for example, an entire volume merely to the year 1919), is available in drastically abridged editions in English and French, and the magisterial work by Screen is available in two English volumes which come with detailed bibliographies. Beyond these, the best sources for Mannerheim are those that he genuinely wrote himself.

Originally printed in an extremely limited wartime run of just 500 copies, *Across Asia* was republished in 1960, and latterly in a lavish revision by Harry Halén which restores several previously cut passages. However, as with Mannerheim's mass market *Memoirs*, the 2007 Finnish edition is abridged, dropping 40 per cent of the admittedly repetitive and data-heavy information that can still be found in the 2008 English-language printing. Mannerheim dropped all reference to Paul Pelliot from the original edition, supposedly for security reasons. He also attempted to excise all mentions of the lumbago that all but crippled him on several occasions. Mannerheim thought it unseemly to record his aches and pains in the published version, and this pursuit of a stiff upper lip removed most mention of the agonising twinges that he called his 'witches' arrows' from editions preceding Halén's. Halén has also uncovered and annotated points where Mannerheim was economical with the truth, such as the awkward day when he preferred to go shooting instead of checking out the precious Dunhuang scrolls. Despite a fiddly user interface, interested readers may also enjoy the more compact CD-ROM edition released by a cluster of worthy organisations. This includes 300 pages of *Across Asia* in digital form, along with pictures tagged to the chronology and occasional illuminating Easter eggs that revisit some locations in modern times. Other readily available primary sources include the aforementioned *Kirjeitä* and a separate volume compiling Mannerheim's correspondence and diary entries from the Russo-Japanese War – all, that is, apart from the pages he ripped out in Vladivostok.

This is, it should be emphasised, a book about Mannerheim, and an attempt to introduce the life of an incredible man to a non-Finnish audience. It is, necessarily, all too brief on several wider issues in Finnish society in the 20th century. For a closer analysis of the resistance to Russia, readers are directed to Polvinen's *Imperial Borderland*; for the great complexities of 1918, here reduced to broad strokes of Red and White, I recommend Upton's *The Finnish Revolution*; for Mannerheim's finest hour, when he led the defence of free Finland, Trotter's *The Winter War*.

Aalto, P, *Oriental Studies in Finland 1828–1918* (Societas Scientiarum Fennica, Helsinki: 1971)

Aittokoski, H, 'Finland shaken 100 years ago by murder of Governor-General Bobrikov', in *Helsingin Sanomat*, 15 June 2004

Akashi, M, *Rakka Ryūsui: Colonel Akashi's Report on his Secret Cooperation with the Russian Revolutionary Parties during the Russo-Japanese War* (Studia Historica 31, Helsinki: 1988)

Baryshnikov, M, *Mannerheim Without the Mask 1940–1944* (Johan Beckman Institute, Helsinki: 2005)

Bergroth, T, 'A Life in Uniform', in Norrback, *A Gentleman's Home*, pp 61–79

Borenius, T, *Field-Marshal Mannerheim* (Hutchinson, London: 1940)

Brantberg, R, *Mannerheim: Tsaarin Upseeri [In the Service of the Tsar]* (Kustannusosakeyhtiö Revontuli, Tampere: 2003)

——, *Mannerheim: Valkoinen kenraali 1914–1918 [The White General]* (Kustannusosakeyhtiö Revontuli, Tampere: 2004)

——, *Mannerheim: Sotamarsalkka 1918–1940 [The Field Marshal]* (Kustannusosakeyhtiö Revontuli, Tampere: 2005)

——, *Mannerheim: Ylipäällikkö ja presidentti 1940–1951 [Commander-in-Chief and President]* (Kustannusosakeyhtiö Revontuli, Tampere: 2006)

Brooke, J, *The Volunteers: The Full Story of the British Volunteers in Finland 1939–41* (The Self Publishing Association, Upton-on-Severn: 1990)

Citrine, W, *My Finnish Diary* (Penguin Books, Harmondsworth: 1940)

Clements, J, *Marco Polo* (Haus Publishing, London: 2006)

——, *Wu: The Chinese Empress who Schemed, Seduced and Murdered her Way to Become a Living God* (Sutton Publishing, Stroud: 2007)

Connaughton, R, *The War of the Rising Sun and Tumbling Bear: A Military History of the Russo-Japanese War 1904–5* (Routledge, London: 1988)

Deacon, R, *A History of the Japanese Secret Service* (Frederick Muller Limited, London: 1982)

Denham, H, *Inside the Nazi Ring: A Naval Attaché in Sweden 1940–1945* (John Murray, London: 1984)

Duus, P, *The Abacus and the Sword: The Japanese Penetration of Korea, 1895–1910* (University of California Press, Berkeley: 1995)

von Fersen, V, 'The Humanitarian Work of Baron Gustaf Mannerheim', in Norrback, *A Gentleman's Home*, pp 114–26.

Flandrin, P, *Les Sept Vies du mandarin français: Paul Pelliot ou la passion de l'Orient* (Éditions du Rocher, Monaco: 2008)

Forsyth, J, *A History of the Peoples of Siberia: Russia's North Asian Colony 1581–1990* (Cambridge University Press, Cambridge: 1992)

Futrell, M, *Northern Underground: Episodes of Russian Revolutionary Transport and Communications through Scandinavia and Finland 1863–1917* (Faber & Faber, London: 1963)

——, 'Colonel Akashi and Japanese Contacts with Russian Revolutionaries in 1904–5', in *Far Eastern Affairs*, 4 (1967), pp 7–22

Halén, H, *An Analytical Index to C.G. Mannerheim's Across Asia from West to East in 1906–1908* (Finno-Ugrian Society, Helsinki: 2004)

——, 'Baron Mannerheim's hunt for Central Asian manuscripts', in Koskikallio and Lehmuskallio (eds), *C.G. Mannerheim in Central Asia 1906–1908*, pp 47–51

——, 'C.G. Mannerheims brev til senator Otto Donner från Kina 1907–1908', in Koskikallio and Lehmuskallio (eds), *C.G. Mannerheim in Central Asia 1906–1908*, pp 53–62

—— and Bent Lerbæk Pedersen, *C.G. Mannerheim's Chinese Pantheon: Materials for an Iconography of Chinese Folk Religion* (Finno-Ugrian Society, Helsinki: 1993)

Hawes, C, *In the Uttermost East: being an account of investigations among the natives and Russian convicts of the island of Sakhalin, with notes of Travel in Korea, Siberia and Manchuria* (Harper & Brothers, London: 1904)

Hedin, S, *My Life as an Explorer* (National Geographic Adventure Classics, Washington: 2003)

Hopkirk, P, *The Great Game: On Secret Service in High Asia* (Oxford University Press, Oxford: 1990)

——, *Foreign Devils on the Silk Road: The Search for the Lost Treasures of Central Asia* (John Murray, London: 1980)

Hudson, M, *Intervention in Russia 1918–1920: A Cautionary Tale* (Leo Cooper, Barnsley: 2004)

Ignatyev, A, *A Subaltern in Old Russia* (Hutchinson & Co, London: 1944; reprinted in Nish, *The Russo-Japanese War*, Vol 8)

Jägerskiöld, S, *Mannerheim: Marshal of Finland* (University of Minnesota Press, Minneapolis: 1986)

——, *Nuori Mannerheim [Young Mannerheim]* (Otava, Helsinki: 1964)

——, *Gustaf Mannerheim 1906–1917* (Otava, Helsinki: 1965)

——, *Gustaf Mannerheim 1918* (Otava, Helsinki: 1967)

——, *Valtion Hoitaja Mannerheim [Regent Mannerheim]* (Otava, Helsinki: 1969)

——, *Mannerheim: rauhan vuosina 1920–1939 [Mannerheim: The Years of Peace]* (Otava, Helsinki: 1973)

——, *Talvisodan ylipäälikkö: sotamarsalkka Gustaf Mannerheim 1939–1941 [Commander-in-Chief of the Winter War: Field Marshal Mannerheim]* (Otava, Helsinki: 1976)

——, *Suomen marsalkka: Gustaf Mannerheim 1941–1944 [Marshal of Finland]* (Otava, Helsinki: 1981)

——, *Viimeiset vuodet: Gustaf Mannerheim 1944–1951 [Final Years]* (Otava, Helsinki: 1982)

Juntunen, A, 'Finland and Siberia', in Lehtinen, I (ed), *Siberia: Life on the Taiga and Tundra* (National Board of Antiquities, Helsinki: 2002) pp 81–7

Kämäräinen, E, *Akseli Gallen-Kallela: Artist and Visionary* (Werner Söderström OY, Porvoo: 1994)

Keene, D, *Emperor of Japan: Meiji and His World 1852–1912* (Columbia University Press, New York: 2002)

King, G, *The Court of the Last Tsar: Pomp, Power and Pageantry in the Reign of Nicholas II* (John Wiley & Sons, Hoboken: 2006)

Kish, G, *North-east Passage: Adolf Erik Nordenskiöld, his life and times* (Nico Israel, Amsterdam: 1973)

Koivisto, T, *Suomalaista sisua villissä Idässä [Finnish Perseverance in the Wild East]* (Gummerus, Jyväskylä: 1947)

Komori, T, *Akashi Motojirō* (Hara Shobō, Tokyo: 1968; reprint Digital Publishing Service 2004).

Koskikallio, P, and Lehmuskallio, Aslo (eds), *C.G. Mannerheim in Central Asia 1906–1908* (National Board of Antiquities, Helsinki: 1999)

Kowner, R (ed), *The Impact of the Russo-Japanese War* (Routledge, London: 2007)

Kurobane, S, *Nichi-Ro Sensō to Akashi Kosaku [The Russo-Japanese War and the Deeds of Akashi]* (Nanso-sha, Tokyo: 1976)

Kuusela, M and Lehtoranta, Raine, *Bakusta Pekingin [From Baku to Beijing]* (Aamulehti, Tampere: 2006)

Lagus, F, *Amurinmaan retki [Expedition to the Amur]* (Werner Söderström OY, Helsinki: 1925)

Lehmusoksa, R and Lehmusoksa, Ritva, *Dining with Marshal Mannerheim* (Ajatus, Helsinki: 2005)

Levine, I, *Letters from the Kaiser to the Czar* (Stokes, New York: 1920)

Luckett, R, *The White Generals: The White Movement and the Russian Civil War* (Longman, London: 1971)

Mäkela, T and Parkkari, Jukka, *Mannerheim ja Ihmissyöjätiikeri [Mannerheim and the Man-eating Tiger]* (Arktinen Banaani, Helsinki: 2006)

Mäkinen, J, 'Aasian halki ratsasti juro Mannerheim' [Across Asia rode a grumpy Mannerheim], in *Helsingin Sanomat, Kulttuuri*, 15 March 2009, p C1

Mannerheim, C G E, *The Memoirs of Marshal Mannerheim* (Cassell, London: 1953)

——, *Suomen Marsalkan Muistelmat [Memoirs of Finland's Marshal]* (Otava, Helsinki: 1954; reprint 2004)

——, *Päiväkirja Japanin Sodasta 1904–1905 sekä Rintamakirjeitä Omaisille [Diary from the Japanese War 1904–1905 with Letters to his Family]* (Otava, Helsinki: 1982)

——, *Kirjeitä Seitsemän Vuosikymmenen Ajalta [Letters from Seven Decades]* (Otava, Helsinki: 1983)

——, *Across Asia from West to East in 1906–1908*, 2 Vols (Anthropological Publications, Oosterhout: 1969)

——, *1906–1908 nian Ma Da-Han Xiyu Kaocha Tupian Shu [Extracts from Mannerheim's Mapping Investigations of the Western Regions from 1906–1908]* (Shandong Huabao, Jinan: 2000)

——, *Across Asia on Horseback CD-ROM* (Finno-Ugrian Society, Mannerheim Foundation, Museum of Cultures, National Board of Antiquities, Försti Filmi, Helsinki: 2000)

——, *Across Asia from West to East in 1906–1908*, revised edition (Otava, Helsinki: 2008)

Mannerheim Sparre, E, *Lapsuuden muistoja [Childhood Memories]* (Otava, Helsinki: 1952)

Matsusaka, Y, *The Making of Japanese Manchuria 1904–1932* (Harvard University Asia Center, Cambridge, MA: 2001)

McKenzie, F, *From Tokyo to Tiflis: Uncensored Letters from the War* (Hurst and Blackett, London: 1905)

Meri, V, *Suomen Marsalkka C.G. Mannerheim* (Werner Söderstöm OY, Porvoo: 1988)

Meyer, K and Brysac, Shareen, *Tournament of Shadows: The Great Game and the Race for Empire in Asia* (Abacus, London: 2001)

Mizuki, Y, *Dōran wa Waga Shōchū ni Ari: Jōhō Gunkō Akashi Motojirō no Nichi-Ro Sensō [Discord is in My Grasp: The*

Russo-Japanese War of Military Attaché Akashi Motojirō] (Shinchōsha, Tokyo: 1991)

Nash, G, *The Tarasov Saga: From Russia through China to Australia* (Rosenberg, Kenthurst, NSW: 2002)

Nevalainen, T, 'Rotuhygienistin painajainen', in Sunday *Keskisuomalainen*, 6 April 2008, p 16

Nidvine, S, 'The Russian Cavalry During the Russo-Japanese War', on the website of the Russo-Japanese War Research Society: www.russojapanesewar.com, 2002

Nish, I, *The Russo-Japanese War, 1904–5: A Collection of Eight Volumes*, 8 Vols (Global Oriental, Folkestone: 2003)

Nomura, Y, *Ōtsu Jiken: Rokoku Nikolai Kōtaishi no Rainichi [The Ōtsu Incident: The Russian Prince Nikolai in Japan]* (Ashi Shobō, Tokyo: 1992)

Norman, A, *Holder of the White Lotus: The Lives of the Dalai Lama* (Little, Brown, London: 2008)

Norrback, M (ed), *A Gentleman's Home: The Museum of Gustaf Mannerheim, Marshal of Finland* (Otava, Helsinki: 2001)

Ollin, K, *Grafton-Affären [The Grafton Affair]* (Olimex, Jakobstad/Pietarsaari: 1999)

Parmanen, E, *Taistelujen Kirja [Book of the Struggles]*, Vols I–IV (Werner Söderström OY, Porvoo: 1936–7)

Pelliot, P, *Carnets de Route, 1906–1908* (Les Indes Savantes, Paris: 2008)

Pentikäinen, J, *Kalevala Mythology* (Indiana University Press, Bloomington: 1999)

Polvinen, T, *Imperial Borderland: Bobrikov and the Attempted Russification of Finland 1898–1904* (C. Hurst & Co, London: 1995)

Seaman, L, *From Tokio Through Manchuria with the Japanese* (D Appleton and Company, New York: 1905)

Screen, J, *Mannerheim: The Years of Preparation* (C Hurst & Co, London: 1970)

——, *Mannerheim: The Finnish Years* (C Hurst & Co, London: 2000)

Selle, E, *Donald of China* (Harper and Brothers, New York: 1948)

Sinerma, M, 'Englannin Sodanjulistus' [The English Declaration of War], in *Mannerheim: Tuttu ja tuntematon [Mannerheim: Known and Unknown]* (Reader's Digest, Helsinki: 1997) pp 222–4

Singleton, F, *A Short History of Finland* (Cambridge University Press, Cambridge: 1998)

Soikkanen, M, *C.G.E. Mannerheim: Suurriistan metsästäjä [C.G.E. Mannerheim: Big Game Hunter]* (Gummerus, Jyväskylä: 1997)

Trotter, W, *The Winter War: The Russo-Finnish War of 1939–40* (Aurum, London: 2003)

Tuomi-Nikula, J and Holmroos, Altti, *Finnish Inland Waters and Archipelago in the Wake of the Czars* (Kristina Cruises, Helsinki: 2003)

Unger, F, *The Authentic History of the War Between Russia and Japan* (World Bible House, Philadelphia: 1905)

Upton, A, *The Finnish Revolution 1917–1918* (University of Minnesota Press, Minneapolis: 1980)

Vlasov, L, *Mannerheim Pietarissa 1887–1904 [Mannerheim in St Petersburg]* (Gummerus, Jyväskylä: 1994)

——, *Mannerheim – upseeri ja tutkimusmatkailija 1904–1909 [Mannerheim – Officer and Explorer]* (Gummerus, Jyväskylä: 1997)

——, *Mannerheimin Elämän Naiset [The Women in Mannerheim's Life]* (Schildts, Keuruu: 2002)

——, and Vlasov, Marina, *Gustaf Mannerheim ja valkoiset emigrantit [Gustaf Mannerheim and the White Russians]* (Schildts, Keuruu: 2007)

Warner, O, *Marshal Mannerheim & the Finns* (Weidenfeld & Nicolson, London: 1967)

Wells, D (ed), *Russian Views of Japan 1792–1913: An Anthology of Travel Writing* (Routledge/Curzon, London: 2004)

Acknowledgements

This book is dedicated to Vesa Mäki-Kuutti, who dragged me around Finland on an insane quest that took us from the Russian border on the Raate Road, all the way to Louhisaari in the south-west, and over to Mannerheim's residence in Helsinki. Even then, he must have known that he was dying, and for him it was a last great adventure. I offered him a job as a researcher on this book, to which he enthusiastically agreed from his hospital bed, but he passed away before work could commence. His funeral took place a cruel week before his daughter married me. Kati Clements has assiduously taken on her late father's task, sacrificing many evenings to pore over letters, reportage and Mannerheim's diaries on my behalf, and discovering in the process that Mannerheim was not at all the stuffy figure she had been led to believe at school.

Many Finns have appointed themselves as my unofficial researchers and helpers, pressing newspaper clippings and dog-eared books into my hands, or discussing their mixed feelings about a national hero: Kaisa Aherto-Lilja, Johanna Ahonen, Mila and Mikko Auvomaa, Janne Hallikainen, Marja-Leena Hanninen, Anna-Leena Lähde, Pekka Kejo, Jyri Kettunen, Pekka Komu, Teemu Korpijärvi, Jussi Komulainen, Pasi Korhonen, Lasse Lilja, Kari, Matias, Pekka, Raija, Seija, Timo and Vitas Mäki-Kuutti, Aaro Mäkimattila, Juha Mäkinen, Elina and Raino Ojala, Annukka Ollitervo, Ritva Parkkonen, Hannu Palmu, Elina Rautasalo, Anni Rihkajärvi, Tomi Sarvanko, Jan Sormunen, Päivi Vestola, Harri Virtanen, and Tino Warinowski. They have been great assistance, and are sure to be my harshest critics – any errors of fact or interpretation in this book are entirely mine. I have been asked to say this, particularly by Uncle Timo, who is concerned that I will say